# Editing by design

# Editing

# by design

A guide to effective
word-and-picture
communication
for editors and designers

By Jan V. White

Second Edition

R. R. Bowker Company
New York and London, 1982

Published by R. R. Bowker Company
1180 Avenue of the Americas, New York, N.Y. 10036
Copyright © 1982 by Jan V. White
All rights reserved
Printed and bound in the United States of America

White, Jan V., 1928-
  Editing by design.

  Includes index.
1. Magazine design.   2. Periodicals.
I. Title.
Z253.5.W47     1982     686.2'24          82-1274
ISBN 0-8352-1508-3                        AACR2

For Clarissa

Charles  Alexander  Gregory  Christopher

# PREFACE

Eight years ago, when the first edition of this book was published, the preface began with these words: "This is intended to be a useful book. A how-to book." The response to the hoped-for usefulness has been so gratifying that here is an updated second edition. Its scope has been enlarged, but its practical orientation remains unchanged.

Among the new material is an analysis of the magazine as a physical object, how it is held and read, and how that must affect the way it is designed. Also, many new patterns for column grids; additional ways of handling pictures; a whole section on what to do with pictures of people; numerous fresh ideas for making the most of spreads; how to blend words with pictures; and, throughout, the effects of change in magazine-making technology. Technology, however, is merely the means to an end. Working editors and designers must, of course, understand it to use its potentials intelligently and work within its limitations comfortably. Yet they must never forget that the only thing that matters is the story, and the context within which the story will be perceived. How the type is set, the halftones produced, the pages assembled, the issue printed are all secondary (albeit essential) side issues. Of prime concern must always be the fundamental function of editing/designing, i.e. communication. That remains the same in spite of changes in technology, fashion, economics, or even computerization. Nothing can ever replace the thinking that only editors and designers can do and without which there can be no product.

Given this confident statement as a preamble, it then seems perfectly logical to return to the original preface, because . . .

This is intended to be a useful book. A how-to book. A primer that gets down to the basic concepts of what a magazine is — and that shows how to turn those concepts to the advantage of the product. It deals with the interrelationship of two functions in the production of publications that are normally thought of as separate: editing and design. It attempts to show that these functions are not separate, but rather two facets of the same act: the thinking underlying both is identical, only the technology differs.

There are many books about editing as a profession. There are also a number of books about design, layout, graphics, typography, and all the other details of an art director's job. There are, alas, few books that recognize that it is essential for the editors to understand what the designers are up to, or that explain to the designers what the editors need. That common ground which is so important to the ultimate quality of their joint efforts is booby-trapped with misunderstandings; this book is an attempt to remove them. It is based on long experience in working with editors and designers in seminars, on the lecture platform, and in day-to-day practice; it is the result of listening to their real-life problems, analyzing their practical questions, and trying to find solutions.

The trouble with many how-to books is that they give you examples of the *what* and lots of ways of *how,* but seldom enough of the *why*. As a result, you have a marvelously useful copybook, assuming that you can just swipe the examples. Unfortunately, the outward form of the examples is often grafted onto material that is unsympathetic to that form, and the result does not turn out as well as expected. WHY, you ask. Surely the pattern was good, and the person who noticed its excellence showed good judgment, and the person who accepted its use was on safe ground. So why did it turn into a disaster?

The reason why that original pattern had been done the way it was done was the ingredient missing from the recipe. What you need to know is the reason behind a design, as well as the characteristics that make it applicable to other situations. It is not enough to show a good solution without defining what makes it good — and what it is good *for*.

That is why this book is organized the way it is; it breaks the material down into the six areas common to all publications: the magazine — object in three dimensions; the page — patterns and potentials; type — the publication's fabric; illustrations — photographs and pictures; illustrations — nonpictorial; and color. Each chapter discusses the general principles, and then analyzes how to make the most of the potential design applications inherent in each of the six areas. These analytical discussions are presented in list form, either as plain lists of ideas or as "do's and don'ts." They are illustrated by examples that are, in turn, analyzed in terms of the specific point being illustrated. The *why* is brought out as clearly as the author's ingenuity allows. Since each point illustrated is a point in itself, there may well be some principles, recommendations, or opinions expressed on one page that are the opposite of the opinions expressed on another page. This is not because the book was carelessly assembled, but because there are many aspects to Truth, many aspects of utility. Some may be better than others in certain circumstances. Some may be totally inapplicable to certain situations. They have all been included because they may be useful solutions to someone's problems.

Some of the illustrations used are not tremendously exciting in terms of "design." This is quite intentional. Since this book is intended to be useful, the examples shown must have a resemblance to the normal sort of problems to be solved. Originality, Creativity, Design, are all Wonderful and Desirable Objectives. But in the realistic world of day-to-day publishing, they often have to be set aside for other, more immediate, more pressing, more important (yes, sorry about that, fellow-designers) aspects of the magazine trade. Besides, the original material is often just plain ugly. And you just cannot make a silk purse out of a sow's ear. You can, however, make a hairy leather pouch out of it! Just as useful for holding coins, if perhaps less pretty.

This does not mean that this book is an apologia for second-rate design, or the good-enough-for-the-mediocre-material-so-let's-relax approach. To the contrary: the very reason for its being is to proselytize for a better product, and surely nothing is more important to the improvement of a product than its appearance.

The book does, however, accept the regrettable fact that the vast majority of today's magazines do not handle the sort of material that is seen in the magazines available at newsstands. Newsstand magazines, be they the old general-interest "horizontal" books or the new, special-interest "vertical" books, are the top of the magazine iceberg. They are the highly visible few, blessed with what appears to be unlimited expertise, money, staff, organization, talent, fascinating subject matter, photographs, artists, filing systems, distribution, and what have you. Their graphic purpose is to create impact, to be fresh, new, exciting, and as with-it as seems most appropriate to appeal to the segment of the market that they serve. They are the pacesetters, the experimenters, the ones that establish the visual climate within which everyone else has to work.

In many instances, their innovative graphics are a cosmetic applied to a standard, conservative base. Sometimes the cosmetic is so strong that it overwhelms the base and becomes an end unto itself. (A dangerous thing to do, but it depends on who is doing it and why, as well as on how it is done; it can provide light-hearted enjoyment.) In any case, the newsstand magazines probably have the advantage of staffs sufficiently well versed in the plain old job of communicating that they can keep the graphic image-making within the appropriate boundaries of tried-and-true communication technique. It is their expertise that makes startling graphics work.

Alas, the other seven-eighths of the iceberg do not have the advantages of capital, talent, subject matter, and so forth. These are the vast majority of publications. The thousands of trade and professional magazines. The numerous employee publications. The hundreds of association publications. The thousands of alumni publications. The newsletters. The high school magazines. And so forth and so on. These are published in spite of frustrating restrictions of budget, space, and typography, and of not-very-good pictures of not-very-interesting subjects. They never have large enough staffs to do the work; they all have too many bosses to please — be they the Publication Committee, or the vice-presidential hierarchy, or the English teacher; they have troubles with printers; their paper stock is not as good as it should be; the postage costs too much; and there is always the competition (who may have just been bought up by a huge conglomerate and is having all sorts of money pumped into it). And there are lots more horror problems to list.

It is very tempting for the editors and designers of such publications to look at the newsstand, see and like an idea here or a trick there, and try to adapt it to their own use. Nothing could be more dangerous: superficial graphic sugar-coating emphatically will not improve a product; rather, improvement results from the excellence with which good publishing techniques, which are the foundation of the entire structure, are understood and applied. And those underlying techniques of course hold true for all kinds of magazines, be they mimeographed four-page in-house memoranda or fat, multicolored national editions.

With this in mind, it occurred to me that it might be good to provide some reasoned and logical approaches to the type of problems most magazine editors and designers inevitably face: what to do with the front cover format; how to design the contents page; what one needs to think of in assembling the scattered department pages in order to make the strongest, cumulative impact with them; how best to handle right-hand starts (always a problem); what the options are in handling editorial pages, new product reviews, late closing news pages. I gathered a compendium of examples of each of these typical difficulties in *Designing for Magazines: Common Problems, Realistic Solutions*, as a companion volume to *Editing by Design*. It carries the philosophy of this book a step further, by showing it in practical applications under realistic circumstances. It, too, is meant to be a useful book.

Westport, Connecticut, February 1982.

# ACKNOWLEDGMENTS

It is impossible to thank individually all the people who have had a hand in this book. That is because it is a collection of ideas and principles slowly accumulated in years of hard labor in the magazine field. To all my clients of yore, therefore, my thanks. You thought, gentlemen, that my fee was ample recompense for services rendered. So it was — usually. But I also received the benefit of experience, discussion, reasoning, and sometimes, battle. All helped to crystallize my views and opinions. This was a priceless recompense.

It would, however, be impossible to omit specific mention of the following editor/friends, whose influence has been, and happily continues to be, vital. My friend Don Holden, who suggested that the lectures I had been giving on editorial presentation just "had to be written down and there you have a finished book." Ha! That was five years ago. My thanks go to Perry Prentice, who not only entrusted this graduate architect with art department work (albeit on architectural magazines), but who also codified the way he wanted his magazines to be edited and designed. The principles in that code are the germ of this book. My deepest thanks go to three editors: Walter F. Wagner, Jr., of *Architectural Record;* John F. Goldsmith of *House & Home;* and Stanley F. Bergstein of *HoofBeats.* My involvement with them transcends the normal client/designer relationship: understanding, trust, and candor prevail when we work together. Nobody needs to prove anything to anyone else; nobody has to outguess or outshine anyone else, which makes working together a joy.

It is rare to find one such paragon of editor-hood in one's working life. To have found three to work with (I nearly said work "for," but that would have been exactly wrong) is fortunate indeed. To them my special thanks for allowing me to experiment in their pages.

The illustrations of spreads and pages from magazines are shown
with the kind permission of the following publications:

*Architectural Record*, McGraw-Hill, New York, pages 22,23,27,29,30,32,36,52,53,66,67,103,134,137
*Casa Claudia*, Editora Abril, Sao Paulo, Brazil, pages 29,37
*Construction Methods & Equipment*, McGraw-Hill, New York, page 81
*Dental Economics*, PennWell Publishing, Tulsa, Oklahoma, pages 50,51
*Engenheiro Moderno*, Informa, Sao Paulo, Brazil, page 43
*Harbus*, Harvard Business School, Boston, page 101
*Hoof Beats*, U.S. Trotting Association, Columbus, Ohio, pages 26,28,29,30,31,32,33,34,35,108,109,135,169
*House & Home*, McGraw-Hill, New York, pages 28,32,33,35,40,41,42,133
*Homebook*, McGraw-Hill, New York, page 36
*Housing*, McGraw-Hill, New York, page 37
*Industrial Engineering*, American Institute of Industrial Engineers, Norcross, Georgia, pages 35,40,41,42,193
*Industrial Marketing*, Crain Publications, Chicago, pages 75,86,87
McGraw-Hill Publications Company, New York, pages 12,13
*Medico Moderno*, Edicom, Mexico City, pages 38,39
*North Shore*, PB Communications, Winnetka, Illinois, page 30
*Oil & Gas Journal*, PennWell Publishing, Tulsa, Oklahoma, pages 72,73

The old movie photographs used to illustrate utilization of
pictures are all by kind permission of the Still File Collection.

# 1

There's more to creative magazine editing than marking up copy: by an aware use of expressive graphic elements, and a purposeful relationship of words, pictures, and space, design becomes communication, not mere ornament.

# EDITING BY DESIGN

# Editing

Editors do more than wield a blue pencil and polish words. Their greater purpose (or one of them, anyway) is to organize the material in such a way that its *significance* shines out. It does not matter whether that significance has world-shattering implications or is just a nugget of knowledge to help readers gain their livelihood more efficiently. What matters is that some message, some point of view, be communicated to the reader.

How does an editor achieve communication that works — that is incisive? By using several tools:

First, obviously, is choice of words.

Second, by organizing the facts and ideas into a logical sequence, so that the trend of thought becomes clear and the tone persuasive.

Third, by expressing the text in typography that reflects the editor's tone of voice — that is, the kind of typography that conveys visually, through size and darkness, the degree of importance attached to any specific area of the magazine or story.

The first two are verbal tools — the most immediate tools of an editor's trade. The third represents another group of tools at his or her disposal: the visual ones. The illustrative ones. It is essential to conceive of all the various illustrative materials as capable of being edited in precisely the same way as words, since incisive "picture editing" is achieved by the same thought process and the same editorial techniques as word editing.

First, obviously, is picking the right pictures.

Second, the illustrations are organized in a sequence that reinforces the flow of the verbal argument, complements it, works with it.

Third, through size and visual emphasis, the relative importance of the content of the illustrative material is indicated, in the same way that tone-of-voice typography reflects the relative importance of the verbally expressed thoughts.

The thought processes involved are identical and their goal is the same: to produce a symbiotic relationship between words and illustrations in which neither element can function without the other and in which each set of elements strengthens the meaning and reinforces the impact of the other.

This objective, however, can only be realized when editor and designer understand each other, their subject, and their respective techniques and aims so well that they manage to make one plus one equal three. Why work so hard? Simply because that is the only way to create a lively product that is memorable and has those qualities so prized in today's rushed world: speed of reading and ease of absorption.

# Design and the designer

With very few exceptions, which are mostly in the general-interest and entertainment areas, magazines that succeed in achieving their own personality, character, excitement, and atmosphere (and that make money for their publishers) are those that do NOT think of design — or "editorial presentation," as it is sometimes called — as the process of "dressing up a story." Those that succeed are the ones that understand that design is an arm of editing, that is, *interpreting* the meaning of, a story.

Where "good looks" are the primary goal, shallowness is too often the result. In fact, design thus motivated is so shallow that it is cosmetic, whereas it ought to be structural and integral.

Editorial presentation is a means to an end, the end of journalistic communication: helping to get a story off the page and into the reader's mind. It is emphatically not "art." In fact Design, with a capital D, is a secondary consideration. The successful layout is the one that helps the story come alive; it is easy to understand, interesting, and therefore memorable. If it happens to be an example of Good Design, so much the better. But that is just gravy; the meat-and-potatoes is effective communication.

The story — any story — exists in space: it needs an area in which the type, which carries the words, and the pictures which carry the images, can be disposed. The story could not exist without that space. Layout — the arrangement of the elements on the page — is integral with the content of the story. The two cannot be split apart. Unfortunately, in practice, they frequently are split apart, and much of the dissatisfaction expressed with today's periodicals' capacity to communicate is traceable to this basic mistake.

Why are form and content so often split apart? Because of the schism that exists between editors and art department people. Editors are trained to be journalists, which is one kind of skill. Designers are trained to be artists, which is another kind of skill. True, both skills are forms of communication, but they are not exactly the same — and so the attitudes involved and the techniques used in thinking differ. As a result, the two have to work together, (the editor and the designer,) often disagree, argue, fight and — worst of all — question each other's motives. If the artist-combatant is to become an effective contributor to the product, he or she must be accepted as a fully active member of the editorial team.

How does the designer become a full-fledged member of the journalistic team? In the chapter on "Illustrations: photographs and pictures," the concept of the story conference is explored in depth. Here suffice it to say that IF the editors and the art director are to work together as a team, the editors and the art director must learn to talk to each other as a team. Editors must not bring a finished manuscript and a bunch of pictures to the designer two hours before deadline and yell, "You have three pages to fit it into — and make it pretty!" Instead, all must discipline themselves to a method of working together that is based on holding formally scheduled meetings at which the story in hand is discussed and, through a meld of each participant's expertise and special experience and interests, a coherent story plan is devised.

Such give and take enables the team to get to know each other as well as to understand the story. Aware of the story's thrust, each member can work on expressing it instead of working at cross-purposes. Moreover, through the story conference the art director becomes involved in the journalistic content of the story, not just its form. In time, he or she is metamorphosed from an artist plain and simple to a journalist first, artist second, applying design talent as a tool in much the same way that the writer/editor uses language-manipulating ability. The pastepot and shears are no less an editorial tool than a typewriter or blue pencil.

# Layout and styling

Layout is the specific, individually tailored solution to a particular story. It is the day-to-day manner in which the tools provided by the magazine's styling are put to use by the designer for journalistic purposes, to make the story clear, interesting, and memorable. It implies working within the strictly defined limitations specified by the styling, retaining the discipline imposed by the styling, but encouraging the application of imagination within the styling's confines. The great bulk of this book concerns itself with the how-to aspects of layout within such restrictions. But before we can begin to explore the details of the practical business of magazine design, we must understand the styling context within which such design operates.

Styling is the permanent, underlying, all-encompassing visual vocabulary of the magazine. It is the result of a set of interrelated decisions made at one time, arrived at logically and with artistic insight. Determining style is an expensive deep-think process based on the editorial future planned for the magazine as well as on its projected economic future. This process takes into account factors such as the direction of market growth, development of audience type, health of the economic sector served, and so on. Styling is based on the equity inherent in the existing product — taking into account such intangibles as the value of recognizable character or elements used in the magazine, reader loyalty, and the magazine's individual personality in its field. Of course, it is also based on purely practical criteria, such as the strengths, weaknesses, and potential capabilities of the staff, the printer, the suppliers, the production capabilities.

Styling decisions are planned to serve the organization for a long time — hopefully a good eight years. If they are to remain viable, their purity must be closely guarded; these decisions must not be diluted or tampered with for short-term purposes, for they are, in effect, the visual vocabulary of the product — and pragmatic changes should never be allowed to corrupt a language.

Getting down to specifics, the styling decisions that provide the tools the editor and designer will use for presenting their stories are decisions about the structure, scale, typographic makeup, and organization of the magazine. They also relate to the artwork, logotype, department headings, type specifications, and all the other details that can be standardized and that are needed for putting a magazine together.

IF the styling is appropriate and sympathetic to the magazine's subject matter, as well as to the people who have to apply it; and IF there is enough capability built into the system to allow variety and freedom of expression; and IF the system is not so strong that it becomes a straitjacket; and IF it is so easy to use that it does not cause more problems than it is meant to solve; and IF — in other words, if it works well, then it will simplify the job of making normal run-of-the-book layouts. Furthermore, it will not be necessary to strive for violent effect in order to gain attention, because the normal mode of expression will be distinctive enough to stand on its own without exaggeration. This normalness, then, will become the special character of the magazine — which is exactly what most magazines attempt to create for themselves and what so few succeed in doing. Obviously it is not easy to achieve, but that does not mean the goal is not worth striving for.

Now, *normalness* (of a distinctive kind, of course) may be all very well, but what about situations that demand special handling? Those Special Reports and extra-exciting articles or issues? Paradoxically, to convey excitement, one has to have dullness first, for excitement exists only in contrast. Mountains get their drama from valleys. If excitement is attempted everywhere, frenetic confusion (a visual babel) results. That is why flamboyance in layout succeeds only when it is presented in the context of nonflamboyance. The best setting for excitement is a styling that creates a climate of normalness.

## Criteria for styling

Here is a list of some of the most important desires of the different people who must be taken into account when a styling process is contemplated. It shows, in capsule form, the many requirements that influence a magazine besides the two obvious ones: to be interesting and to make money.

The balancing of those various desires, the compromises that have to be made in satisfying them, the diplomacy (or is it brashness?) required to reach any agreement at all, are problems best left to the specialist. Just look at what a magazine has to contend with:

**Reader satisfaction**

Ease of legibility (a universally demanded characteristic, asking simply for large enough type in columns of the right width — comparatively simple to provide, but the cause of tremendous arguments).

Instant communication (page arrangements that signal at a glance what is important and what is less so, so that the reader does not have to read everything to make up his own mind).

Memorableness (presenting the words and pictures so adroitly that no effort is required to remember them because the very deftness makes their point stick).

Understandableness (simplicity of language and design, so the reader does not have to work hard to grasp the meaning).

*Result:* Service (the reader consciously feels better off for having spent some valuable time on your product and feels good about it, has a satisfied glow about it — and may even quote something from it the next day).

**Editor satisfaction**

Aptness to the subject matter and the audience (this is a question of defining their character and expressing it in the choice of sympathetic graphic materials).

Capability for tone-of-voice typography (to express through visual means the varying degrees of importance of the thoughts; consists of flexible typography and layout in a context of flexible space allocation).

Simplicity of application of the system (anything that creates complications will be resented and remain unused; time is always too short and there are never enough people to do the work).

Efficiency of operation (solving in advance as many problems as can be foreseen, and working out a system that will accommodate them easily; mechanizing the operation even to the point of computer programming).

*Result:* The editor is freed from the chores of small-scale decision making, and can thus concentrate his or her efforts on more worthwhile pursuits that will be more useful to the product: development of stories in greater depth, spectacular content, broader scope.

**Publisher satisfaction**

A product that is identifiable, recognizable, and has a reputation (all of which make it easier to sell as a vehicle for advertising).

A product that distinguishes clearly between the editorial matter and the ads (which is good for both: the editors get recognition for the amount of material they have packed into the issue — which makes the readers happy; this can only come about if the editorial matter has its own recognizable character; the advertisers are happy because the contrast between the editorial material and their own is so clear that it reinforces the support that the edit gives the ad when they appear next to each other).✱

---

## ✱ Why must editorial matter look all-of-a-piece?

Because the subscribers are spending their hard-earned cash to buy the content.

Because the advertisers are investing their ad budgets in a vehicle that has the right sort of readership — and it is likely that some of the subscribers just cited are an advertiser's best prospects.

Because the advertisers are looking for optimum exposure for their ads, and are likely to get the best editorial support through maximum contrast between edit and ad.

Because the advertising agency media specialist probably does not understand the technicalities in the magazine's subject matter (and finds it hard to judge the quality of editorial matter, specially in the specialized press). But he or she can certainly judge the amount and the impact of the editorial matter just by looking, without study.

In business magazines, it is especially difficult to make the editorial matter stand away from the ads, since by and large they both treat the same subject. The similarity is merely in the pictorial material; the headline often uses the same words. It therefore becomes doubly important to differentiate between the two kinds of uses to which the blank page is put. Three basic techniques:

Creation of a regularity in the basic geography and structure of the issues, so that readers know the issue's sequence and where in the issue they are most likely to find what they are looking for. This habit-pattern is a valuable asset not only because it helps foster product loyalty in the reader, but also because it speeds communication between editor and reader.

Invention of a typographic styling responsive to all the needs of the magazine. This responsiveness should not only allow tone-of-voice expressiveness, as outlined earlier, but must also permit differentiation between the various areas of the magazine. Thus, areas that require maximum flexibility (the editorial "feature" section, in the middle of the book) should have that capacity built in, whereas areas that ought not to have such flexibility (such as the front and back of the book's scattered pages or "mixed" pages, where part of the page is editorial and part devoted to advertisement) should have maximum restrictions. Yet both areas should have strong family resemblance to each other, so that the magazine is tied into a visual unity.

Imposition of a simple, regimented regularity to the scattered spaces in the front and back of the book (the spaces that are overwhelmed by the flamboyance of the advertisements that surround them, yet must be there to provide the "editorial support" so dear to advertisers' hearts). It is impossible to outshout the ads, so it is much wiser to make the editorial matter as visually UNinteresting as possible. Such dullness, by contrast, creates maximum visibility. This logical approach sounds acceptable in theory, but in practice, editors find it goes against their training to make things appear dull on purpose, and so it leads to unsatisfactory compromises based on "just this once let's do such-and-such."

Since footnotes get very high readership (if there are not too many of them), this VERY IMPORTANT material is presented in the guise of a footnote. But it is the key to the whole thesis of this book.

Simplicity of operation and efficiency in production (which tend to save money — and there is not a publisher alive who would not like to do that!).

*Result:* A product so well organized that it does not have to overcome internal hurdles; as a result, the publisher can concentrate his or her effort on external problems of economic competition. The product also sells itself by being so much better than its competitors that less effort is needed to cajole subscribers on the one hand and advertisers on the other.

## Art director satisfaction

Graphic materials and effects that work well together and with the subject matter that needs to be expressed (so the wheel does not have to be reinvented every time another story is started on).

Precisely worked-out standards for handling the materials (so the mechanical "dull" parts of the job can be passed to an assistant, or the person who handles the "traffic" in the office, or even the printer).

Maximum flexibility with a minimum set of tools (it is important to have available as wide a set of choices as possible for placing the various elements on the page, yet to place them within carefully predetermined positions that are part of a pattern which helps give the issue an overall unity).

*Result:* Freedom from mechanical puzzles, allowing time to think creatively, journalistically, in depth — all the way from story conferences through to final layout — about the inter-relationship of the content and the form of the story. Ultimate result: a better product.

## Team satisfaction

Any set of rules implies a parallel set of restrictions. If the styling is to be successful, it must be used with consistency, which means that there must be self-discipline on the part of all concerned, to maintain and safeguard those rules. Therefore everyone involved must fully understand the reasons for the rules and must agree with the underlying principles. Most especially, they must realize that the rules are a help, not a hindrance to their work. This awareness will counteract the desire to make changes or tamper with the techniques the rules demand.

2

THE MAGAZINE: OBJECT IN THREE

# DIMENSIONS

A favorite toy 100 years ago was the little book with pictures that seemed to move as the pages were riffled: the policeman chasing a dog; the guardsman marching outside the palace; the delivery boy pedaling away on his bicycle. One story was printed on the right-hand pages, and the book had to be turned upside down to see the other story. The faster the pages were flipped, the faster the action became — and the greater the hilarity produced.

This simplistic example indicates how an apparently two-dimensional object, such as a printed page, can be used to far greater effect when it is multiplied, repeated, and bound into a book. The page's isolated flatness is transmitted into just one event in a series — preceded and followed by others. The single page has height and width, but backed up by another one, it suddenly gains depth as well. The depth — the thickness of the sheet of paper — is not great, but it exists, and that sliver of thickness makes all the difference between the palace guardsman standing frozen and appearing to have motion and life.

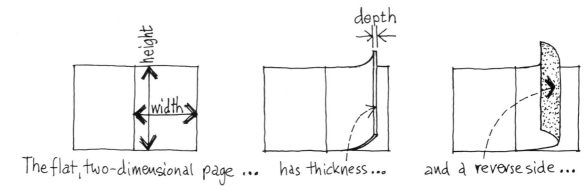

The flat, two-dimensional page ... has thickness ... and a reverse side ...

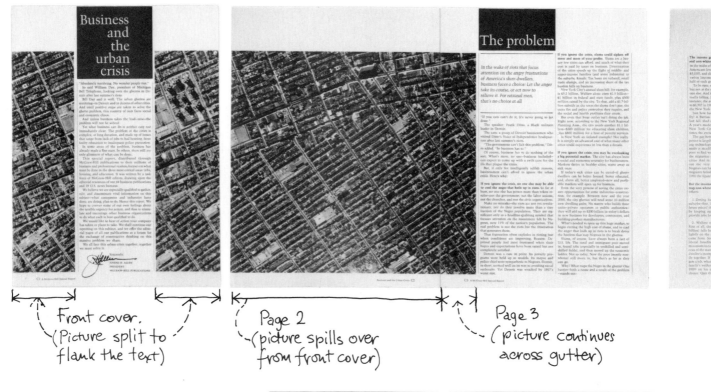

Front cover.
(Picture split to flank the text)

Page 2
(picture spills over from front cover)

Page 3
(picture continues across gutter)

One important aspect of this third dimension, however, requires special emphasis and clarification: *time* is involved in the appreciation of a page and of every other page that follows in sequence. A magazine is, in effect, a series of events that follow one after the other as the pages are turned, exposing spread after spread.

This space/dimension/time relationship is probably the least-used and least-understood capability that the medium has to offer. It is a capability that is, admittedly, somewhat esoteric; furthermore, it operates at a level about which the busy working editor and art director seldom have time to think or opportunity to act. They usually have to concentrate so hard on the story they are currently dealing with (and which is just an element to be imposed on a few of those marvelously fertile blank pages) that they forget about dimension and time that might well be exploited for the benefit of their product as a whole.

If they were more consistently aware of the third and fourth dimensions, they could use other tools in achieving a more varied

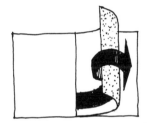

... with a potential interrelationship that should be exploited

Pages 4 and 5 and rest of piece

Back cover (glimpse of picture from front cover)

Front cover

and effective result: They could build in contrast between stories (following a "fast" story full of pictures and short on text with a "slow" one full of heavy-going technicalities; then following that one with a "personality" story that is not quite as slow as the one before, perhaps, but certainly looks and feels different; and so on).

They could vary the scale of elements from story to story, thus achieving more variety in the overall presentation (by using a three-column makeup on one story and following it with a story based on two-column makeup — with change of visual scale in picture-sizing that reflects the two different page breakups).

They could insert elements in strategic positions that carry surprise (an unexpectedly large picture, perhaps, or a startlingly out-of-scale element, or a full-bleed color page — or whatever might be unexpected).

They could deliberately build in curiosity-arousing elements that pull the reader from spread to succeeding spread (with questions at the bottom right-hand corner of the right-hand page, perhaps).

They could create carefully contrived patterns and rhythms to build up a series of smaller stories into a larger, more important-appearing major statement (through judicious use of repetition of graphic elements, page arrangement, space allocation, or who knows what else they might dream up?).

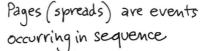

Pages (spreads) are events occurring in sequence

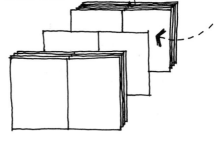

They do not exist singly, but only in context of the group.
It takes time to perceive them, one after the other.

The reader has the memory of what he has just seen

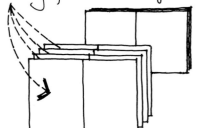

... as well as curiosity about what he is going to see.

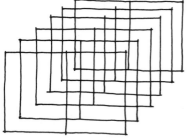

So the magazine should perhaps be thought of as a "transparent" series of events

The physical properties of the magazine — its size, shape, weight, stiffness, floppiness, fatness, and the way it is bound —

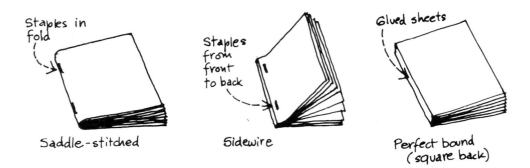

Staples in fold

Saddle-stitched

Staples from front to back

Sidewire

Glued sheets

Perfect bound (square back)

all affect the way it's held in our hands. That, in turn, affects the way we perceive it as we leaf through it. We hold the object by the spine when we first pick it up to find out whether it is for us

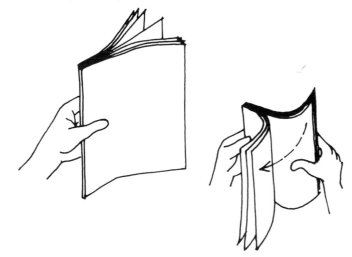

or not — when we riffle through it fast. It doesn't matter whether that riffling be done left-to-right or right-to-left. The fact remains that in holding it by the spine we hide the area near the gutter because that's where the hand is doing the holding. Thus, for all practical purposes, the inside half of each page is useless in that first, crucial viewing of our product. Few people even bother

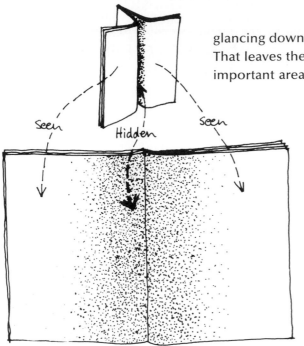

glancing down at the lower portion of the outer half of the page! That leaves the upper, outside corners of the pages as the vitally important areas seen by everyone.

In spite of the fact that we may design and assemble our magazines in carefully crafted, logical, and subtly paced sequences of impressions, most readers typically hunt-and-peck, choosing to pay attention at random to that which interests them. To make matters even more distressing, they most probably do this back-to-front! It is therefore common sense to try to catch their attention with hooks on every page. Is it not also logical to position those hooks in the areas most likely to be seen?

Drawing attention to and then making the value of the contents of a package irresistible to the consumer are packaging design goals that move cornflakes off supermarket shelves. Making the value of a magazine's contents visible and selling it is no different from selling cornflakes. We must use every trick and merchandising insight at our command, turning them all to our advantage, responding to the reader's habits with layouts that work. The principle here is embarrassingly simpleminded: *don't bury good material in the gutter.*

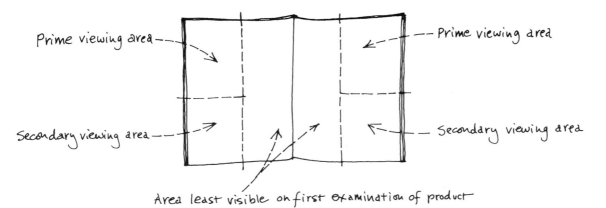

There is a second principle closely related to this one: *don't worry about the foot of the page.* Nobody bothers to look there. It is the top of the page that matters. We should control the tops

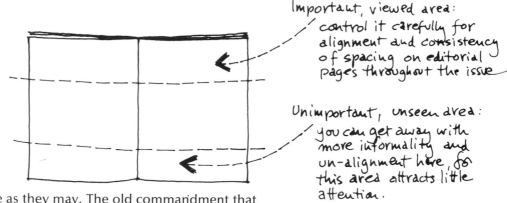

Important, viewed area: control it carefully for alignment and consistency of spacing on editorial pages throughout the issue.

Unimportant, unseen area: you can get away with more informality and un-alignment here, for this area attracts little attention.

and let the bottoms come as they may. The old commandment that dictates perfect alignment at the foot of the page is nonsense. It does make the pages "neater," but in order to achieve such a character it succeeds in making life difficult; furthermore, too often it forces us to make compromises where it matters (i.e., at the top) for the sake of areas that don't matter (i.e., at the foot of the page). Wherever there is a choice, it is wiser to opt for the top.

# How we look at, then read, the product

Readers see the magazine twice: the first time when riffling through the pages to determine whether it is interesting; then the second time, slowly and deliberately, when they have committed attention to it.

## Riffling the pages

This process results in two distinct sets of impressions: (1) a cumulative *muchness*, and (2) a set of memorable highlights. These highlights stand out in contrast to the overall background texture and their function is to beguile the superficial page flipper into becoming an involved participant — a reader.

Clearly, take both of these very different characteristics into account when making the magazine. To succeed, it is essential to conceive of the product as a three-dimensional entity.

The impression of cumulative muchness is built up by repeated signals that act as beacons in the reader's travels through our microworld of space (on the many pages) and time (needed to see them all). Recognizable, repetitive character is what these beacons must have in common, no matter what their actual shape may be: department headings, perhaps; or graphic elements such as portrait sketches of columnists; or big numbers denoting sequencing of chapters; or boxes around repetitive units of some sort; or merely the typographic handling of display type — to name but a few.

The cumulative impression is also built up by the color and texture of the body copy typography (the black marks on the paper) and — no less vital to the visual flavor — the margins and the spaces between the type (the white paper not printed on). Here, too, the secret is in repetition and careful attention to consistency. Cheating — even just once — cannot help but diminish the desired overall effect. Is such a departure worth it? The decision must be based on cold analysis of the cost/benefit ratio.

The memorable highlights mentioned above contrast against this regular, controlled background. This is usually where the fun of magazine making is, for the flamboyance of idea married to appropriate rendering can lead to effective communication value, reader involvement, and even design awards. But it is essential to be ruthless in editing ideas for excitement down to just those that are truly effective in doing two things simultaneously: (1) getting the inherent editorial meaning across, while (2) being visually irresistible. Cuteness, decorativeness, even startlingness for its own sake often backfire because the viewer quickly senses the shallowness of thought beneath an amusing graphic surface.

The trick is to find the active balance between the flamboyant (needed to hook page rifflers into becoming readers) and the repetitive background patterning (needed to make potential readers realize that the product they are holding is worth their investment of money and — even more precious — time).

## Reading the stories

When the page riffler has been persuaded of the value of the product on that first go-round, he or she starts to examine it a second time. This time, however, it is much more slowly, deliberately, with greater attention, for he or she has become an involved reader. At this point the value of flamboyant attention-getters recedes into the background. They have done their work of bringing in the reader. Now what was background becomes foreground: other, even more vital characteristics come into their own — first and foremost, good clear writing. Good, clear illustration that reinforces the words with apt images. Good, clear organization that encourages the flow of ideas in logical sequence. Good, clear presentation that acts as a lubricant, helping to slip those ideas off the page into the reader's mind. . . .

The way a publication lies on the table and opens up is the reason for the preference for right-hand pages in the front of the book and left-hand pages in the back of the book...

... the heavier part lies flat, giving easier visibility and avoiding reflected highlights on the paper, whereas the lighter part is curved, shiny, and thus less inviting to read. The centerfold is neutral.

# Essential equipment to encourage thinking in 3-D

Get rid of that ordinary desk in the art department and replace it with a kitchen counter at least ten feet wide; this will let you place ten pages' worth of dummy sheets in line next to each other, so that you can work several pages simultaneously (doing a story as a whole).

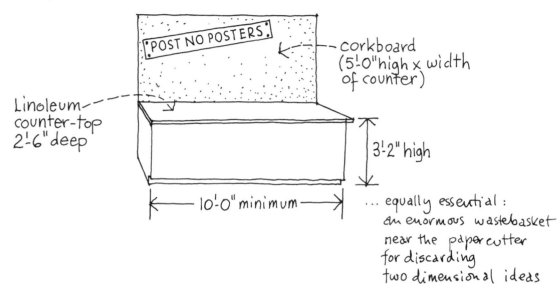

POST NO POSTERS!

corkboard
(5'-0" high x width
of counter)

Linoleum
counter-top
2'-6" deep

3'-2" high

|← 10'-0" minimum →|

... equally essential:
an enormous wastebasket
near the paper cutter
for discarding
two dimensional ideas

The tabletop should be at least as high as the normal kitchen counter, preferably higher, so you can work comfortably standing up. You may also buy a bar stool to go with the counter, provided that you do not perch on it except to rest a while: the very act of walking from page to page and back again helps you to perceive each page in the context of its neighbors and as an arrangement of units that will ultimately be printed back to back folded into an inescapable sequential interrelationship.

Keep that tabletop clear of encumbrances; never use it for storage; and never cover the wall behind the table with graphic flamboyances and esthetic inspirations. They will only distract your attention from the functional relationships in front of you. The more antiseptic your working area, the clearer your view of the job in hand.

Plan the book visually, using preprinted forms arranged in such a way that you are forced to think in horizontal sequential flow, just as in the product itself. There should be two kinds of preprinted forms available:

It is wise to have these forms well printed on good stock in colored ink — gray would be most suitable; you will need to, *want* to use these forms and use them with pleasure. (Nobody relishes using shoddy mimeographed blots on scratchy paper.) If such preprinted forms seem like a luxury, train yourself to draw thumbnail sketches of the pages in horizontal sequence — to remind yourself of the necessity to think in three dimensions.

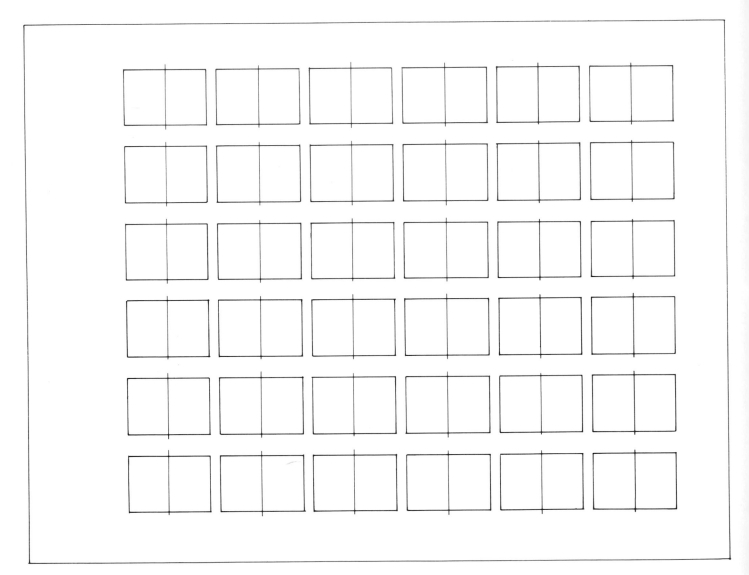

*First,* a form that shows the entire magazine on a single 8½″ × 11″ sheet. This is needed for broad planning, space allocation, organizing, housekeeping, checking assignments — NOT for designing the book.

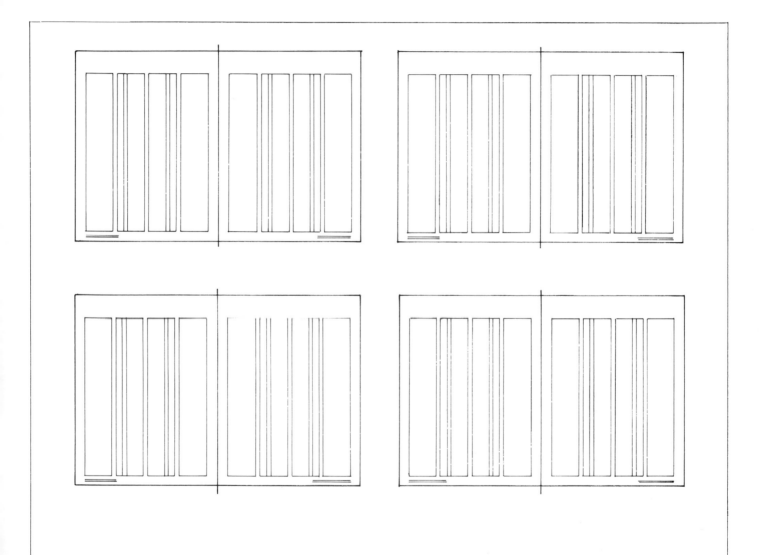

*Second,* a form that is a miniature of the magazine's dummy sheet, showing columns and other preordained positions with which you have to work. The exact size of these miniatures depends on personal preference, based on the amount of annotation and detail you will be putting down — and on the size of your handwriting! A most useful scale is one that allows four full spreads to be accommodated on a standard 8½″ × 11″ sheet. This is large enough to allow ample annotation, yet small enough not to demand too much accuracy.

# Assembling the issue in miniature

Spend the extra money to have miniature photostats of each spread made as it is produced (one half of original size is ideal). Trim off the excess paper and then pin the stats in correct sequence on the wall above the work counter. As work proceeds on an issue, it is impossible to remember what the story that was finished two weeks ago, and that went to the printer day-before-yesterday, looked like. Yet it is essential to take its appearance into account as you make decisions about the story on the board today.

Miniaturization also has the effect of showing up the pattern within a story while playing down the minor details — thus enabling you to become more clearly aware of that which matters most in the magazine: the basic pattern of each story.

A further advantage of miniaturization: you can inspect the upcoming issue — for characteristics that can only be perceived when the whole book has been laid out — before it is irretrievably

Miniature photostatic copy of a layout, shown here full size: the details disappear, the broad strokes remain

5

committed to paper by the thousands. You can change story sequence, improve the contrast in story types, get better picture story/ text story rhythm, and in general improve the pacing of the issue.

The cost of such photostats is not inconsiderable, and if your magazine is not highly illustrated, then perhaps sketches of each spread, or better yet, the neatly rendered miniature dummy forms described earlier, may prove adequate. However, some sort of visual record of the details of the issue is absolutely essential, and every effort should be made to produce the miniatures in spite of the normal busyness. A useful aid in the production of the "mini-wall" is to have rectangles permanently marked on the wall into which the miniatures are placed as they are produced. A further refinement: use thumbtacks with numbers printed on them, which are available at all map stores, for indicating page numbers. The mini-wall thus becomes a very useful tool for the entire staff, especially if a production schedule and check-off system are added to the basic concept.

How about Polaroids? Or reducing copies made on a Xerox copier? (64% of a 64% is an ideal size).

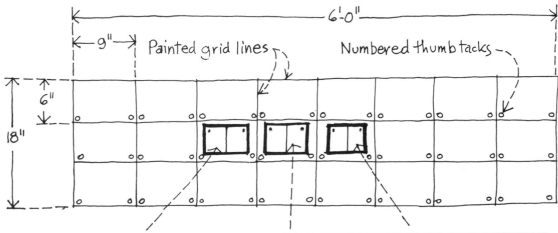

# Exploiting the third dimension

## The spread

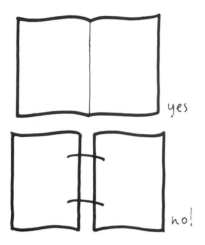

yes

no!

Think in terms of horizontal spreads, instead of vertical single pages. The normal magazine shape is vertical; the text in its columns is vertical; so the temptation is to subdivide the space in vertical slivers. But, once the readers get beyond the front cover and have opened up the issue, they see a horizontal shape interrupted by the gutter in the middle. However, they perceive only one page at a time, because they are used to seeing pages split away from each other and because the available space is normally organized as two contiguous vertical elements. (One automatically thinks of an ad as a single-page vertical element — and the same holds true for frontispieces, chapter openings, and so forth.) It is incumbent upon the editor and designer to break out of this straitjacket wherever opportunity allows; hence, they must conceive of the two-page spread as a large horizontal module with a minor interruption down the middle, instead of as two smaller vertical modules that happen to be glued together in the middle.

The resulting effect on the reader is of a broadened, widened, more expansive aura in the product as a whole; and — when big pictures are used — a feeling of enormous enclosure, like the experience of the audience at a Cinerama presentation.

Remember that the horizontal spread shapes are part of a steady flow of such shapes, independent on the dummy sheets while being worked on, but folded together back-to-back accordion-style when they reach the reader.

Here are eight pages – the way they are normally visualized :

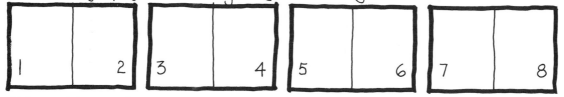

This working pattern only exists as a convenience for production, however.

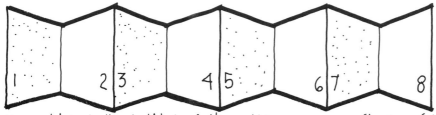

It would be better to think of them this way – as a flowing, folded space

But this is the way the reader sees them

Design each story, no matter how long or how short, as a unit. Do not fall into the trap of working on one page of a multipage story until you have solved the basic pattern for the entire story, start to finish. This is where the value of that kitchen-counter worktable is most evident: use it to organize the raw material into piles co-ordinated to the pages on which the material is planned to fall; then work out an overall design that will accommodate the material within the story's matrix.

Material to be accommodated on each spread          Dummy sheets in a row to help define sequence

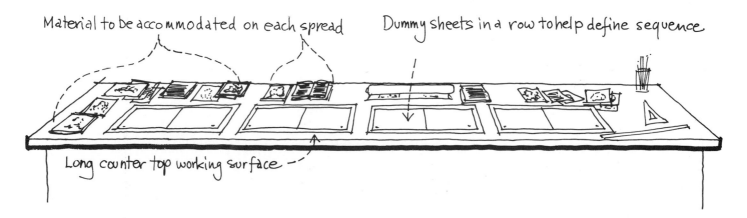

Long counter top working surface –

# Horizontal alignment

Emphasize horizontals: on the single page, on the spread, on the series of spreads. Horizontal alignment (so long as it is adhered to with precision) is the simplest and most effective instrument with which to create horizontal patterns within a basically vertical mass.

The "magic line" is the principle of alignment carried out as a deliberate design technique throughout a story. It is a predetermined position on the page — an edge — a frontier — used as a line from which the various elements (graphic or typographic) are hung. It is invisible, since no actual physical mark is made on the paper; it is merely a demarcation line that gives structure to the individual pages and ties whole stories together by virtue of that repeated structural capacity. The more pictorial the story, the more effective the use of the magic line becomes, since there are more edges of more elements to help define it. Each story dictates its own magic-line position, since the placement of that position is dependent on the optimum use of the material available in the story; there can be more than one such line in any story. It is a tool, however, that must be used very simply and forthrightly, or it fails.

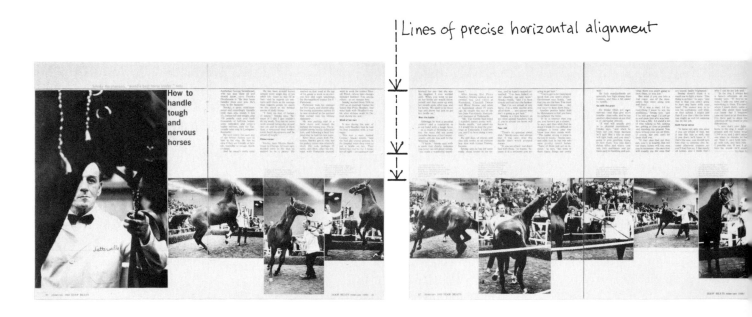

Lines of precise horizontal alignment

# Horizontal modules

Establish horizontal modules for the publication, in much the same way that you have vertical modules for the type (i.e., columns). This may take a little doing — and may be unpopular in situations where maximum flexibility is required. A number of European magazines have adopted such systematization, basing their modules on mathematical proportions coordinated with picture shapes and type lineage. In practice, such systematization may be useful for only a few highly specialized publications (such as catalogs that use picture/caption presentation), but the principle is sound, and should be made use of when it is applicable.

Multipage story based on a series of
horizontal modules (A, B, C) and two
additional special positions (D, E).

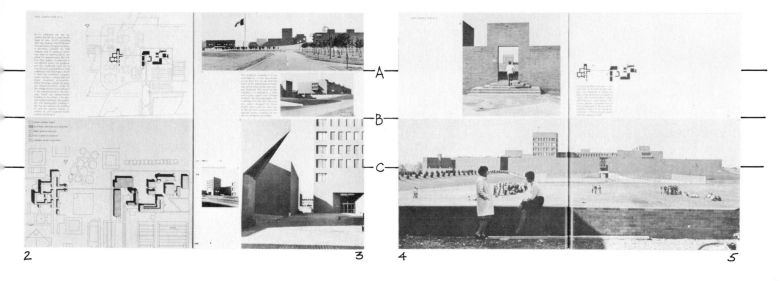

A
B
C

2        3        4        5

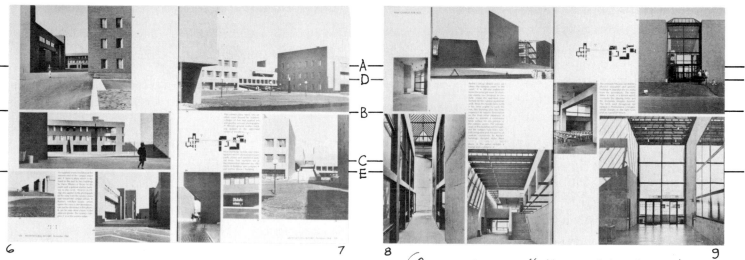

A
D
B
C
E

6        7        8        9

(On page 8 : two off-the-module mistakes)

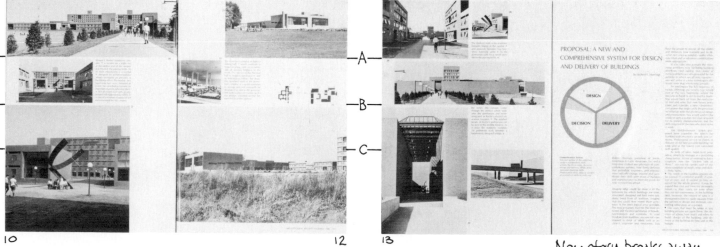

A
B
C

10        12        13

New story breaks away
from modules

27

# Making the spread appear wider

Use tricks to make the spread appear wider than it is. The simplest example of this is, of course, the full-bleed two-page picture which can create an impression of enormous size.

A single picture is wide enough, but splitting the space horizontally emphasizes the width even more.

It may be useful to remember that running pictorial matter on the outer edges (left and right) of the spread makes the spread stretch wider in appearance; interestingly enough, the same effect can be achieved by pictorial matter placed in the gutter only. By the same token, a homogenized mass of pictures and text neatly disposed in the normal rectangular text space on each page makes the spread thoroughly uneventful and as small as it can be (assuming that anybody notices it).

The segment of the photo at far right was simply split away from the rest of the image and pushed over for effect.

## Family apartments

### There's a huge demand for them ...

... but it's a tough market to build for

Demarcating the head- and foot-margins by a black rule emphasizes the horizontality of the spread.

The focal point in the center of the spread is expanded by means of pictorial "callouts." This shows that it is indeed possible to achieve an effect of size using a bunch of small pictures.

The startlingly large figure breaks out of the confines of the photo, invading the space alongside. The scale is what does the trick here. (see p.162)

A full-bleed photo is undoubtedly impressive, for the vastness of the space defined in the picture extends indefinitely beyond the edges of the page because of the bleeding. But the impact is heightened by the contrast of the tiny inset photo.

# Jeremy Jacobs—
## quiet man behind the bustling conglomerate

TEXT BY DON EVANS

The box interpenetrating both the white space of the left-hand page and the photo at right knits the two disparate elements into a unified — large — image. The line is run in bright red!

## The Opulence
BY LAURIE LEVY
PHOTOGRAPHY BY MICHAEL ROBERTS

On the runway, it is a golden age. Opulent is the word for Fall Fashion '81.

Designers are showing a renewed affection for rich fabrics, unrolling endless bolts of lush velvets, cashmeres, easy tweeds and blanket wools in the form of sweeping skirts and culottes, the dramatic cloth-conscious shawls that prove to be the

Using the inner area of the spread and leaving the left and right edges empty makes the spread look larger. Here the silhouette captures its surrounding white space and turns it into an active background; the effect is heightened by the parallel handling of the text.

Make use of graphic techniques that tie the pages together and so help to emphasize the horizontal-spread shape. There are as many ways of doing this as there are clever designers, but to illustrate the kind of thinking involved, here are some of the most obvious stratagems:

Jump the gutter with a big picture.

Jump the gutter with a background tint block.

Jump the gutter with a strong graphic device .

Jump the gutter with clear white space (clearly edged, so it appears as though it was supposed to be there, rather than that the printer forgot to fill the hole with a picture).

Jump the gutter with a string of like-size elements.

Government subsidized housing: Sleeper market of the Seventies

It's a sleeper because unless you've had something to do with government housing programs, you may not realize how big the subsidy market has suddenly become. This year, subsidized units will total about 450,000 units—roughly double what it was last year and a whopping 25% of all housing starts. And according to HUD Secretary George Romney, it's going to get even bigger—possibly well beyond 600,000 units a year in the next few years. Apparently the government is now committed to backing its housing programs with enough money to make a real dent in our shortage of low-income housing. If so, the long-term result could be a market that is both big and much less vulnerable to tight-money problems. Few builders can afford to ignore such a market.

Jump the gutter with strong headline typography.

Link facing pages by similarity of shape or mirror image of the shape.

Overwhelm the gutter by the strength of the patterns that cross it.

Link facing pages by implication of meaning.

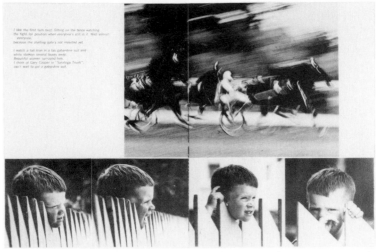

Overwhelm the gutter by playing up the meaning of the pictures that cross it.

Link facing pages by placing everything at an angle.

Link facing pages by using an angle in the major illustration as a basis for placement of all the other elements.

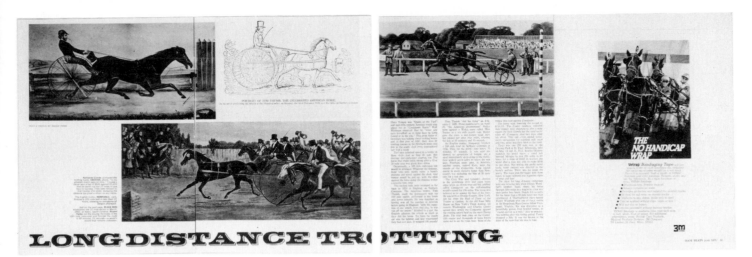

# LONG DISTANCE TROTTING

Jump the gutter and expand the concept of flow from page to page
by carrying the illustration, or other recognizable element, from
this spread overleaf to the succeeding one.

At the foot→ or at the head↓ of the page

Carry white space overleaf from this spread onto the next, aligning
the elements carefully, because only when it is precise and accurate
does this device become believable as a deliberately applied
technique.

Align pictures, both in outline shapes as well as within the images: here the horizon and the scale all relate smoothly to each other.

Run a frieze across the tops of a sequence of pages. It is a useful contrast to the rigidity of the text beneath.

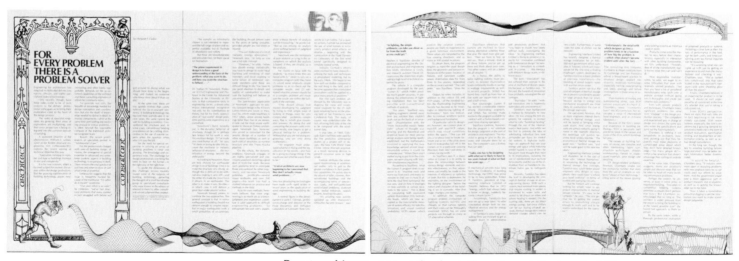

Run two friezes: one at the foot, the other at the head of the pages — for defining a story within the issue.

Do something special with the pictures which then becomes
characteristic of the spreads (here shadow boxes lit from below.)

Surround the entire page with a frame of some sort (here a notebook)
to give a personality and to tie several pages into coherent patterns.

Use a symbolic background to unify little pictures and yield
overall impact to an otherwise less-than-fascinating subject.

# Making the most of the scattered pages

## Interrelationship of all editorial spaces

Be aware that the scattered pages are parts of a whole, in spite of being separated by ads. It is therefore essential to think of them graphically as interrelated. Since they are widely scattered, the problem of giving them immediate recognition quality is very difficult, and the wisest course is to make them as standardized as possible. In areas of the magazine where advertisements vie with each other for attention, with flamboyance, color, and screaming typography, it is best to underplay the presentation of the editorial pages — since it is obviously impossible to outshout the ads. A contrast of "dull" editorial matter against "exciting" ad will be advantageous to both, especially to the editorial pages, since all these scattered pages will, cumulatively, stand out by this contrast, and will become more visible — and much more effective — than if they were designed to be more "noticeable."

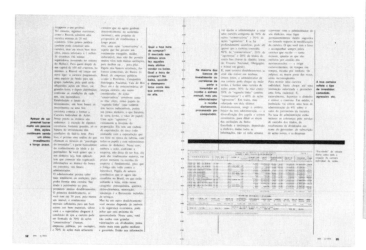

Since this Mexican medical magazine's policy is to give maximum editorial support to the ads by placing edit pages in the midst of the ads throughout, the editorial product is made visible by its special character: simplicity, restraint, plain type; specially tailored page arrangements are standard. Heads and logos are coordinated. Discipline is evident everywhere, including the feature story openers.

# Rhythmic repetition

Repeat elements on each page in the same position; where, for instance, an interview story carries over for several pages scattered among ads in the front of the magazine, a photograph of the personage centered precisely in the middle of each center column becomes a trademark of that entire story and ties it into a very strong whole. The photographs can — and should — vary, though they must all be of the same subject to achieve recognition quality. But this effect would be totally lost if the placement of the portrait varied from page to page (even if the pictures were identical). It is not the content of the picture so much as the shape and placement of the graphic element that does the work of tying pages together.

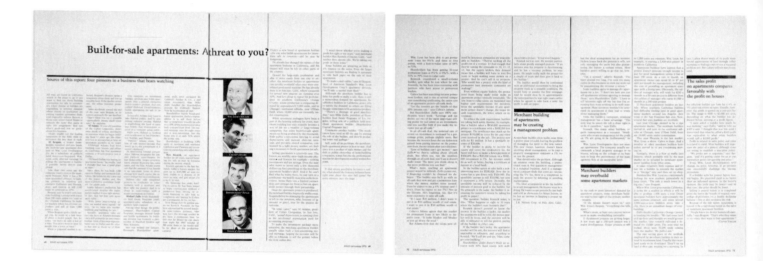

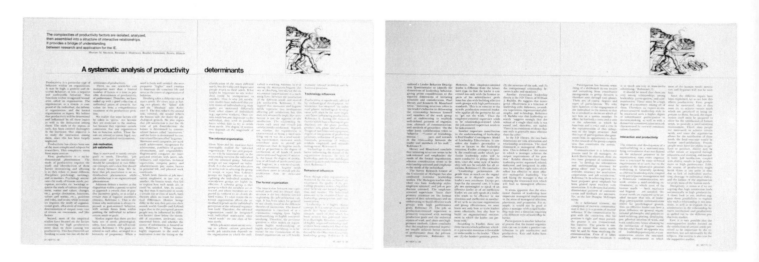

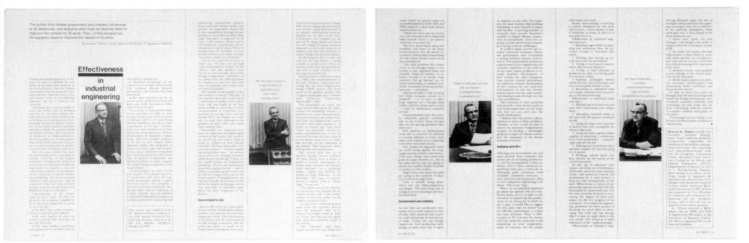

The most obvious form of repetition. (see text, opposite)

The rhythmically repeated element does not have to be photographic. This example shows that the same results can be achieved with plain vertical and horizontal lines. The counterpoint of the thin verticals against the heavy horizontals (which, in turn, are tied to the subheads) carries the eye from spread to spread and ties the whole story together.

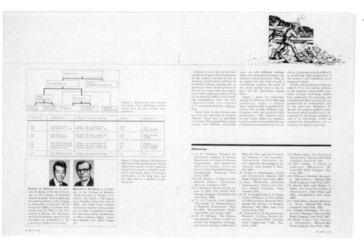

This is as visually dull as can be: no illustrations except the diagrams and a couple of mugshots on page 5. "Productivity" is the subject — so a man working is the obvious illustration. What makes this use of the obvious a little more interesting is that the potential 3D of the publication was used: the little wood chopper appears in the same position in all three spreads — and as you go through the story, his pile of chopped wood grows bigger.

# Graphic signals

Invent graphics and use them as signals. This is where "department slugs" come in: these are simply standing headings for regular departments of the magazine appropriate for filling scattered space in the front and back of the magazine. The names of such departments are usually set in type and then decorated with a greater or lesser degree of dressing up. As a general rule, they should be as simple and visible as possible, not only as contrast to the graphic irregularities of the surrounding ads, but also because their function is to be noticed — fast — by the reader who is skimming through these areas of the book. Most important, they must have a strong family resemblance: a file drawer whose contents have all been labeled by different hands in different inks on different color labels may be a most decorative file drawer, but you have a much harder time finding what you are looking for in it than in a dull old drawer where all the headings are on nice neat white stick-on labels, all in the same place on all the tan file folders.

## or:

Organize all the scattered editorial spaces within a box or frame that helps to define the material within as editorial matter. Repeat this frame in all such spaces and in each issue.

# Deep head margins

Leave an extra-heavy top margin on all scattered spaces, using that startling white wasted space to do the "I am editorial space" signaling for you.

*In this publication all stories start with a four-line abstract. It is placed in a space defined by horizontal hairline rules, and the byline is run beneath the lower rule. The abstracts, in their deep space, are useful visual signals — and easy for future retrieval. The format is echoed in all department slugs.*

The "departments" of this Brazilian engineering publication are headed by distinctive typographic labels (which match the headline typography in style and strength). But the feature stories also carry a numeral in the same position that a slug would be looked for. Result: the issue has a rhythmically occurring visual signal that both ties it together into a unified product, and imparts a special visual character to the product.

# 3

# THE PAGE: PATTERNS AND

# POTENTIALS

To achieve a unified editorial product, it is necessary to have a clearly defined and clearly patterned breakup of the space on all editorial pages. This rhythmic patterning (which is based on structural foundation of columns spaced within their surrounding margins) becomes a signal that helps distinguish editorial pages from advertising pages.

# Margins

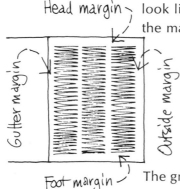

Head margin
Gutter margin
Outside margin
Foot margin

Possibly the most crucial element that can make the editorial spaces look like editorial spaces is the frame that surrounds the type — the margin around the "live-matter page."

The great majority of ads are not designed to parallel the edge of the space that has been purchased; they have instead an irregular outline with no visible means of support. Besides, each ad is designed to be as different from its neighbor as its creators can

This is the standard 7" x 10" ad area

The margin surrounding most ads is not defined

...because most ads have varied edges and their outline is irregular

devise it to be. But each editorial page has a major asset in the fact that it is one of a series, just one link in a long chain of events. It must take advantage of that asset by making sure that its outline is as regular as possible, in order to contrast with the irregular perimeter of the ads.

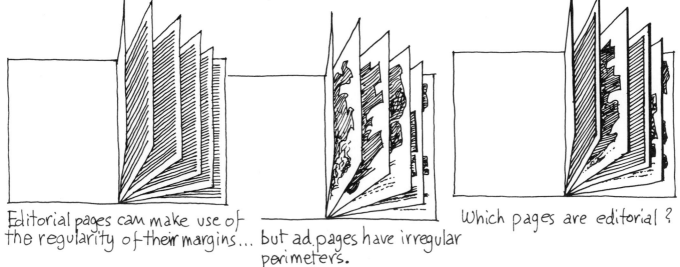

Editorial pages can make use of the regularity of their margins... but ad pages have irregular perimeters.

Which pages are editorial?

Most magazine pages are based on 8½″ × 11″ size, trimmed to save paper and most full-page ads are 7″ × 10″. Smaller ads are sold in shapes proportional to the column structure — as vertical thirds, two thirds, halves, etc. — and since an advertiser often has to use the same artwork in several competing magazines, it is wise not to tamper with ad-space sizes, since such tampering might well prevent him from buying our space. This might be unpopular with the publisher.

Some common sizes:

| | |
|---|---|
| 8½″ × 11″ | 9″ × 12″ |
| 8⅛″ × 10⅞″ | 9″ × 11″ |
| 8¼″ × 11¼″ | 8″ × 12″ |
| 8″ × 11″ | 10″ × 13″ |
| 8¼″ × 10⅞″ | 5½″ × 8½″ |
| 8³⁄₁₆″ × 10⅞″ | 7½″ × 9¼″ |

Standard ad shapes:

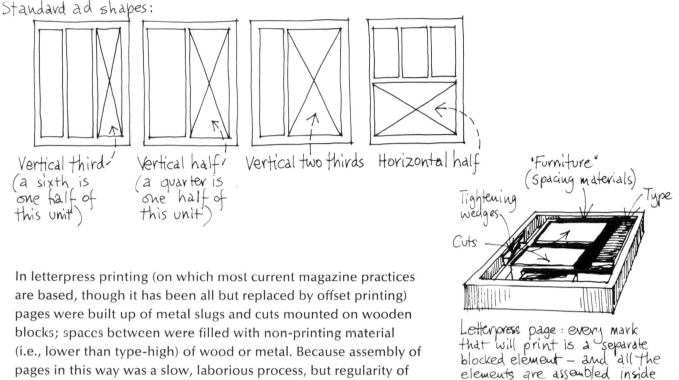

Vertical third (a sixth is one half of this unit)

Vertical half (a quarter is one half of this unit)

Vertical two thirds

Horizontal half

"Furniture" (spacing materials)

Tightening wedges

Type

Cuts

Letterpress page: every mark that will print is a separate blocked element — and all the elements are assembled inside a steel frame. Spacers are inserted between them as required, and the assembly is tightened by means of wedges on two sides

In letterpress printing (on which most current magazine practices are based, though it has been all but replaced by offset printing) pages were built up of metal slugs and cuts mounted on wooden blocks; spaces between were filled with non-printing material (i.e., lower than type-high) of wood or metal. Because assembly of pages in this way was a slow, laborious process, but regularity of pattern was advantageous to the printer, the basic 7″ × 10″ ad size was also used as the basic size for the editorial live-matter page. Coincidentally, this 7″ width works out very well when broken up into three columns or two columns of type:

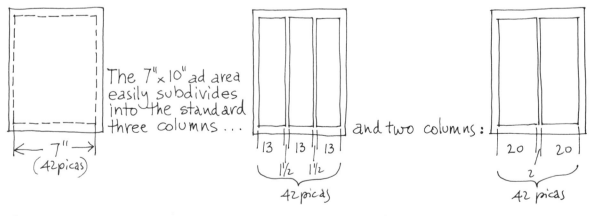

The 7″×10″ ad area easily subdivides into the standard three columns ...

7″ (42 picas)

13  13  13

1½  1½

42 picas

and two columns:

20  20

2

42 picas

These arrangements are very easy, efficient — and dull. In offset printing, however, pages are assembled by stripping pieces of film together, and the letterpress-metal-building-block restrictions can be ignored, with the result that the margin/column/space arrangement can be re-examined with new freedom. The freedom can make the live-matter page image varied and characteristic of a particular publication. Needless to say, the developing electronic page-assembly technologies promise even greater freedom of options, as well as speed.

Narrower than usual... wider....... higher than expected... deep sinkage

Released from the standard 7″ × 10″ straitjacket, we can handle the margins as we see fit: by broadening the live-matter page (reducing the margins) to gain an aura of fully packed usefulness; or by narrowing down the live-matter page (increasing the width of the margins) to create an impression of lavishness and conspicuous consumption. We can raise the live-matter page, giving the foot margin extra space for a more interesting folio-and-footline treatment (including, perhaps, the continued line). Or — as is most often done, since the payoff is most obvious — we can deepen the head margin and let the extra white space at the top of the page signal the "editorialness" of the space below. Obviously the decision about what to do with the space depends on the kinds of problems that have to be solved. In any case, the margins must not be allowed to lie fallow; they must be put to work.

# Columns

Live-matter page column structure has traditionally been the two-column and three-column breakup. There is nothing wrong with this arrangement — it works very well, people are used to it, and it is coordinated with the ad spaces that have been sold, so that it is an economical system. The traditional three-column makeup is also ideal for running-text stories in fast-closing news magazines, or for stories where there is neither the time nor a need for special layout treatment. But its very efficiency and overuse makes this format unexciting unless particularly clever graphic materials are added to play down the makeup pattern and play up the content. Alas, the majority of publications cannot draw upon the talent that goes into the design and illustration of three-column-makeup magazines such as the literary monthlies or *New York Magazine,* for instance. Instead, they must work within their areas of material and capabilities, and find their differentness through other means, one of which is different column arrangements.

There is no functional reason why a four-column page-arrangement should not be perfectly usable, even on a standard

8¼"-wide page. Even five columns are perfectly practicable. Nor is there any reason why all columns must be of equal width or why various column widths cannot be mixed, so that a number of different page arrangements can be achieved.

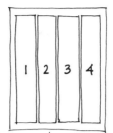

A four-column structure allows variations such as these

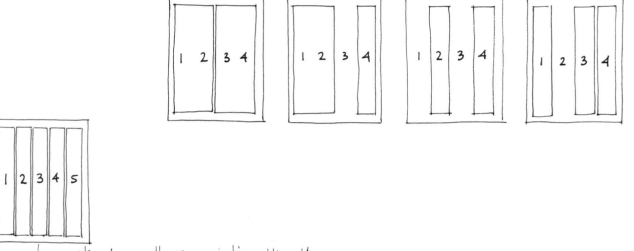

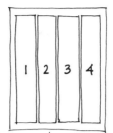

A five-column structure allows variations like these:

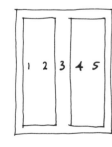

A group of miscellaneous page arrangements

The most interesting results are obtained from a layout sheet that combines a two-column with a three-column arrangement, adds a four-column arrangement, and has a five-column capability.

Here is an example of a publication's skeleton and, shown in miniature opposite, are a few of its inherent pattern possibilities.

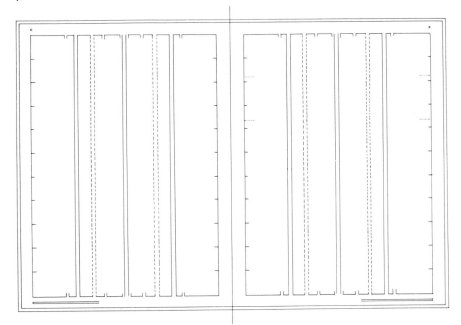

The advantages of having more than two allowable page arrangements (the two-column or three-column standards) are — obviously — the variety and scale that can automatically be built into the publication's design. Different degrees of scale, different type sizes (coordinated to the appropriate column width), and different illustration sizes become possible. This expanded variety of means of expression fosters more creative thinking in the journalistic sense, too — and everyone gains. The only extra cost involved is the initial cost of designing an appropriate system that will be most apt for the specific publication's material, manner, and methods of publishing.

Example: combining three-column and two-column makeup

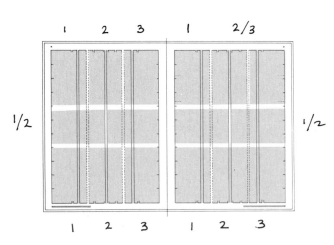

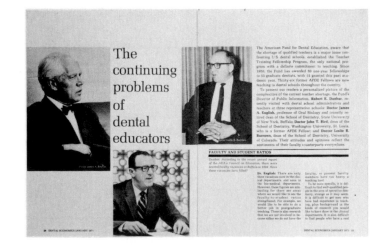

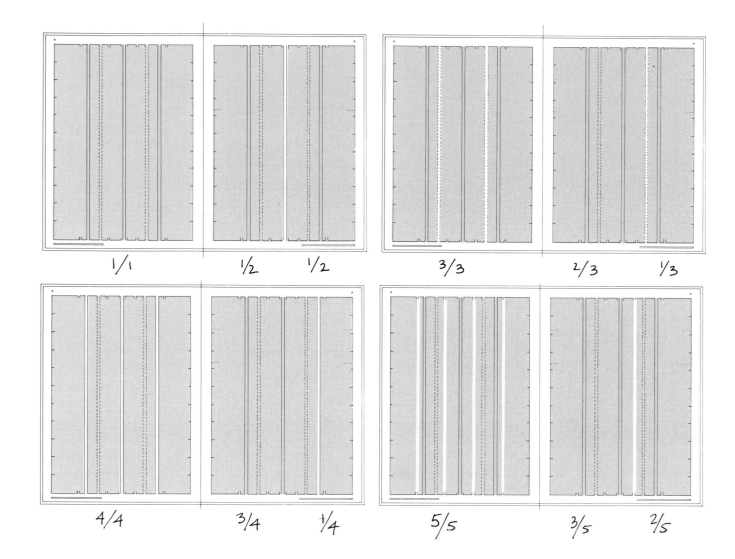

1/1    1/2    1/2    3/3    2/3    1/3

4/4    3/4    1/4    5/5    3/5    2/5

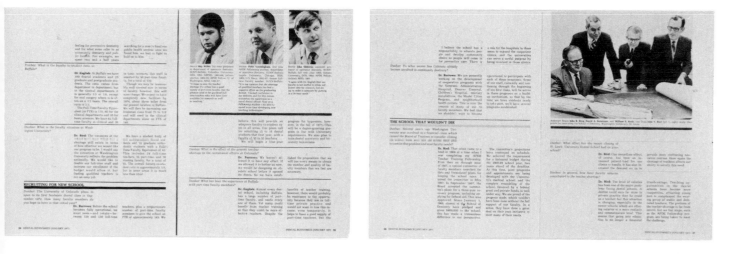

Example: two-column makeup

1    2    1    2

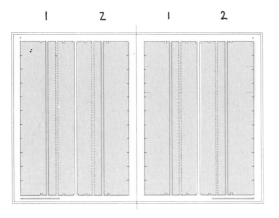

Example: five-column makeup based on a central axis

1  2  3  4  5    1  2  3  4  5

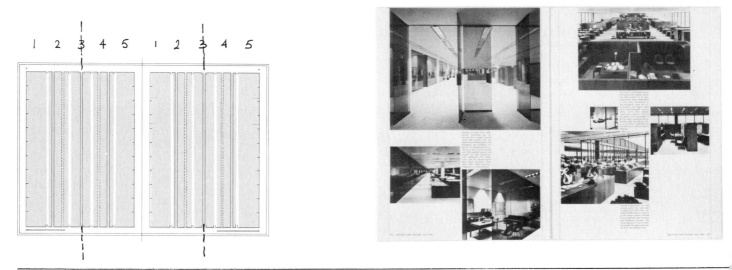

Example: four-column makeup (with departures from the rigid grid)

1    2    3    4    1    2    3    4

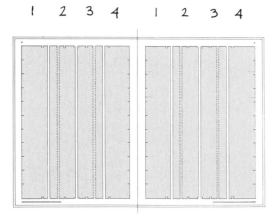

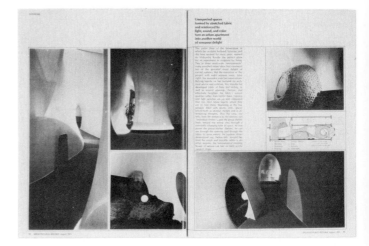

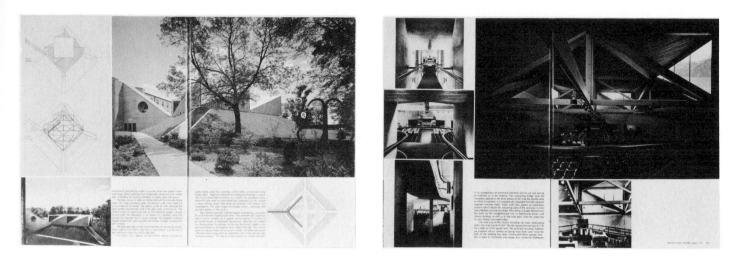

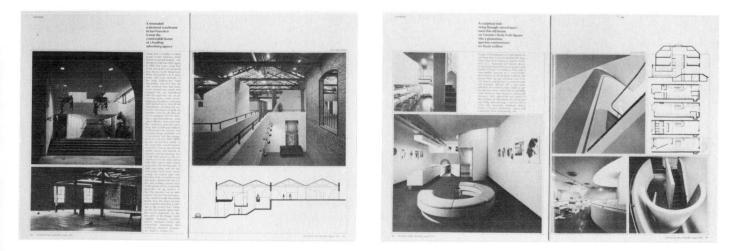

This page breakup scheme appears complicated but is, in fact, very simple: by making the columns narrower than the maximum, the saved space can be added either to the outside margins or to the gutter margins. This allows text columns to be placed on the page in two sets of positions: either close to the gutter or close to the outside. The variety of picture-sizing possibilities and page arrangement options this provides is nigh on endless. Try it.

A two-column per page scheme. The very narrow columns are intended to be left blank, invaded only by subheads, callouts, breakouts, quotes, mugshots, captions, by-lines, and whatnots. Pictures can also, of course, be sized to span the full half-page width.

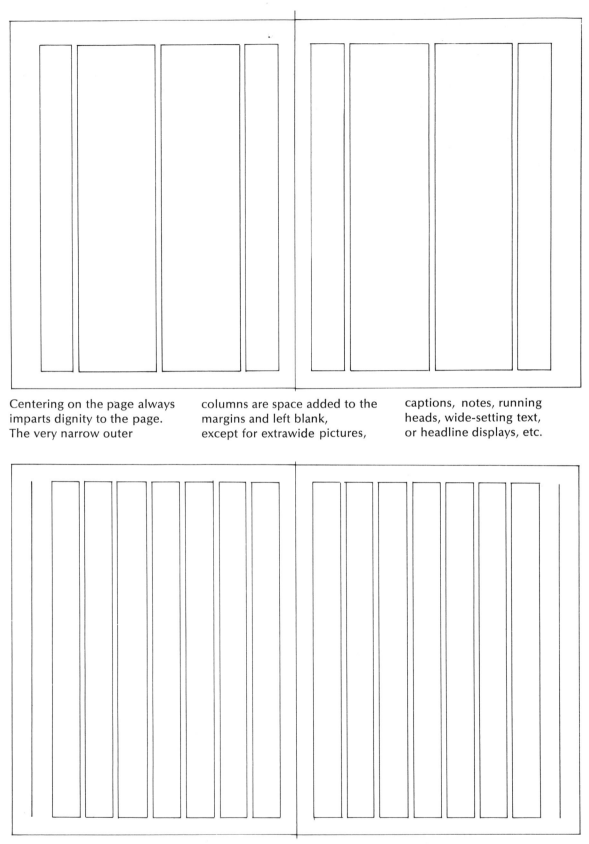

Centering on the page always imparts dignity to the page. The very narrow outer columns are space added to the margins and left blank, except for extrawide pictures, captions, notes, running heads, wide-setting text, or headline displays, etc.

This looks like a forest, but it is a highly flexible system allowing rich variety of page formats. A single column is useless by itself, but doubled-up or tripled-up and placed in the variety of positions that seven columns allow, a whole range of interesting page formats can be invented. Note the extra "half-bleed" position shown in the outside margins — that, too, becomes useful. Four examples based on this scheme are shown on the next two pages. . . .

Examples of the seven-column page shown in the diagram at the bottom of page 55:

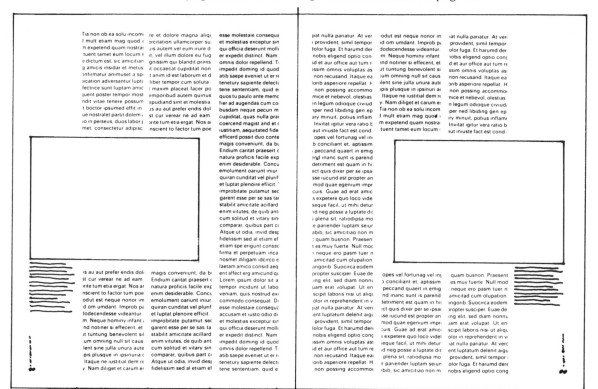

Concentrating the text toward the center of the spread leaves the outside margins free. The generous white space gives the pictures high visibility as they intrude into the text from the outside. Space for captions is found in the outermost column added to the normally open margin.

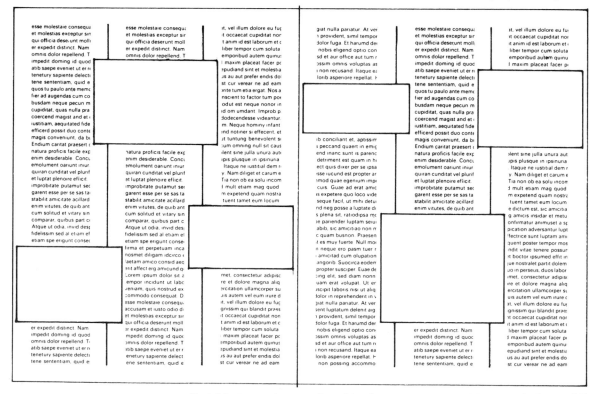

Outside text columns placed in the outermost positions, with the middle column centered between them. Vertical rules are run up the center of the space between; pictures "overlap" the rules. In spite of fullness, the pages have a pattern that overcomes the possible feeling of crowding.

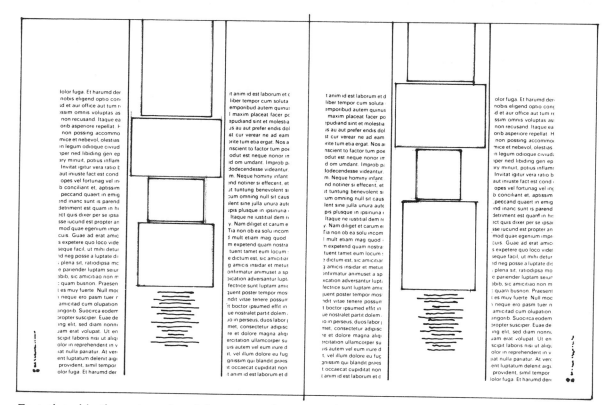

Text placed in the outer pairs of the seven-column page leaves the central three free for pictures and captions. Vertical rules bleeding at head of page help to define that leftover space and give the pages a crisp, planned, precision.

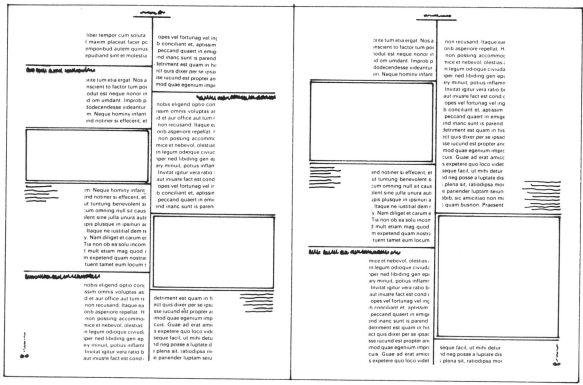

The text (set at the normal double-column width) is placed alongside the vertical rule that carries a bar above, on top of which the running head is placed. Headlines and pictures extend out into the wide spaces, but are tied to the central axis by horizontal "branch" lines.

# The grid

It is possible to subdivide the page into horizontal modules of predetermined size in the same way as one can split the page into vertical ones — i.e., columns. The most efficient way to do so is to split the column into horizontal slivers whose height corresponds to a given number of lines of type (like this example, which is based on four lines of type per rectangle with a blank line in between).

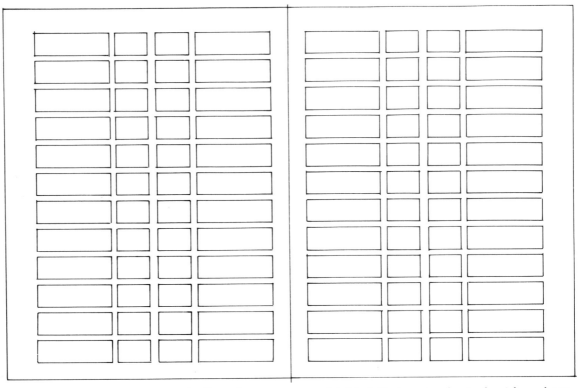

At first glance one would think that such a logical grid ought to make life easier for all concerned: the writer, who can better calculate how many lines to write more creatively; the designer, who can correlate the sizes of illustrations with the text more accurately; the stripper, who can assemble the film for the pages more meticulously; the editor, who can estimate space allocation more precisely . . . alas, this is a misleading hope. Things never seem to fit, unless they be forced into the mold, so much so that what started out as a tool of great potential quickly turns into a straitjacket.

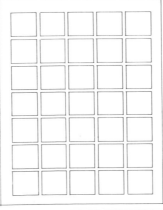

So, in spite of the fact that patterning, repetition, and regularity throughout the issue are crucially important to effective magazine making, only in special situations can the rigidities imposed by grids make sense in practical day-to-day working terms.

# Working with the page

White space

This is the most misused, misunderstood, abused material on the page. White space is hard to become aware of. It is emphatically NOT the random nothing-area that is *left over* after the "important" stuff has been imposed on the page. Nor is it the no-man's land between lines in the head, between the head and the blurb, or the other bits of flotsam and jetsam that float around the ill-designed page.

Genuine white space is an active participant in the design of the page (i.e., functional design — that works to get ideas off the page into the reader's mind). It is not just negative background, but is a positive attribute of the page. Like the margins, which are not merely edges of blank paper surrounding the live-matter area but also work as patterned signals throughout the publication, all the other areas of the page that are not covered with ink should have a utilitarian purpose. The ideal is analogous to the yin and yang principle, where the black cannot exist without the white.

Being aware of white space as a potential tool facilitates using it. The white space is used most effectively — most noticeably — if it has a clearly defined geometric shape. When its edges have been demarcated in some obviously intended way, then the reader perceives that it is supposed to be that way, and no longer has the uneasy feeling that perhaps the printer has left out a picture.

A clear area of white space can be as dramatic as a picture (especially if the picture is mediocre, as many often are). It gives the eye a place to rest. It can be a foil to the text: an "empty" contrast to the "full" areas that thereby makes the full areas appear even fuller. It can help to organize the material on the page. It can tie successive pages together by repetition of identifiable areas. White space, if used well, is the cheapest addition to the publication's roster of weapons. Here is a typical example:

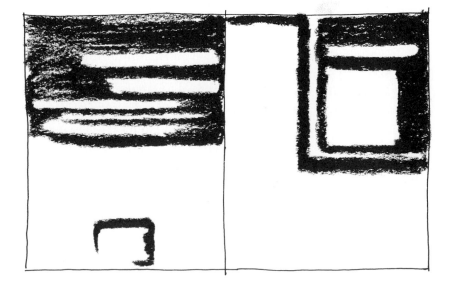

This is a perfectly acceptable layout, with lots of white space in it. But it has little personality or drama. Why? Because it matters little how many square inches of blank paper there are — what matters is the *shape* of the white space and where it appears on the page. In the case above, the square inches of space have been split up and wedged between the various elements in the top half of the spread, thereby loosening and disintegrating the fabric. The grey areas in this drawing show the enormous expanses of white space available, yet how cut up it is. It is not an ocean, it is a group of interconnected fjords — none of which counts for very much. Here is the same spread, with the same material, rearranged to make maximum use of the potential inherent in white space. First, the text has been tightened into a clearly defined rectangle and the boxed matter has been incorporated within it. Second, the display matter (head, blurb, byline) has been stretched across both pages, to parallel the horizontality of the six-column text beneath.

The space above the text area can be relied upon to dominate the top half of the spread, because it is so large; the headline and blurb are placed at the TOP of the space — on its outermost

edges — to help define its extent and increase its apparent size. Besides, placing the headline way up there makes it quite obvious that we mean the white space to be there, it is not an error, we are proud of that wonderful white space and want it to be seen — and the presentation is the better for it.

Finally, the little whimper of an initial letter in the "before" version has been enlarged into a bang that does something more than just attract the eye to the starting point of the text.

Extra cost of the improved presentation? None, besides the effort of recognizing white space and using it properly.

## Concentration of elements

To help speedy recognition of what the page contains, it is necessary to organize the various elements into subgroups as clearly as possible. The layout must communicate a sense of order and conciseness. It must appear to have been planned in a coherent, forthright way. The material on the page should be broken up into bite-size chunks, which are quickly noticed and absorbed, and are inviting to the eye. (People don't mind reading small pieces of copy: the shorter, the more irresistible.) The reasoning behind this principle is the same as that which makes a bowl of regular shredded wheat hard to plough through, whereas the same amount of the bite-size shredded wheat is easily coped with.

Having decided what major elements in a story need to be stressed, pull everything related to each of these points into proximity with that point, since closeness implies relationship. Separate unrelated elements from each other by squeezing out the excess space from within each subgroup and adding it to the space around the subgroup — so that the closeness becomes closer still and the separateness becomes more separated by moats of white space.

Wherever possible, pull subsidiary elements into the body of each of the subgroups, so that odds and ends, such as bylines

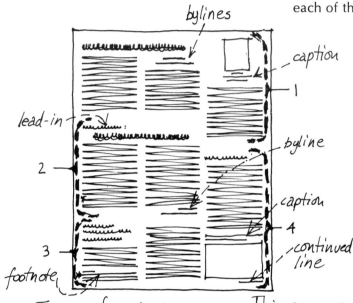

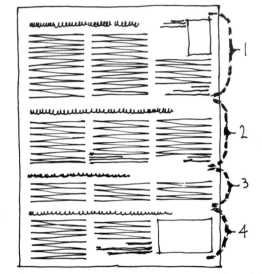

There are four short pieces on this typically gray page.
PLUS: two pictures, bylines, captions, lead-ins, footnotes, continued lines to add to the confusion

This arrangement contains the same material, but it squeezes each unit into a self-contained rectangular space. All the odds and ends floating around have been

captured and held within the rectangular spaces. The page is no less gray, but it is much simpler to analyze at a glance. Thus — hopefully — much more "attractive" to read.

and continued lines, do not invade what should remain clear, undisturbed white space. This procedure gives rise to a peculiar problem involving perception: editors, close to their product, think in terms of the groupings all the time. Aware of each group's frame of white space, they unconcernedly drop a continued line in the middle of that space, reasoning that a continued line is a relatively minor element, and the white space is still doing its work. But the reader does not know at first glance (which is crucially important) which of the various elements is primary in importance. If the precious white space frame is interrupted in any way, it no longer functions as a frame; its character is altered by the intrusion and the clear moat effect is ruined. That is why it is important to eliminate as many visual nuisances as possible (by editing them out, if feasible, or at least sinking them into the fabric of the type areas).

There are two basic approaches to page design, from which all the rich variations grow: the flow-through, and the deliberate.

## Flow-through page makeup

In this way of thinking, the copy flows through as it comes, starting at the top left-hand corner of the page and ending diagonally opposite. Pictures or illustrations are dropped in as they, too, come. Usually they are coordinated with the text as single-column or two-column cuts falling somewhere near where their subject is being discussed in the text. They are placed arbitrarily on the page, to relieve it of its three-column tedium (usually in a corner, which is the least likely place for a picture to "break up" the page: if you want to break something up, you do it in the middle, not at an edge . . . but never mind, breaking up a page by inserting a picture — any picture — should not be done often, anyway, so it is not wise to spend too much effort on it). Most of the regrettable publication "design" can trace its ancestry back to this newspaper-reduced-to-magazine-size approach.

The philosophy behind flow-through makeup is very simple: there are X pages to fill with material. There are Y column-inches of text to be shoehorned onto those pages and, by damn, we won't cut a line of copy if we can avoid it. After all, the reader is so fascinated by our stuff (aren't we the "Bible of Our Industry"?) that we don't need to make the stuff visually appealing, journalistically organized, or even simple to take in or remember. All we have to do is to slap it down as it comes. The reader is intelligent (our readership surveys say he is in the highest income bracket and has 2.7 children and lives in a suburb and had 4.2 years of college) and has been loyally reading us this way for 60 years, so why rock the boat?

This sort of thinking conduces to the following sort of (slightly exaggerated) disaster:

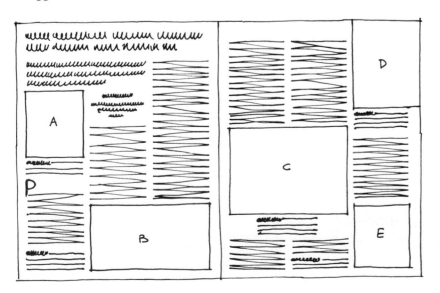

Typical three-column makeup with copy running through, it
includes pictorial elements inserted for "variety" — to make the
layout more "interesting looking." The reader's eye is asked to travel
an unbelievably complicated route through that body copy. Below,
the outline shows the perimeter of the text areas, and the heavy
arrows show the actual reading matter to plough through;
the dotted arrows show the motion the eye must make to jump
from the end of one text area to the start of the succeeding one. The
four obvious confusion points are indicated by question marks.

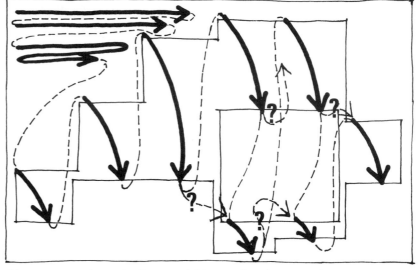

Pictures, captions, byline, and biographical material are all placed
strategically to be as uncrossable a set of hurdles as possible.

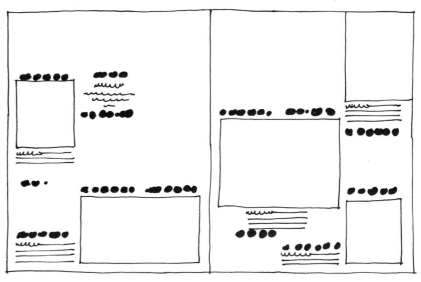

This effect would be laudable, in an exercise to stimulate the eye
muscles. But the objective is actually speedy, effective
communication, and every time the eye encounters a hurdle,
the flow is interrupted. Since such interruptions also impede thought
processes, obstacles are out of place in page design.
Here is an alternate arrangement of the same material, accommodat-
ing the same illustrations, sized the same, with the same number
of text lines. This layout would not win an award for beauty or

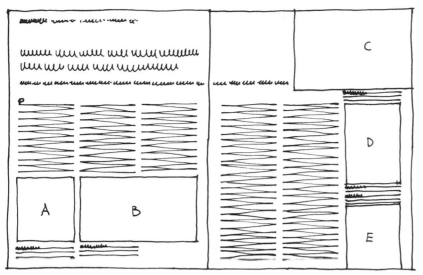

originality, but it is clearer to follow than the first one. The text shape is much simpler. The pictures have been pulled from the stream of type and grouped around the perimeter of the page. The captions have been moved from the text area to the picture areas, where they belong.

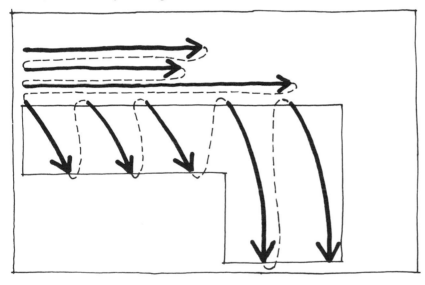

The preceding example of "lazy man's flow-through page makeup" shows little thinking. It is mechanical. ( The "after" version is a slight improvement.) Lest you consider flow-through page makeup *verboten*, however, on the next page is an example where it works very well, because it is used to communicate a flow-through subject. In this translation of an audible illustrated lecture into the inaudible medium of print, the words are interspersed with related pictures, the pictures are grouped according to relationships of meaning, and the story flows from page to page in logical sequence. The entire presentation (half of which is shown here) is held together by the black background, which acts as both binding agent and conveyor of darkened-lecture-hall atmosphere.

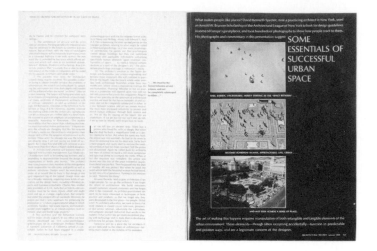

Example: flow-through page makeup that is based on following the trend of the storyline, expressing it through grouping and placement on the page. There is a logical progression from item to item, in the sequence desired by the editors.

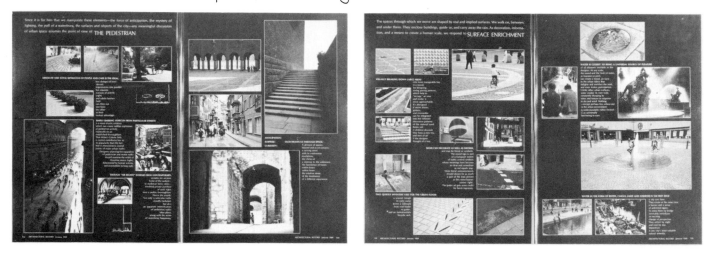

see detail opposite

Since it is for him that we manipulate these elements—the force of anticipation, the mystery of lighting, the pull of a waterfront, the surfaces and objects of the city—any meaningful discussion of urban space assumes the point of view of **THE PEDESTRIAN**

**ABSOLUTE AND TOTAL SEPARATION OF PEOPLE AND CARS IS THE IDEAL,** but changes of level (above), organization into parallel but separate avenues of activity (right) and subtle barriers (left) can filter out one from the other to their mutual advantage.

**SIMPLY BARRING VEHICLES FROM PARTICULAR STREETS** is a more drastic solution which can create sudden explosions of pedestrian activity, especially on an established thoroughfare. That Milan's Galeria (left) is roofed contributes less to its popularity than the fact that it interconnects several points of major urban traffic.

Designers planning the separation of pedestrian and motor traffic should examine the width of Venetian streets (right), determined by human activity, not automobile turning radii.

**THOUGH "AIR RIGHTS" SCHEMES SEEM CONTEMPORARY,** arcades are ancient. Some of the earliest— in medieval Swiss cities— involved private purchase of such rights over a public thoroughfare. Hence the arcade. Not only is vehicular traffic visually excluded, but also an apparent intensification of pedestrian traffic takes place, along with the sense of something happening.

## Deliberate page makeup

This kind of page makeup starts from the premise that each story and/or each story's component parts require handling as a fresh problem demanding journalistic analysis and a visual interpretation of that analysis. Each story is a carefully thought through unit of the magazine, handled as best suits its size, content, and importance, and the space available. Obviously this approach entails more work than the flow-through method, but it results in a better (whatever that may mean) magazine. This strong recommendation must not be interpreted to imply that cut-and-dried layouts are never to be used and that three-column makeup is FORBIDDEN. Such layout schemes should be used where they make sense, but occasionally more expressive schemes are called for.

The most important device in planning this sort of story presentation — and the most useful ploy in working it.out — is the playing off of one element in the story against another. This contrasting device does two useful things: first, it creates visual interest; second, it helps clarify the story, and enables the reader to see its component parts, so he can decide the sequence as well as the detail in which he is going to read it.

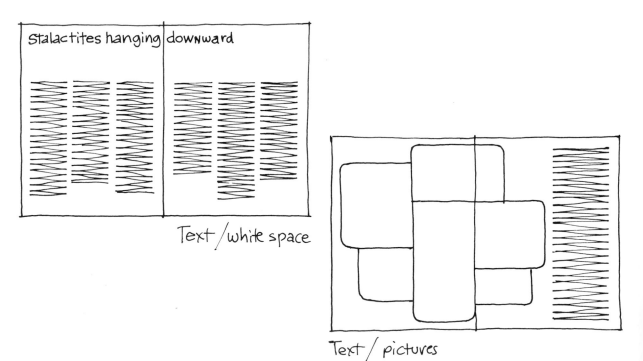

Text / white space

Text / pictures

These examples are some drops in the bucket of possibilities for contrast. Whatever arrangement is used, one criterion must remain constant: that of *simplicity*. Unless the design is simple in both concept and execution, it will not be noticed. The greater the complexity, the easier it becomes for the confused reader to miss the point the editor is driving at. If the technique of contrast is to be used, it must be applied with the obvious impact of a sledgehammer, or it will be missed.

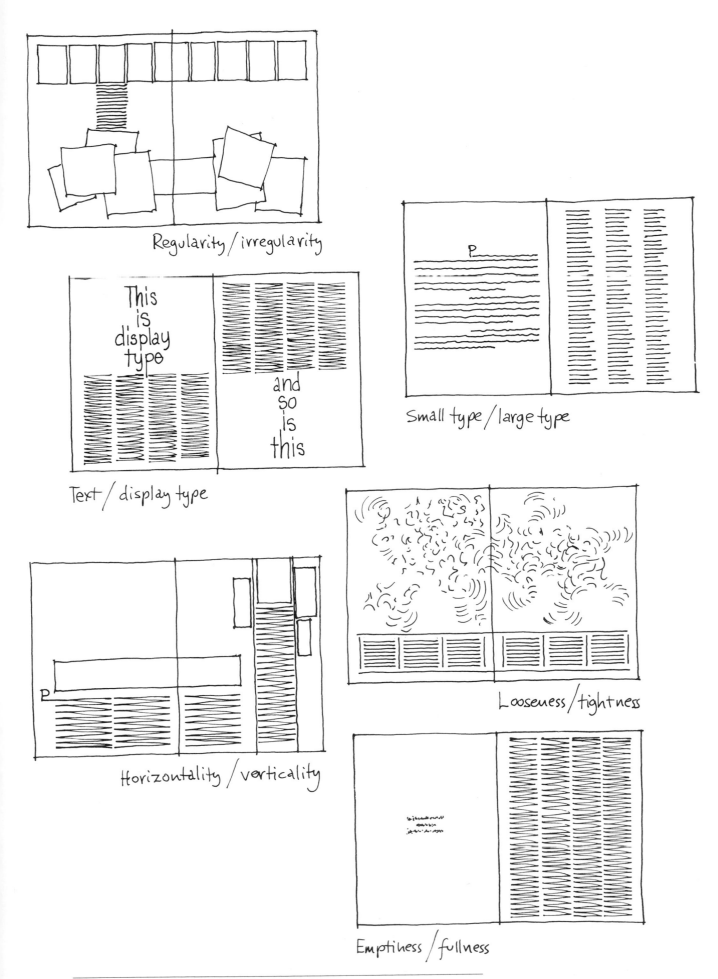

Regularity / irregularity

Text / display type

This
is
display
type

and
so
is
this

Small type / large type

Horizontality / verticality

Looseness / tightness

Emptiness / fullness

# Camouflaging

It is often impossible to organize material on a page in an orderly arrangement. For example, the individual elements might be pieces of text of different lengths (that must, logically, remain so); or they might consist of diverse images in various graphic techniques, forcing the designer to run a collection of drawings, diagrams, and photos, all meriting equal size and attention, yet unsympathetic in style to each other.

Such situations demand ingenuity, plus a bit of arbitrary patterning. The arbitrary pattern must be devised (and courageously used) so that it becomes the dominant visible element on the page, with the material slotted into it becoming less noticeable. Naturally, the pattern must harmoniously accommodate the largest as well as the smallest unit, and do it so subtly that they obviously "belong." That is where the ingenuity comes into play.

A very simple example: six pieces of copy and headlines, all of unequal length. Without a masking structure, they would look like this on the spread:

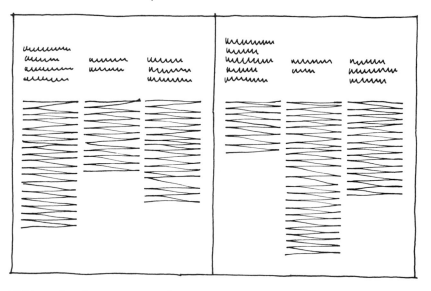

With a simple structure of vertical rules (long enough to accommodate the longest unit, plus a bit over) the unequal pieces of copy

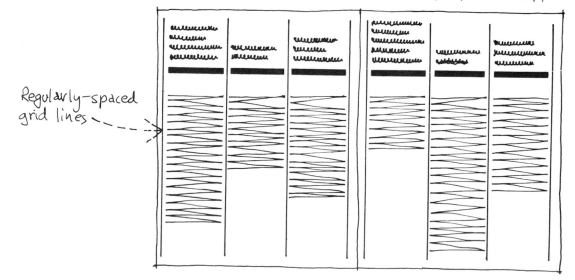

Regularly-spaced grid lines

blend into an all-encompassing whole, which creates the visual impact. The unequal hunks themselves disappear. The inequality has been masked.

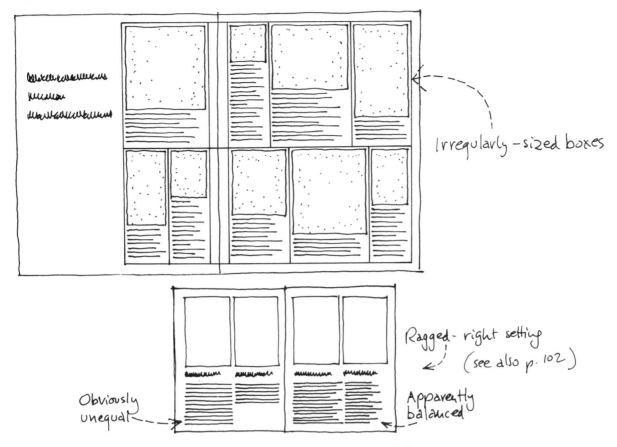

Irregularly – sized boxes

Ragged- right setting
(see also p. 102)

Obviously unequal

Apparently balanced

A technique that is much more difficult to apply successfully, but less hackneyed than the framing camouflage, is the focal-point trick. It exploits the fact that when the eye is drawn toward an interesting element, it tends to ignore the surroundings. So, gigantic initials set in the text (perhaps two to a page), or greatly out-of-scale numerals, or any graphic spot that is both unexpected and visually decorative or symbolic can, if startling enough, effectively mask the shortcomings around it.

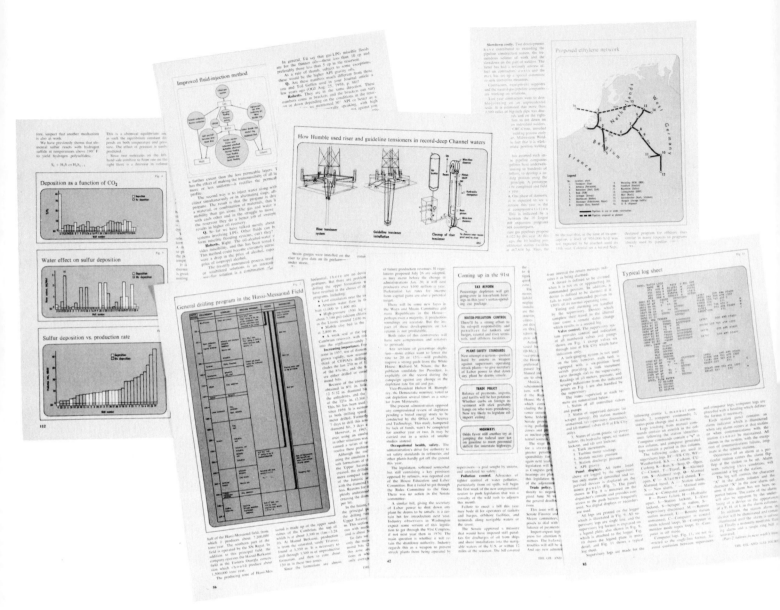

Here is an example of the camouflage principle applied in strictly graphic terms. A major weekly newsmagazine in a specialized field runs a number of different kinds of illustrations: maps, charts, diagrams, photos, technical drawings, etc., all in black and white or with color. Being a weekly, it requires a large art staff to produce this artwork. Despite the basic house style to which all artwork must conform, the variety of subject matter as well as of illustrative methods and illustrators used to fragment the image of the publication. To overcome this problem without creating restrictions that would impose a hardship on personnel, a set of frames was devised into which each piece of artwork is fitted. The frames camouflaged the differences between the various pieces of art. The frames are standardized, but the contents decidedly individual. The frames are modular, sized in increments of columns in width, and in increments of several text-lines in height (see drawing); they also include space for all the required information, such as heading, source, figure number, copyright line. The

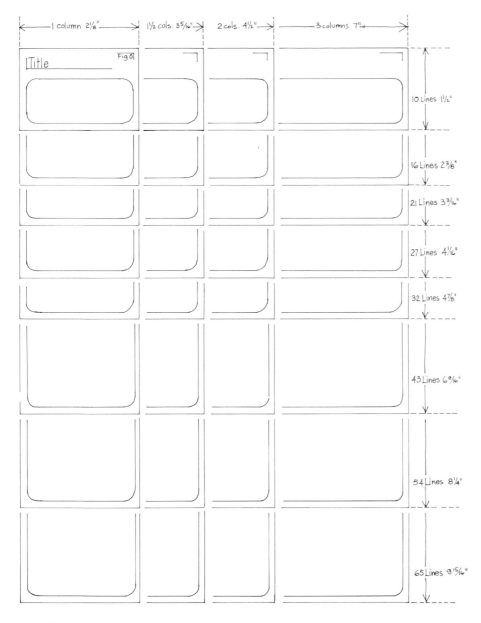

In the figure, the following labels appear:

- 1 column 2⅛"
- 1½ cols. 3⁵⁄₁₆"
- 2 cols. 4½"
- 3 columns 7"
- [Title] Fig 0]
- 10 Lines 1½"
- 16 Lines 2⅜"
- 21 Lines 3³⁄₁₆"
- 27 Lines 4¹⁄₁₆"
- 32 Lines 4⅞"
- 43 Lines 6⁹⁄₁₆"
- 54 Lines 8¼"
- 65 Lines 9¹⁵⁄₁₆"

publication has used the system for several years — proving its effectiveness — and it is a major factor in creating the publication's own recognizable character.

## Predetermined character

This area is fraught with danger of the sort that is usually recognized only when the issue is off press and the office copies have arrived. Suddenly the idea that seemed so bright and original is seen for the cliche it is. How come? Probably because the detail handling of the graphics was not done with the requisite skill or finesse. An old trick must be extremely well done if you are to be forgiven for doing it at all.

On the other hand, it is important to remember there is nothing new under the sun; someone, somewhere, has had the same idea, and carried it out more or less successfully. Hence, the originality of an idea is generally less important than its aptness to its journalistic purpose and the excellence of its realization.

It's not what you do, but how and when you do it, that matter.

Here are several of the most often-used clichés, which might prove useful as idea starters.

## Oldness

Use sepia-colored duotones (black and brown) to make photographs look like faded 19th century tintypes. Imperfections, such as dark spots, heighten verisimilitude. Black-and-process yellow do not work very well; the result is a little too greenish. If process colors must be used, think in terms of black-and-red duotones printed over a screen of process yellow.

Rely on full four-color separations of black-and-white original photos to make the reproductions look rich and painting-like, especially if the original photos are not plain black, but have a color tint, such as sepia.

Crop the photos into peculiar shapes, such as ovals or cartouches.

Put photos in old-fashion "frames" — real ones or specially designed ones.

Use mezzotints or horizontal line-screen renditions in lieu of normal halftones.

Make the whole page brownish with ink for oldness; use mauves and pinks for Victorian flavor.

Make fake burned edges (or coffee-stains) on the page.

Employ old-fashioned typefaces, of course. Demure — or circusy.

## Engineeringness

Strive for crisp layout: alignment of edges of elements, lots of ruled lines, possibly even a box around each page.

Simulate blueprints: run the whole page in blueprint blue with all linework "dropped out" in white; or use a fake Ozalid process with a mottled background and the stripped-in linework run in solid dark blue.

Use Leroy or other mechanical stencil lettering, simulating the kind seen on drawings.

Place the title block in the lower right-hand corner of the page, as on a drawing.

Set the headlines in solid capitals (since most engineering lettering is done in all caps).

Use graph-paper backgrounds in color.

## Nostalgia (album style)

Try a full-page bleed background simulating album paper (in black ink or, better, in color). Most convincing is a halftone reproduction run in black or colored ink, showing the mottled texture of typical album paper.

Show uncropped snapshots (with white border frames). The subjects must be crudely photographed: wherever people are shown, they must be *in front of* a significant background (as most snapshots show); some person must be moving, cut off at the knees, etc.

Have pictures overlapping at odd angles.

Display pictures with corner holders.

Incorporate handwritten annotations, including arrows, dates, some questions or uncertainties.

---

## Memorandums

Use background paper tinting of some sort (paler than that suggested for the album pages); lined notepaper, perhaps, or graph paper.

Specify typewriter type (which can, of course, be set as type by the printer). If the illusion of a memorandum is to be successful, the type must be large enough to appear to be true typewriter type, and 10 point is the smallest. It is equally important to restrict *all* type in the "memo" to typewriter type — which entails such presentation problems as the difficulty of making large headlines.

Incorporate handwritten annotations or scribbles or underscores or crossing out.

Use scribbled diagrams roughly drawn.

---

## Business

Use ticker-tape type.

Utilize preprinted forms from stationery stores and/or rubber stamps.

Ornament with signatures and notarial seals of various kinds.

Employ punchcard images (holes, shapes, stacked cards, etc.)

Specify computer type.

Use stock market tables as background mood-creator.

---

## Unexpected realism

Use children's ABC blocks (with pictures pasted on, perhaps).

Include photographs of a package with string and address label.

Use pictures of pictures in color, with the shadows they make on the background paper.

Use airline tags  with destinations on them; labels of all sorts.

Use models constructed of appropriately symbolic materials.

John Martinez

# Unusual devices

If there is enough lead time and advance planning, there is no need for even the most budget-conscious publication to rule out the flamboyance of an unexpected trick or two. Production people enjoy solving peculiar problems and love to be asked for advice (it gives them a chance to show off their expertise, and it is a change of pace for them, too). It is wise, however, to consult them more than two days before closing time.

Remember that any gimmick will probably have to be printed as a separate "form" and bound into the book as an "insert." The number of positions where this can be done is limited, because it must be done between "signatures" (i.e., between the normal groups of 8-page or 16-page folders on which the run of the book is printed, folded, and bound). Therefore, the rest of the editorial pages have to be planned around the position of the intended insert.

Gatefold (single foldout)

Half-page foldout

Accordion foldout

Double foldout

Full vertical booklet

Stepped partial pages

Small stitched booklet

Full horizontal booklet

## Gatefolds

The simplest and commonest device is a single-page foldout (also known as "gatefold"), either left-hand or right-hand. Such a foldout has to be printed as a separate six-page form, and requires special folding equipment before being inserted into the book. (Note that the pages that fold must be narrower than the trimmed width of the entire publication, so that the fold itself will not be cut off when the issues are trimmed after binding.) Because this procedure is comparatively expensive, a gatefold should be used only in editorial situations warranting that expense, and where the impact of the extra width can be most advantageously used. Generally, gatefolds are indicated for panoramic photographs spanning all three pages, or for tabular material requiring such special width. It is foolish to use a gatefold for normal-sized, normal-shaped, or normal-looking editorial matter.

A double foldout is a very rare explosion of attention-requiring material. The half-page foldout's advantage is that of surprise: when the half page is lifted up, the relation of the image on the half page and the image that had been covered comes off as a one-two punch. It is an ideal before-and-after visualizer.

The vertical gatefold, a most unusual device, is very expensive because of the die cutting required. Thus, if a skyscraper must be shown, run it sideways on the page (across the gutter) instead of upward.

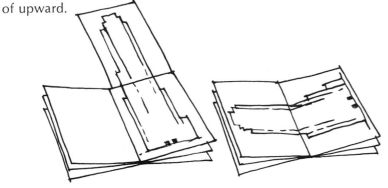

Often a special story warrants using special paper. If planned for in advance, the cost may not be prohibitive. Such inserts are normally handled as in four- or eight-page signatures (always starting with a right-hand page and ending with a left-hand page). The stock may be colored; textured; or plain, but heavier-weight white. Colored stock is especially useful as a signal for a series of special stories running in successive issues.

Colored stock has an extra advantage in that printing in a second color on a colored paper can produce unexpectedly rich effects. Some stocks are even designed to give the effect of four-color process printing when a specific ink color is used on it. The printer becomes the editor's best friend in planning and achieving such effects.

Anything is feasible (given money, time, imagination, and a desire to experiment):

Metallic inserts for added sparkle, or for a literal interpretation of the Definitive Treatise on the Latest State of the Art in Aluminum or Steel.
Transparent inserts of plastic stock, used to show, in overlay form, the stages that make up a technical process, a petroleum cracking plant, or the insides of a frog.
Die-cut holes for a looking-through-the-keyhole effect.
Perforations in the paper for purposes other than tearing out coupons.
Tip-ins, or glued-on pieces of something on the page; unless the material is printed, the post office may have objections to using actual samples, so it is wise to check with them first before investing money and planning time.

# 4
# TYPE—
# THE PUBLICATION'S
# FABRIC

Futura Light (I) when combining text and display faces, first decide whether you are seeking harmony or contrast. Then consider size, style, weight or color, white space within and around the type area, relative position of text and display type, and relationship to other graphic elements, including

Univers Light #685 (M) when combining text and display faces, first decide whether you are seeking harmony or contrast. Then consider size, style, weight or color, white space within and around the type area, relative position of text and display type, and relation-

Cairo Light (I) when combining text and display faces, first decide whether you are seeking harmony or contrast. Then consider size, style, weight or color, white space within and around the type area, relative position of text and display type, and

*Garamond Italic (I) when combining text and display faces, first decide whether you are seeking harmony or contrast. Then consider size, style, weight or color, white space within and around the type area, relative position of text and display type, and relationship to other graphic elements,*

*Baskerville Italic (I) when combining text and display faces, first decide whether you are seeking harmony or contrast. Then consider size, style, weight or color, white space within and around the type area, relative position of text and display type, and relationship to*

Baskerville (I) when combining text and display faces, first decide whether you are seeking harmony or contrast. Then consider size, style, weight or color, white space within and around the type area, relative position of text and display type, and relationship to other graphic ele-

Granjon (Li) when combining text and display faces, first decide whether you are seeking harmony or contrast. Then consider size, style, weight or color, white space within and around the type area, relative position of text and display type, and relationship to other graphic elements, in-

Garamond (I) when combining text and display faces, first decide whether you are seeking harmony or contrast. Then consider size, style, weight or color, white space within and around the type area, relative position of text and display type, and relationship to other graphic elements,

*Optima Italic (Li) when combining text and display faces, first decide whether you are seeking harmony or contrast. Then consider size, style, weight or color, white space within and around the type area, relative position of text and display type, and*

Optima (Li) when combining text and display faces, first decide whether you are seeking harmony or contrast. Then consider size, style, weight or color, white space within and around the type area, relative position of text

Melior (Li) when combining text and display faces, first decide whether you are seeking harmony or contrast. Then consider size, style, weight or color, white space within and around the type area, relative position of text and display type,

*Bodoni Book Italic (I) when combining text and display faces, first decide whether you are seeking harmony or contrast. Then consider size, style, weight or color, white space within and around the type area, relative position of text and display type, and relationship to other graphic*

Bodoni Book (I) when combining text and display faces, first decide whether you are seeking harmony or contrast. Then consider size, style, weight or color, white space within and around the type area, relative position of text and display type, and relationship to other graphic

Bookface (I) when combining text and display faces, first decide whether you are seeking harmony or contrast. Then consider size, style, weight or color, white space within and around the type area, relative position of text and display type, and relationship to other

Palatino (Li) when combining text and display faces, first decide whether you are seeking harmony or contrast. Then consider size, style, weight or color, white space within and around the type area, relative position of text and display type, and relationship to other

*Bookface Italic (I) when combining text and display faces, first decide whether you are seeking harmony or contrast. Then consider size, style, weight or color, white space within and around the type area, relative position of text and display type, and relation-*

News Gothic (I) when combining text and display faces, first decide whether you are seeking harmony or contrast. Then consider size, style, weight or color, white space within and around the type area, relative position of text and display type, and relationship to

I = Intertype   Li = Linotype   M = Monotype

Reprinted from *Typographic i* © and published by the International Typographic Composition Association, Inc.

Century Expanded (I) when combining text and display faces, first decide whether you are seeking harmony or contrast. Then consider size, style, weight or color, white space within and around the type area, relative position of text and

*Times Roman Italic (Li) when combining text and display faces, first decide whether you are seeking harmony or contrast. Then consider size, style, weight or color, white space within and around the type area, relative position of text and display type, and relation-*

Times Roman (Li) when combining text and display faces, first decide whether you are seeking harmony or contrast. Then consider size, style, weight or color, white space within and around the type area, relative position of text and display type, and relation-

Univers Medium #689 (M) when combining text and display faces, first decide whether you are seeking harmony or contrast. Then consider size, style, weight or color, white space within and around the type area, relative position of text and display type, and rela-

Caledonia (Li) when combining text and display faces, first decide whether you are seeking harmony or contrast. Then consider size, style, weight or color, white space within and around the type area, relative position of text and display type, and relationship to

*Caledonia Italic (Li) when combining text and display faces, first decide whether you are seeking harmony or contrast. Then consider size, style, weight or color, white space within and around the type area, relative position of text and display type, and rela-*

Akzidenz Grotesk (Li) when combining text and display faces, first decide whether you are seeking harmony or contrast. Then consider size, style, weight or color, white space within and around the type area, relative position of text and

Futura Medium (I) when combining text and display faces, first decide whether you are seeking harmony or contrast. Then consider size, style, weight or color, white space within and around the type area, relative position of text and display type, and relationship to other graphic

*Bodoni Italic (I) when combining text and display faces, first decide whether you are seeking harmony or contrast. Then consider size, style, weight or color, white space within and around the type area, relative position of text and display type, and relationship to*

Trade Gothic Cond. #18 (Li) when combining text and display faces, first decide whether you are seeking harmony or contrast. Then consider size, style, weight or color, white space within and around the type area, relative position of text and display type, and relationship to other graphic elements, in-

Helvetica (Li) when combining text and display faces, first decide whether you are seeking harmony or contrast. Then consider size, style, weight or color, white space within and around the type area, relative position of text and display

Century Schoolbook (I) when combining text and display faces, first decide whether you are seeking harmony or contrast. Then consider size, style, weight or color, white space within and around the type area, relative position of text and dis-

Bodoni (I) when combining text and display faces, first decide whether you are seeking harmony or contrast. Then consider size, style, weight or color, white space within and around the type area, relative position of text and display type, and relationship to other

Clarendon (Li) when combining text and display faces, first decide whether you are seeking harmony or contrast. Then consider size, style, weight or color, white space within and around the type area, relative position

**Univers Bold #693 (M) when combining text and display faces, first decide whether you are seeking harmony or contrast. Then consider size, style, weight or color, white space within and around the type area, relative position of text**

**Futura Demibold (I) when combining text and display faces, first decide whether you are seeking harmony or contrast. Then consider size, style, weight or color, white space within and around the type area, relative position of text and display type, and**

**News Gothic Bold (I) when combining text and display faces, first decide whether you are seeking harmony or contrast. Then consider size, style, weight or color, white space within and around the type area, relative position of text and display type, and rela-**

**Times Roman Bold (Li) when combining text and display faces, first decide whether you are seeking harmony or contrast. Then consider size, style, weight or color, white space within and around the type area, relative position of text and display type, and relation-**

**Trade Gothic Bold Cond. #20 (Li) when combining text and display faces, first decide whether you are seeking harmony or contrast. Then consider size, style, weight or color, white space within and around the type area, relative position of text and display type, and relationship to other graphic ele-**

**Futura Bold (I) when combining text and display faces, first decide whether you are seeking harmony or contrast. Then consider size, style, weight or color, white space within and around the type area, relative position of text and display**

**Helvetica Medium (Li) when combining text and display faces, first decide whether you are seeking harmony or contrast. Then consider size, style, weight or color, white space within and around the type area, relative position of text and**

There is just too much raw graphic material to choose from: all those typefaces the printer has; the special ones from the type-setting house; the new, fashionable ones that are becoming available for photographic setting; the plethora of cold-type and pressure-sensitive faces available for homemade typesetting; plus the variations of all the faces made by the different manufacturers for the mechanical or photographic typesetting machinery. This veritable babel of visual voices explains the confusion and lack of cogent direction evident in much of today's typography.

Fine, innovative typography is a subtle and sophisticated art that takes years to understand. Such training can be acquired only through actually working with type: studying it, specifying it, designing with it, playing with it, enjoying it, loving it. It is the kind of artistic medium that one wisely leaves to the experts. In any case, typographic trailblazing is emphatically not an area in which the editor and art director ought to expend their energies. Not only because it is such an esoteric art, but — and this is far more important — because the normal magazine depends on its typography to *hold it together*. Typographic fireworks, albeit fun and games in themselves, cannot help but *tear it apart*. Words (i.e., type) are the one element occurring on all pages, and they must be used to help unify those pages into a common package. To achieve this unity — which is actually nothing but easy recognition — it is essential to retain a basic simplicity throughout.

Like typographic fireworks, too many small-scale variations can also destroy a magazine's overall image. Too many minor changes in type size, style, and setting merely dilute the overall impact by creating too many unnecessary visual diversions.

Such minuscule subtleties are lost on the fast reader, who perceives only visual confusion; that reader's verdict is likely to be, "Huh, what a mess; not a very good issue." They are equally lost on the slow reader, who is so enmeshed in the subject matter that he or she cannot understand the editorial reasons behind the "peculiarly presented" story; that reader's verdict will be "hard to read."

The editor has been trained to believe that it is essential to *help the reader* by "breaking up the text," by "using variation in type size to express degrees of importance," by using the capabilities of type to echo "tone of voice" — all of which is perfectly right and true. But one can easily "break up the text" to the point where it disintegrates; and expressing degrees of importance through type size can result in a page that looks like a printer's type sample. (Multiply this hodgepodge by a magazine's worth of pages and you have quite a mess on your hands.)

To avoid such embarrassment — and misplaced effort — the magazine should be designed as an overall product, given a styling, and subjected to a set of rules of appropriate behavior.

# Principles of effective magazine typography

Use the least possible number of typefaces and type sizes. Naturally you need to have at your disposal enough graphic material to permit flexibility in expressing what has to be said in an appropriate way — but you ought not have more than that. Once you have settled on your means of expression, stick to it. Resist the temptation to add different material, even on special occasions, because you are building equity in this restrained visual vocabulary and you must guard its purity at all times. That "special" solution may be "attention grabbing," and may thus help the story for which you choose it, but what is its effect on the overall image of the product?

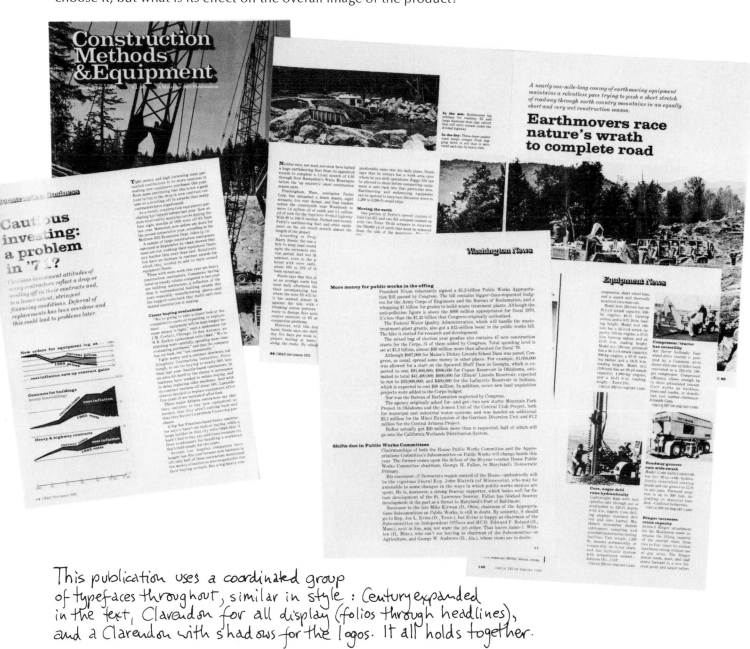

This publication uses a coordinated group of typefaces throughout, similar in style: Century expanded in the text, Clarendon for all display (folios through headlines), and a Clarendon with shadows for the logos. It all holds together.

## Keeping in the family

Use the same typeface for display as for the text. Doing so results in a smoother, more unified product that has a more "designed" appearance. Most normal typefaces have sufficient variation within the family to encompass the differences in size, weight (i.e., black-ness), and emphasis necessary for the editor to express the relative importance of the words.

What is a "family"? Simply a group of typefaces designed as variations on a basic face, all bearing the same generic name. There are literally dozens of variations of, for instance, Bodoni: fat ones, thin ones, slanted ones, big ones, small ones; but all quite obviously related to each other in character. Here is an example of a sans serif family: the top line is the "normal," or "original," version.

Helvetica
*Helvetica Italic*
Helvetica Thin
Helvetica Light
*Helvetica Light Italic*
**Helvetica Medium**
***Helvetica Medium Italic***
**Helvetica Bold**
***Helvetica Bold Italic***
Helvetica Regular Condensed
**Helvetica Extra Compressed**
**Helvetica Bold Condensed**
Helvetica Extended
Helvetica Med. Outline
Helvetica Bold Outline
Helvetica Bold Condensed Outline
Helvetica Shaded Center
Helvetica Medium Shaded Right

The others are variants. It might be a little confusing to use *all* the variants in one issue of one magazine (assuming that the supplier has them all available, which he probably hasn't). But it is convenient to be able to pick three or four and play them against each other in different areas of the book or different stories. The overall character is not harmed, since the family resemblance sustains the basic unity of image; yet there is enough variety to lend sparkle and liveliness.

This is seven point trump roman regular, set two points leaded to a width of nine picas. It is specified as seven on nine by 9 picas. The character count at this width is twenty-nine characters per line. This nine-

*5 columns*

This is eight on ten trump by eleven picas, set in the four-column measure appropriate for all front and back of the book matter ex-

This is nine point trump set on an eleven point body; it is nine on eleven trump roman set at eleven picas wide per line. The character count per line is thirty, and the maximum number of lines per column is seventy-two. This is nine on

*4 columns*

This is nine point trump regular roman set on an eleven point body at a set width of fifteen picas per line. It is specified as nine on eleven trump by fifteen. The average character count per line at this width is forty-two characters, and there are seventy-two lines per column. It is the standard

*3 columns*

This is nine point trump on a twelve point body or as it can be specified: nine on twelve trump, by twenty-two and a half picas wide. This set width is the correct width for two-column makeup of the magazine. Its character yield per line is fifty-six, and there is a maximum of sixty-six lines in the column. This is nine on

This is ten on thirteen trump roman regular by twenty-two and a half picas. It is ten point trump three points leaded and set on a slug that is twenty-two and a half picas wide, which is the correct measure for two column makeup. The number of characters per line is an average of fifty-six, and the maximum number of lines per column is sixty. This is ten point trump leaded three points

*2 columns*

This is ten point trump roman four points leaded and set to a width of thirty-one picas. This width spans two columns in the three-column page arrangement. The character count is seventy-six characters per line, and there are fifty-six lines per column. This is ten on fourteen trump by thirty-one picas.

*2-out-of-3*

This is ten on fourteen trump roman by thirty-five picas. It is ten point trump leaded four points and set to a width of thirty-five picas, which spans three of the columns in a four-column page arrangement. The character count at this width is eighty-seven characters per line, and there are a maximum of fifty-six lines in every column. This is ten

*3-out-of-4*

This is ten point trump leaded five points between the lines and expressed as ten on fifteen trump. It is set at a set-width of forty-seven picas, which is the width of the full live-matter page, spanning all the various page arrangements possible: two-column, three-column, four-column and the five-column picture spacing. There are one hundred and seventeen characters in every line of type and there are a total of fifty-two lines of such spacing possible per page. This is ten point

This is twelve point trump upper and lower case roman, leaded six points; this can be specified as twelve on eighteen trump. It is set to a measure of forty-seven picas which is the full live-matter page width and spans all the possible page formats and column arrangements. *This is twelve point trump italic up*
**This is twelve point trump semibold upper and lower case, leaded six points; this can be specified as**

*Full page*

Restrict typesetting to columns that are standardized in both width and placement on the page, and depart from this format only in the most unusual circumstances. The pattern created by the columns carries a rhythm throughout the magazine and is therefore a major contributing factor to product unity.

# Standardization of type specifications

Develop a standard type specification for each type size, and correlate it with the various column widths available on the page. The spacing between lines must also be taken into account. The purpose of this standardization is twofold:

1. To provide the most legible typography in the spaces available. Legibility of a line of type is affected by the typeface, the size of the type, and the length of the line in which it is being used. There is a rule of thumb that a line of type ought not to exceed 1½ alphabets in number of characters, but this stricture is not necessarily binding, since in specific situations many factors come into play that are peculiar to each magazine, each typeface, each readership, the color of the paper, the quality of printing, and so forth. It is wiser to forget such rules and work to meet the exigencies of the problem at hand. One fact, however, stands true in all cases: the longer the line, the harder it becomes to read. This difficulty can be overcome, and the eye aided in traveling the line's full length, by isolating each line from the one above and below it. The longer the lines are, the more space that has to be inserted between them. This extra space is called "leading," after the sliver of metal (usually lead, but sometimes brass) that was manually inserted between the lines when all typesetting was done by hand — letter by letter, line by line. Machine setting — both hot metal and photographic — accomplishes this "leading out" mechanically. But the machine must be instructed precisely how much leading (vertical space, expressed as points) to insert. So, the legibility of a piece of type design depends on the ratio of the apparent size of the type to the length of the line it is set in *and* to the spacing between lines.

2. To provide an evenness of "color" throughout the magazine's editorial spaces. Every typeface has a certain degree of grayness — its color. This color is more discernible in large masses than in a single alphabet. The object in preparing standardized typography in a magazine is to maintain the same degree of grayness in all situations, whether the columns be narrow (and therefore set in small type) or extra wide (and therefore set in a much larger size). A reader's first impression of each page ought to be the same, as far as lightness or darkness of the body type is concerned.

Thus, a coordinated system of typography is a complex aesthetic and functional calculation requiring the balancing of a number of factors. If it is well worked out, it becomes a basic — and important — visual tool as well as a constant definer of the magazine's personality.

This is nine point trump set on an eleven point body; it is nine on eleven trump roman set at eleven picas wide per line. The character count per line is thirty, and the maximum number of lines per column is seventy-two. This is nine on eleven trump regular roman by a set width of eleven picas. This is the basic standard type setting for the four-column makeup and should be used throughout the book under normal circumstances. This is nine point trump set on an eleven point body, it is nine on eleven trump roman set at eleven picas wide per line. The character count per line is thirty, and the maximum number of lines per column is seventy-two. This is nine on eleven trump regular roman by a set width of eleven picas. This is the basic standard type setting for the four-column makeup and should be used throughout the book under normal circumstances. This is nine point trump set on an eleven point body, it is nine on eleven trump roman set at eleven picas wide per line. The character count per line is thirty, and the maximum number of lines per column is seventy-two. This is nine on eleven trump regular roman by a set width of eleven picas. This is the basic standard type setting for the four-column makeup and should be used throughout the book under normal circumstances.

an eleven point body; it is nine on eleven trump roman set at eleven picas wide per line. The character count per line is thirty, and the maximum number of lines per column is seventy-two. This is nine on eleven trump regular roman by a set width of eleven picas. This is the basic standard type setting for the four-column makeup and should be used throughout the book under normal circumstances. This is nine point trump set on an eleven point body, it is nine on eleven trump roman set at eleven picas wide per line. The character count per line is thirty, and the maximum number of lines per column is seventy-two. This is nine on eleven trump regular roman by a set width of eleven picas.

*lines. The character count is thirty characters per line and the maximum number of lines in a column is seventy-two. This is nine on eleven trump italic set eleven picas wide. It is nine point trump italic with two points of lead between the lines. The character count is thirty characters per line and the maximum number of lines in a column is seventy-two. This is nine on eleven trump italic set eleven picas wide. It is nine point trump italic with*

*lines. The character count is thirty characters per line and the maximum number of lines in a column is seventy-two. This is nine on eleven trump italic set eleven picas wide. It is nine point trump italic with two points of lead between the lines. The character count is thirty characters per line and the maximum number of lines in a column is seventy-two. This is nine on eleven trump italic set eleven picas wide. It is nine point trump italic with*

This is nine point trump regular roman set on an eleven point body at a set width of fifteen picas per line. It is specified as nine on eleven trump by fifteen. The average character count per line at this width is forty-two characters, and there are seventy-two lines per column. It is the standard size and face to be used for the three column makeup of the magazine page, on occasions when such three-column makeup is editorially appropriate. This fifteen pica width should be reserved for unusual circumstances and used on rare occasions only. This is nine point trump regular roman set on an eleven point body at a set width of fifteen picas per line.

This is nine point trump regular roman set on an eleven point body at a set width of fifteen picas per line. It is specified as nine on eleven trump by fifteen. The average character count per line at this width is forty-two characters, and there are seventy-two lines per column. It is the standard size and face to be used for the three column makeup of the magazine page, on occasions when such three-column makeup is editorially appropriate. This fifteen pica width should be reserved for unusual circumstances and used on rare occasions only. This is nine point trump regular roman set on an eleven point body at a set width of fifteen picas per line.

This is ten on thirteen trump roman regular by twenty-two and a half picas. It is ten point trump three points leaded and set on a slug that is twenty-two and a half picas wide. The number of characters per line is an average of fifty-six, and the maximum number of lines per column is sixty. This is ten point trump leaded three points and set to a set width of twenty two and a half picas. This is ten on thirteen trump roman regular by twenty-two and a half picas. It is ten point trump three points leaded and set on a slug that is twenty-two and a half picas wide, which is the correct measure for two column makeup. The number of characters per line is an average of fifty-six, and the maximum number of lines per column is sixty.

*This is ten on thirteen trump italic by twenty-two and a half picas. It is ten point trump italic leaded three points and set on a slug that is twenty-two and a half picas wide, which is the correct measure for two-column makeup. Character count is fifty-six characters per line and there is a maximum of sixty lines per column. This is ten on thirteen trump italic by twenty-two and a half picas. It is ten point trump italic leaded three points and set on a slug that is twenty-two and a half picas wide, which is the correct measure for two-column makeup. Character count is fifty-six characters per line and there is a maximum of sixty lines per column. This is ten on*

This is ten point trump leaded five points between the lines and expressed as ten on fifteen trump. It is set at a set-width of forty-seven picas, which is the width of the full live-matter page, spanning all the various page arrangements possible: two-column, three-column, four-column and the five-column picture spacing. There are one hundred and seventeen characters in every line of type and there are a total of fifty-two lines of such spacing possible per page. This is ten point trump leaded five points between the lines and expressed as ten on fifteen trump. It is set at a set-width of forty-seven picas, which is the width of the full live-matter page, spanning all the various page arrangements possible: two-column, three-column, four-column and the five-column picture spacing. There are one hundred and seventeen characters in every line of type and there are a total of fifty-two lines of such spacing possible per page. This is ten point trump leaded five points between the lines and expressed as ten on fifteen trump. It is set at a set-width of forty-seven picas, which is the width of the full live-matter page, spanning all the various page arrangements possible: two-column, three-column, four-column and the five-column picture spacing. There are one hundred and seventeen characters in every line of type and there are a total of fifty-two lines of such spacing possible per page. This is ten point trump leaded five points be-

*This is ten point trump italic leaded five points between the lines and expressed as ten on fifteen trump italic. It is set at a set-width of forty-seven picas, which is the width of the full live-matter page, spanning all the various page arrangements possible: two-column, three-column, four-column and the five-column picture spacing. There are a total of one hundred and seventeen characters per line in this measure and there are a total of fifty-two lines of such spacing possible per page. This is ten point trump italic leaded five points between the lines and expressed as ten on fifteen trump italic. It is set at a set-width of forty-seven picas, which is the width of the full live-matter page, spanning all the various page arrangements possible: two-column, three-column, four-column and the five-column picture spacing. There are a total of one hundred and seventeen characters per line in this measure and there are a total of fifty-two lines of such spacing possible per page. This is ten point trump italic leaded five points between the lines and expressed as ten on fifteen trump italic. It is set at a set-width of forty-seven picas, which is the width of the full live-matter page, spanning all the various one hundred and seventeen characters per line in this measure and there are a total of fifty-two lines of such spacing possible per page. This is ten point trump italic leaded five points between the lines and expressed as ten on fifteen trump*

This is ten point trump roman four points leaded and set to a width of thirty-one picas. This width spans two columns in the three-column arrangement. The character count is seventy-six characters per line, and there are fifty-six lines per column. This is ten on fourteen trump by thirty-one picas. This is ten point trump roman four points leaded and set to a width of thirty one picas. This width spans two columns in the three-column arrangement. The character count is seventy-six characters per line, and there are fifty-six lines per column. This is ten on fourteen trump by thirty-one picas. This is ten point trump roman four points leaded and set to a width of thirty one picas. This width spans two columns in the three-column arrangement. The character count is seventy-six characters per line, and there are

*This is twelve point trump italic upper and lower case, leaded six points; this can be specified as twelve on eighteen trump italic. It is set to a measure of forty-seven picas, which is the full live-matter page width and spans all the possible page formats and column arrangements. This is twelve point trump italic upper and lower case, leaded six points; this can be specified as twelve on eighteen trump italic. It is set to a measure of forty-seven picas, which is the full live-matter page width and spans all the possible page formats and column arrangements. This is twelve point trump italic upper and lower case, leaded six points; this can be specified as twelve on eighteen trump italic. It is set to a measure of forty-seven picas, which is the full live-matter page width and spans all the possible page formats and column arrangements. It is set to a measure of forty*

Dummy type sheets used for assembling layouts show the various type sizes used in the appropriate column width settings.

Be consistent in the placement, spacing, and use of type throughout the magazine. Standardize everything that can possibly be standardized: space between various elements, such as headline and text, and deck and headline; spacing around subheads; space between picture and caption. The purpose of this consistency is to achieve a designed regularity, a thought-through *rightness*. (Besides, you do not want to have to reinvent the wheel every time; the more presolved problems you don't have to concern yourself with, the more time you have for concentrating on what really matters: the content of the book.) Probably more than anything else, this organized and regular atmosphere is the secret of a magazine's unified personality.

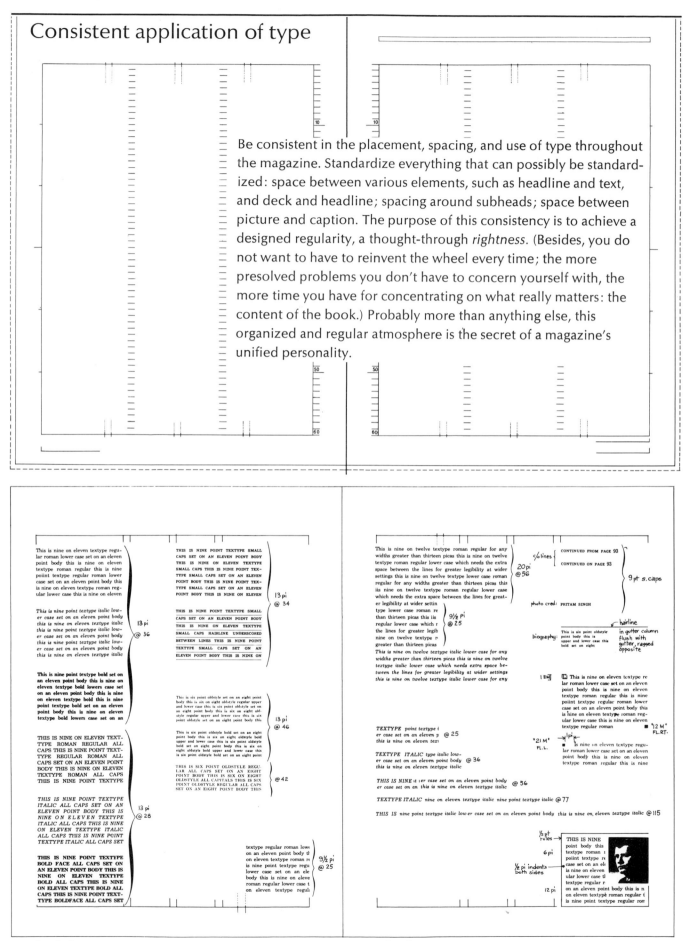

**body type**

**misc.type**

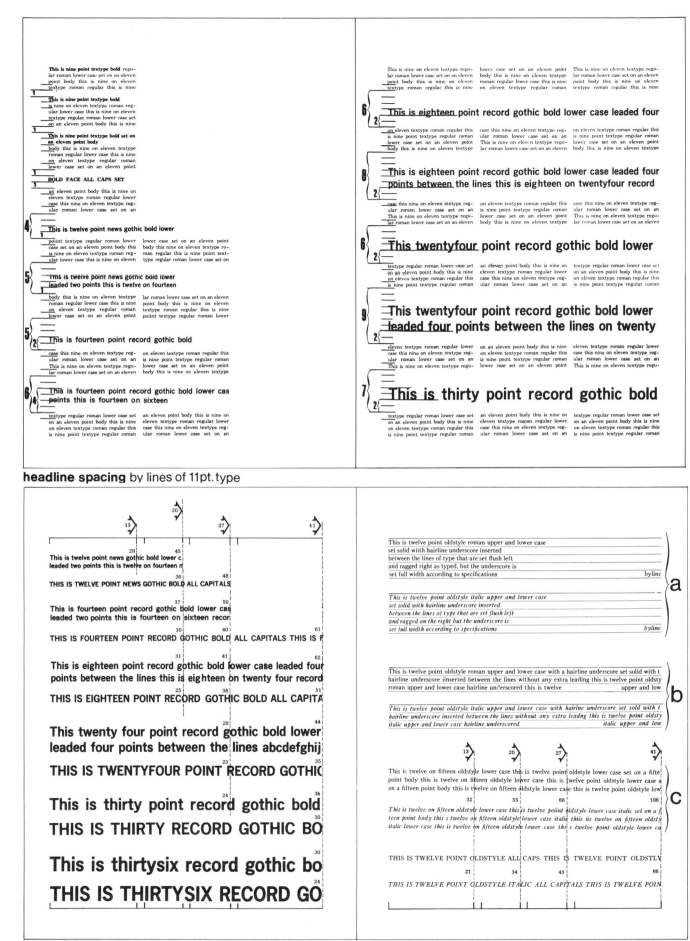

**headline spacing** by lines of 11pt. type

heads

decks

Type is measured by points (12 to the pica; six picas to the inch). Unfortunately the sizing system bears little relation to the actual size of the marks that appear on paper, since the point size is the measurement of the height of the piece of metal that supports the actual letter that prints. The *apparent* size of a piece of type depends on the design (the relationship of the "x height" to the ascenders and descenders in the lowercase letters). There is no system of measuring type the way it actually appears on the page. Editors often fall in the trap of believing that when they call for a ten-point size of type, they automatically get a large dimension. Alas, it depends on what face they are calling for a ten-point size in. These are all set in ten point:

This copy is set in ten-point Garamond to a width of twelve picas. It is set solid, with no extra space inserted between the lines, so that the comparison of apparent size can be made between this and the other two examples on this page. It is set in ten point, but it certainly looks smaller than the other ten-pointers, doesn't it?

This copy is set in ten-point Century Expanded to a width of twelve picas. It is set solid, with no extra space inserted between the lines, so that the comparison of apparent size can be made between this and the other two examples on this page. It is set in ten point, but it appears much larger than the Garamond at left.

This copy is set in ten-point News Gothic to a width of twelve picas. It is set solid, with no extra space inserted between the lines, so that the comparison of apparent size can be made between this and the other two examples on this page. It is set in ten point, but it looks bigger than the Century Expanded, and enormous compared to the ten-point Garamond.

These three groups of letters are set in the same typefaces as the paragraphs above them: Garamond, Century Expanded, and News Gothic. The letters' overall height is the same, which is why they can be labeled "60 point." But in this large size it becomes quite obvious why they appear to have different sizes, even though they all take up the same amount of space on the page. It is the relationship of the x height to the space taken up by the ascenders and descenders that makes the difference.

The moral: Never specify type by guessing at the point size number. Play it safe by looking the typeface up in the type sample; determine visually what size will be most suitable, and then use the point size — as a reference figure only.

Note, also, that in this procedure it is essential to use the type sample book from the typesetter who will do the work. There are so many variations of each face available on the various machines that a Garamond, say, from a supplier who still uses hot metal type will look very different from the Garamond supplied by a competitor who uses photographic typesetting. They both supply "Garamond" (or a reasonable facsimile), but the customer may be in for quite a surprise when he receives first proofs, expecting one version and gets the other.

## Type as tone of voice

Bear in mind that typography is an art capable of great expressiveness and variety. To make the most of its capabilities (when the time is right), it is necessary to to use ingenuity, tempered with taste and restraint. To illustrate a minuscule fragment of this range of adaptability, here is a simple example: set by themselves, unadorned, in plain type, the words can be understood, and the mind can accept what it is they are saying; but the message is not nearly as vivid, memorable, or quickly absorbed — as in the variations that follow.

Typography can crystallize a tone of voice: it can be raised or lowered; it can appear to shout—or it can appear to whisper

Typography can crystallize a tone of voice: it can be *RAISED* or *lowered*; it can appear to SHOUT—or it can appear to WHISPER

**Typography can crystallize a tone of voice: it can be RAISED or LOWERED; it can appear to *SHOUT*—or it can appear to** *whisper.*

*Typography can crystallize a tone of voice: it can be raised or lowered; it can appear to shout—or it can appear to whisper.*

Typography can crystallize a tone of voice: it can be raised or lowered; it can appear to shout—or it can appear to whisper

Typography **can** crystallize a tone of voice: it can be raised or lowered; it can appear to shout—or it can appear to whisper.

## Italics: pros and cons

Use italics sparingly. There is no question about it — they are harder to read than their roman counterpart. Most magazines misuse italics, depending on them for emphasis: this is quite wrong, since they are a development of an informal, handwritten style, and so are lighter and paler and weaker — which are precisely the characteristics you don't want for emphasis. But there it is: an illogical convention we will continue living with.

Since they are a gentler, less formal style, italics lend themselves best to informal use as contrast to the more formal roman: as large, floating lines, unaligned at left or right; or perhaps as blurbs or quotes run ragged right, a few lines at a time.

*Italics are paler, gentler, quieter than roman of the same face, size, and leading*

*This is nine on eleven trump italic by fifteen picas wide. It is nine point trump ital with two points of lead between the lines and it is set to a width of fifteen picas which is the normal width for three column makeup of the page. The character count is forty-two and the maximum number of lines per column is seventy-two. This is nine on eleven trump italic by fifteen picas wide. It is nine point trump ital with two points of lead between the lines and it is set to a width of fifteen picas which is the normal width for three column makeup of the page. The character count is forty-two and the maximum number of lines per column is seventy-two. This is nine on eleven trump italic by fifteen picas wide.*

This is nine point trump regular roman set on an eleven point body at a set width of fifteen picas per line. It is specified as nine on eleven trump by fifteen. The average character count per line at this width is forty-two characters, and there are seventy-two lines per column. It is the standard size and face to be used for the three column makeup of the magazine page, on occasions when such three-column makeup is editorially appropriate. This fifteen pica width should be reserved for unusual circumstances and used on rare occasions only. This is nine point trump regular roman set on an eleven point body at a set width of fifteen picas per line. It is specified as nine on eleven trump by fifteen.

*Two good ways to use italics:*

*This is ten point trump italic
which has five points of lead between the
lines. It is set flush left and ragged
right, which makes its application rare:
reserved for situations where a very special
feeling of background sophistication
needs to be imparted to the beginning of
a story. It is a technique which is useful in
its capacity to make some of the normal
and ordinary type feel extraordinary.
It is no longer a trademark of "poetry"*

*This is ten point trump italic leaded five points between the lines and expressed as ten on fifteen trump italic.
It is set at the width of the full live-matter page, spanning all the various page arrangements possible:
two-column, three-column, four-column and the five-column picture spacing.
There are a total of one hundred and seventeen characters per line in this measure*

Use all-capital setting only when the lines are very short — as label headlines, perhaps, or single words popping up above normal lowercase. The average reader is not used to reading long lines of capitals. (Only architects and engineers are happy with them, because capitals are used for most labeling on drawings.) In bulk, they are hard to read (even for architects and engineers), but this characteristic may well be useful for specific situations where it is important to the subject matter that the reading speed be slowed down and an aura of dignity be created (as in an OPEN LETTER TO THE PRESIDENT).

*HIS IS TEN ON FIFTEEN OPTIMA ITALIC CAPS THIS IS TEN ON FIFTEEN OPTIMA ITALIC CAPS THIS IS TEN ON FIFTEEN OPTIMA ITALIC CAPS THIS IS TEN ON FIFTEEN OPTIMA ITALIC CAPS THIS IS TEN ON FIFTEEN OPTIMA TALIC CAPS THIS IS TEN ON FIFTEEN OPTIMA ITALIC CAPS THIS IS TEN ON FIFTEEN OPTIMA ITALIC CAPS*

HIS IS TWELVE ON TWENTY OPTIMA CAPS THIS IS TWELVE ON TWENTY OPTIMA CAPS THIS S TWELVE ON TWENTY OPTIMA CAPS THIS IS TWELVE ON TWENTY OPTIMA CAPS THIS IS WELVE ON TWENTY OPTIMA CAPS THIS IS TWELVE ON TWENTY OPTIMA CAPS THIS IS TO

**HIS IS FOURTEEN ON EIGHTEEN OPTIMA SEMIBOLD ALL CAPS HAND SET THIS IS OURTEEN ON EIGHTEEN OPTIMA SEMIBOLD ALL CAPS HAND SET THIS IS FOURTE**

Never Set Headlines Using Capital Initials And Lowercase On Every Word — unless your intention is to create visual hiccups. This is a bad and outmoded convention left over from nineteenth-century newspapering days, when there was not enough large display type to go around and headlines using the small type that was available in the shop had to be invented. This practice does, indeed, make the words appear different in texture (so it does achieve its purpose of gaining attention), but such heads are extremely difficult to read and there is no longer any functional reason (other than tradition) to continue using them. A headline set in bold and black type is different enough from the body copy to signal its importance, and it is lily-gilding to make it important-important by capitalizing the initials. Unfortunately, because the typewriter is limited in its mode of typographic color expression, the practice is retained in typing, and as a result it gets translated into typeset type, because editors are used to seeing it.

# Color and texture of type: justifying lines

B  A  D
T  Y  P  E
SPACING

Avoid using type in such a way that the printer will have to destroy the color of the type by being forced to "open up" between words or characters. This requirement not only ruins legibility, but also conduces to an amateurish appearance. There is a natural, optimum setting for all type, regardless of the machinery used to do the actual setting (whether it be hand-set, metal character by metal character, in the manner invented by Gutenberg in 1456; or machine-set line by line on the Linotype, or Monotype, or Intertype; or set by computer-generated film typography at 60,000 characters per minute). The technology of typesetting has much to do with the *economics* of the printing business, but it should not be allowed to affect the *readableness* of the product. Technically many things are possible to achieve. The question that matters is: Are they right for the product?

To avoid problems and disasters in the normal workaday world of the publication, therefore, it is wise to avoid:

Avoid: Headlines  that  must  be  justified  flush  left  and  right  in  too  wide  a  space  with  too  few  words.

*The spacing in this line looks right. But just compare it to the others!*

Avoid: Columns  that  are  too  narrow  and  therefore require too  much  letterspacing  in order to "justify"  or fill out each line.  (Any  type  specifier  who calls for fewer  than  28  characters  per line  is playing  with  fire.)

*This is the only acceptable line in the whole paragraph.*

Avoid: *Blurbs that are less than  half  a  page  wide.  In  cases  where  they must,  of  necessity, be  narrow-  er,  let  the  lines  be  set  unjustified  (i.e.,  irregu-  lar in  length).*

*This is bad throughout.*

The purpose is to retain the spacing between characters appropriate to the way the typeface was designed, since it looks best, and therefore reads best, that way.

*In cases where blurbs must be narrow, let the lines be set unjustified (i.e., irregular in length), flush left or flush right, centered, or staggered.*

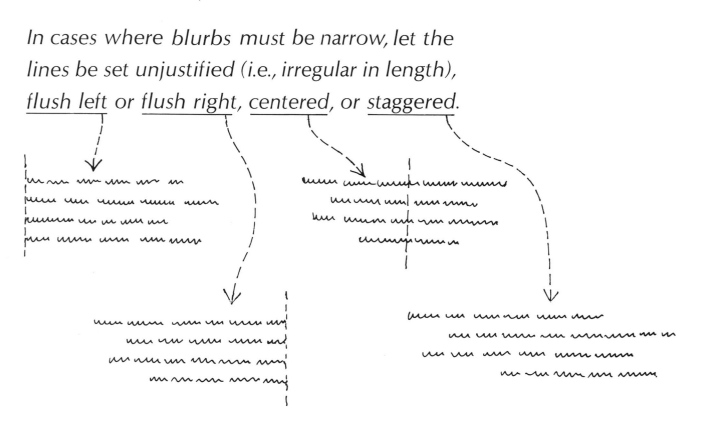

## Color and texture of type: justifying columns

Be painstakingly accurate in filling columns with the correct number of lines. Never allow the printer to justify columns by opening up between lines. This technique is the best way to destroy the color of the type — and to downgrade the visual standard of the product. A magazine is not a newspaper; it cannot claim "pressure of time" as an excuse for shoddy workmanship.

## Breaking up the text

Break up unrelieved text columns to create events along the way for the reader's eye — and to make it look like less work to read all that type. (But don't overdo it.)

Some of the more common ways to achieve this breakup with typographic materials

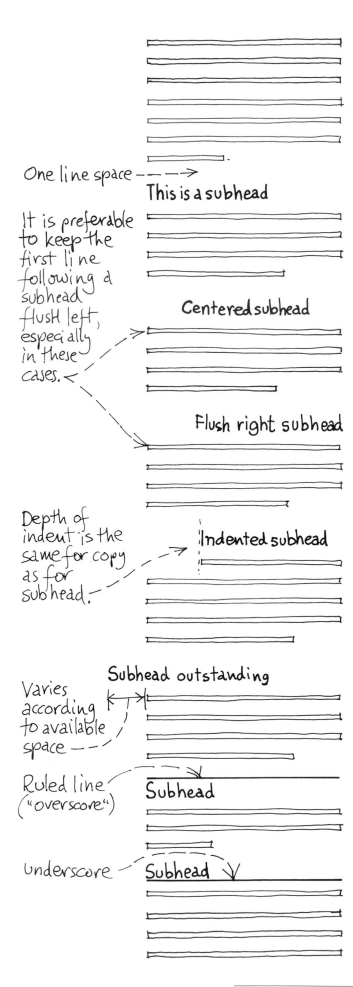

One line space ---->

This is a subhead

It is preferable to keep the first line following a subhead flush left, especially in these cases.

Centered subhead

Flush right subhead

Depth of indent is the same for copy as for subhead.

Indented subhead

Subhead outstanding

Varies according to available space ---

Ruled line ("overscore")

Subhead

underscore

Subhead

The type used for setting subheads varies with the style, meaning, relative importance, and function of the words, and with the way the stories are written. Thus, if the subheads are merely text-breaks to make the mass of reading-matter less unpalatable, then they should be small and discreet. If, however, they are miniature headlines, signaling the structure and content of the story, their importance should be reflected by size and graphic handling.

Subheads can be set in same size as the text, in the same face:

Roman, upper- and lowercase
ROMAN, ALL-CAPITALS
Italic, upper- and lower case
ITALIC, ALL-CAPITALS
ROMAN CAPS AND SMALL CAPS
Roman bold, upper and lower
ROMAN BOLD, ALL CAPITALS

Or they can be set larger.

Or they can be set in a contrasting typeface.

The examples shown here merely indicate placement in the column and a few of the commonest graphic devices for handling subheads.

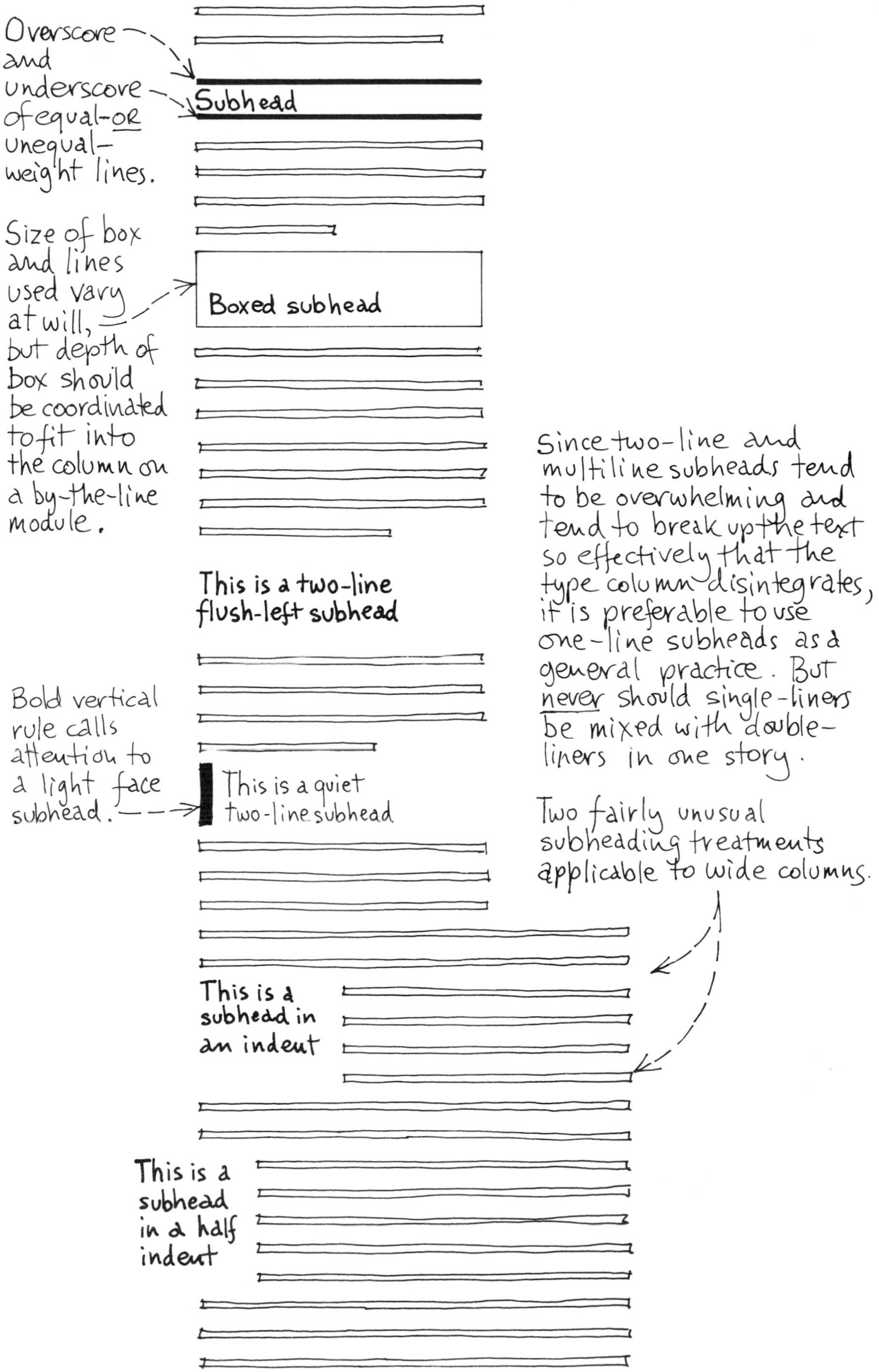

Overscore and underscore of equal-_or_ unequal-weight lines.

**Subhead**

Size of box and lines used vary at will, but depth of box should be coordinated to fit into the column on a by-the-line module.

Boxed subhead

**This is a two-line flush-left subhead**

Bold vertical rule calls attention to a light face subhead. ——

This is a quiet two-line subhead

This is a subhead in an indent

This is a subhead in a half indent

Since two-line and multiline subheads tend to be overwhelming and tend to break up the text so effectively that the type column disintegrates, it is preferable to use one-line subheads as a general practice. But _never_ should single-liners be mixed with double-liners in one story.

Two fairly unusual subheading treatments applicable to wide columns.

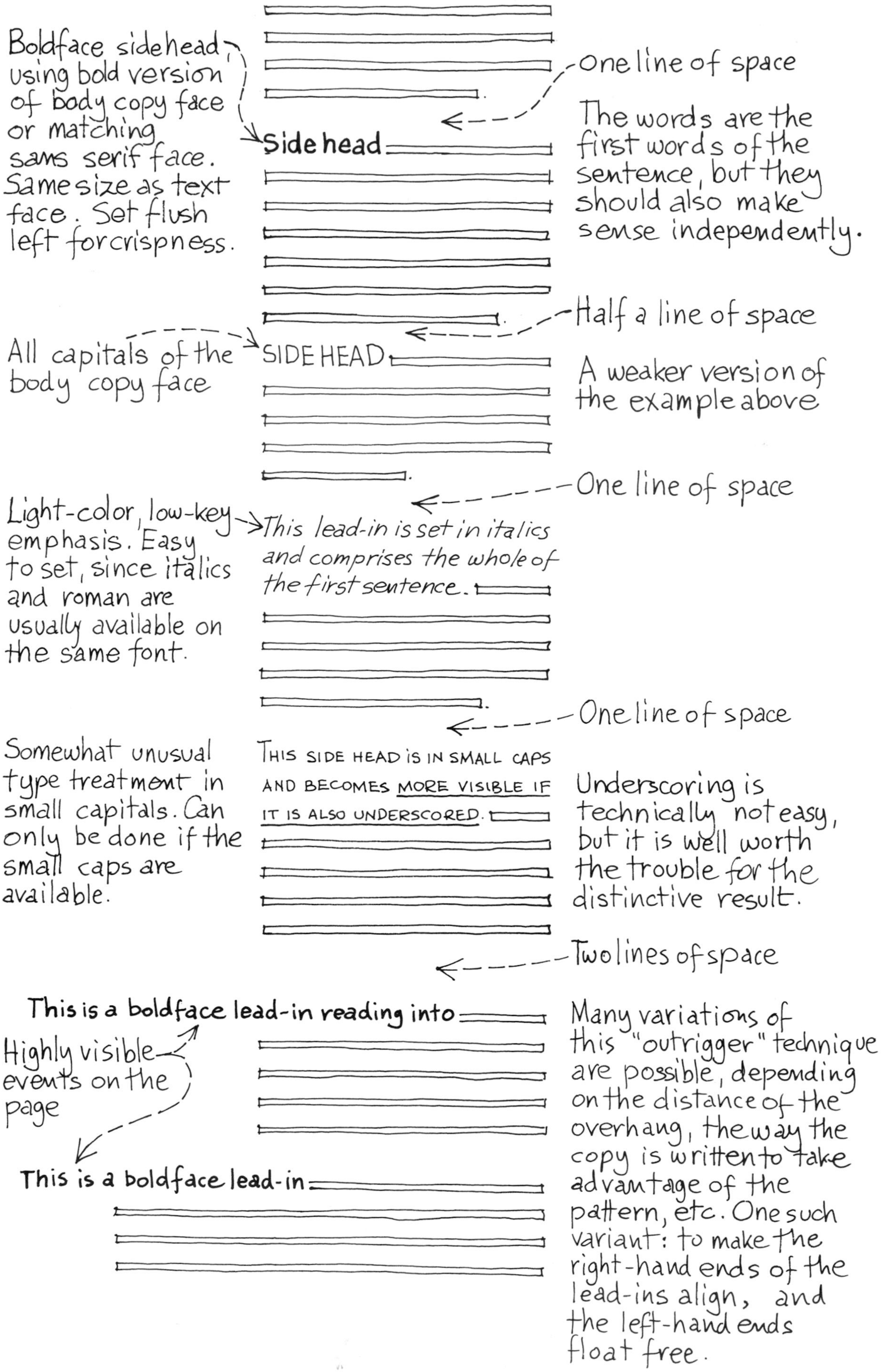

Boldface sidehead, using bold version of body copy face or matching sans serif face. Same size as text face. Set flush left for crispness.

One line of space

**Side head**

The words are the first words of the sentence, but they should also make sense independently.

Half a line of space

All capitals of the body copy face

SIDE HEAD

A weaker version of the example above

One line of space

Light-color, low-key emphasis. Easy to set, since italics and roman are usually available on the same font.

*This lead-in is set in italics and comprises the whole of the first sentence.*

One line of space

Somewhat unusual type treatment in small capitals. Can only be done if the small caps are available.

THIS SIDE HEAD IS IN SMALL CAPS AND BECOMES MORE VISIBLE IF IT IS ALSO UNDERSCORED.

Underscoring is technically not easy, but it is well worth the trouble for the distinctive result.

Two lines of space

**This is a boldface lead-in reading into**

Highly visible events on the page

**This is a boldface lead-in**

Many variations of this "outrigger" technique are possible, depending on the distance of the overhang, the way the copy is written to take advantage of the pattern, etc. One such variant: to make the right-hand ends of the lead-ins align, and the left-hand ends float free.

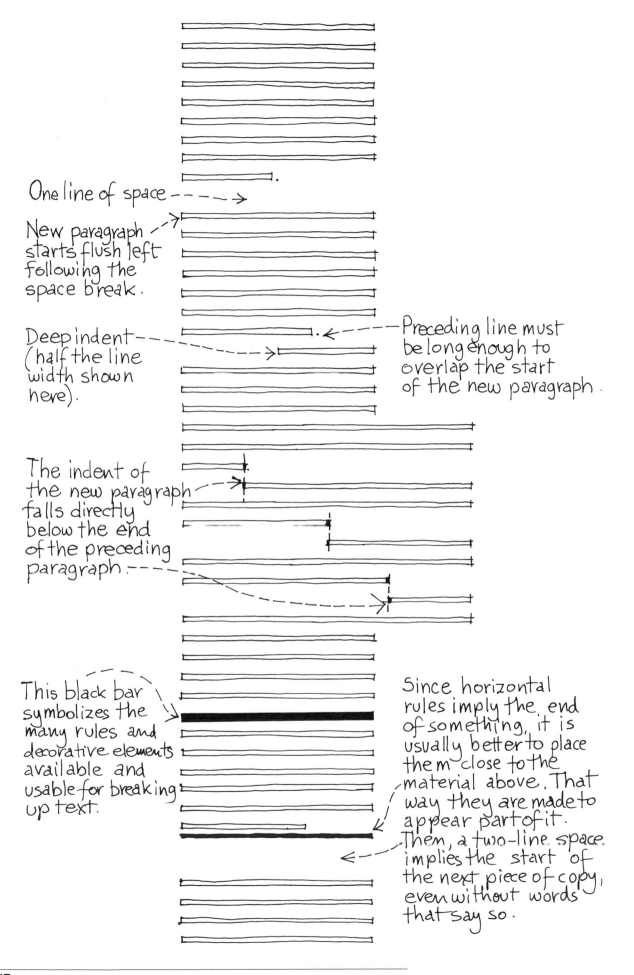

One line of space - - - - →

New paragraph starts flush left following the space break.

Deep indent (half the line width shown here).

Preceding line must be long enough to overlap the start of the new paragraph.

The indent of the new paragraph falls directly below the end of the preceding paragraph - - -

This black bar symbolizes the many rules and decorative elements available and usable for breaking up text.

Since horizontal rules imply the end of something, it is usually better to place them close to the material above. That way they are made to appear part of it. Then, a two-line space implies the start of the next piece of copy, even without words that say so.

The top of the
initial aligns with
top of the first
line.
The bottom
aligns perfectly
with the bottom
of the third line.

The outer edge
extends into the
margin, to make it
appear to align
visually.

Top line must
extend into mortise
to allow the first
word to appear
complete.

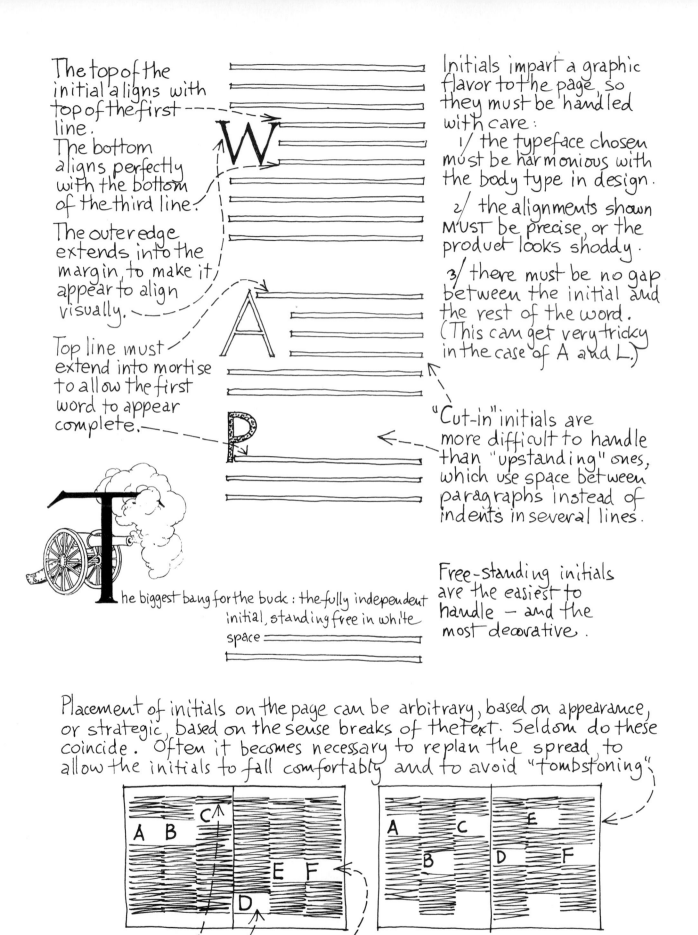

Initials impart a graphic
flavor to the page, so
they must be handled
with care:
1/ the typeface chosen
must be harmonious with
the body type in design.
2/ the alignments shown
MUST be precise, or the
product looks shoddy.
3/ there must be no gap
between the initial and
the rest of the word.
(This can get very tricky
in the case of A and L.)

"Cut-in" initials are
more difficult to handle
than "upstanding" ones,
which use space between
paragraphs instead of
indents in several lines.

Free-standing initials
are the easiest to
handle — and the
most decorative.

The biggest bang for the buck: the fully independent
initial, standing free in white
space

Placement of initials on the page can be arbitrary, based on appearance,
or strategic, based on the sense breaks of the text. Seldom do these
coincide. Often it becomes necessary to replan the spread, to
allow the initials to fall comfortably and to avoid "tombstoning".

Insufficient text
above or below

Bad alignment
in columns

Never allow less than three lines of text at the top or bottom of a column above or below a subhead or other text interruption; that way you quarantine it and make sure that it belongs to the running text, instead of beginning or ending a separate textual element.

There should be at least three lines of type here

This is a headline

## Indenting first paragraphs

Ensure a crisp, squared-off white space around the headline by avoiding an indent of the first paragraph. This is a critical area where clarity and precision are essential to ensure attention. A discreet (i.e., small) initial or square can be used to signal the start of the text, so long as it does not take away any of the attention-getting quality of the headline or the blurb.

## Indenting elsewhere

Indent paragraphs in the normal fashion (or more deeply), and do not be afraid of "widows" (short last lines of a paragraph) — like the indents, they serve to let a little air and variety into the type, even though they do sometimes make it appear a little messy. Type is to be read; these small interruptions help to vary the pattern and so make it more interesting to the eye. Type must not be allowed to become a pale gray rectangle — handsome but sterile. However, never allow a widow to appear as the first line at the head of a column or page. It looks shoddy and unkempt.

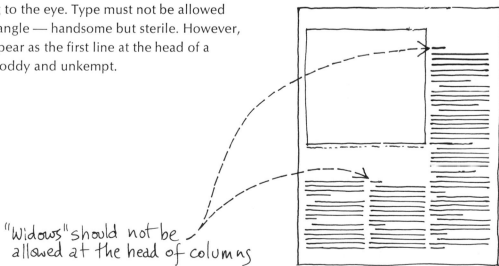

"Widows" should not be allowed at the head of columns

# Long headlines

Use headline type in such a way that you have ample space to say enough to make the headline meaningful, useful, catchy. It is wise, therefore, to make use of type that is smaller, and at the same time bolder, than you might at first deem appropriate. That way you get the necessary eye-catching blackness that a headline needs to be noticed, and you get enough characters to say something in.

*This gains attention by blackness and bigness.*

# This is an important headline!

## This headline says much more in the space

*This headline trades off bigness of type for more words. The blackness remains the same, so the eye is attracted the same way.*

If the subject requires a shorter headline (in the form of a label, perhaps), then add a hefty blurb to explain what the story is about, and what its significance to the reader is.

# Two-word label

*This, dear reader, is what the label is all about. Furthermore, here is the reason you should spend your precious time reading the article.*

*— — — — — — The blurb explains in detail what the label-headline leaves out.*

# Setting the headline stacked in several lines is a welcome change of pace

*← — —* Use a stacked headline, with many but very short lines, as a variant on the normal page-wide headline.

If you use a two-line headline, make sure that the second line is shorter than the first, to bring the end closer to the beginning of the text below.

*The first line is longer than the second)*

Restrain headline typography; do not shout too much. This way the attention-getting capacity of type is reserved for situations that deserve such treatment for editorial reasons. By shouting out loud everywhere, you end up by not being heard at all, since all that shouting cancels itself out. A small-size headline in plenty of surrounding white space is often much more effective than that same space filled to the brim with bloated words.

Before and after example shows how effective heads can be, even if "small", when they appear in clearly-articulated spaces.

# Ragged-right setting

Be aware of the advantages of ragged-right/flush-left setting.

It looks and feels different from the conventional, expected, justified column treatment. This differentness can be made use of in situations that demand special stress, such as pronouncements, introductions, editorial statements or comments, etc. Or it can be useful as a foil to the regular setting in purely decorative terms.

It "opens up" the rigid column structure and lets in some air.

It certainly looks different from the surrounding ads.

The fabric of the type retains a smoother texture, since the need to justify the lines does not exist. As a result, the typesetter does not need to insert arbitrary extra spacing beween words or characters and thus he does not have to spoil the color and evenness of the type. This very smoothness, together with the signaling quality that each line has at the end (since each end of a line comes at a different position), actually makes this kind of typesetting easiest of all to read.

Editors tend to fear it, since to them it "looks like poetry" (which is what their copy is NOT). But it has been used on non-poetic subject matter often enough and widely enough by now to have destroyed that particular prejudice.

On a purely practical plane, it has an additional advantage that has nothing to do with aesthetics or ease of reading, but everything to do with ease-of-getting-the-book-out.

Ragged-right setting allows great leeway in writing, since the difference in line length allows variation in word count per line, without such variations appearing to be mistakes. That way you can, for instance, have several copy blocks that have an equal number of lines — so they appear to be the same length — yet by varying their line lengths, some can have a smaller number of words than another. This attribute is particularly useful in captions, new-product reports, or any other form of listing of a variety of elements that call for picture/caption treatment, where some are more important than others or there is more to say about some than there is about the others — yet all of which need to be handled equally for some other reason.

Flush right and left setting makes inequality of text painfully obvious

Ragged right setting allows the lines of the right-hand column to be shorter, thus filling the total NUMBER of lines and balance the left-hand column. The disparity in VOLUME of text is thus masked and becomes acceptable.

In the example opposite, the pages appear similar, even though the amount of text on each varies widely.

## REFLECTIONS ON ENVIRONMENT

Architecture, of all possible things
on earth, has by nature
such a wonderful potential
for aliveness.

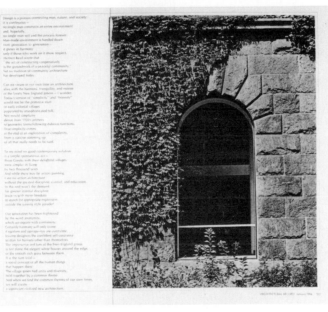

"Design is concerned with
a sympathetic attitude;
a desire to save, to build
to regenerate, to not spoil
what is already there."

## Flush left feels right

Make use of the natural propensity of type to be set flush left; it feels most comfortable that way. When headlines or subheads are centered in the space in which they ride, they become free-standing, unallied elements. They have dignity and importance — but they appear alone. Move them over to align flush left with other elements on the page, especially the type blocks, and immediately they take on a dynamic quality, an air of belonging in the surroundings — of being designed-in — and a much more active and lively presentation results.

Headline centered on the page

Dignified headline treatment, somewhat stuffy and aloof. Static and quiet.

Headline placed flush left with text

Active, participating headline reflects on a larger scale the way the text is positioned on the page, and the rhythms work together.

## Captions and pictures

Captions must be closely allied to the picture they refer to: they should not float in space, but instead should meld with the picture into a visual unity. They are subordinate to the picture, explaining it, pinpointing its meaning within the story, expanding the ideas generated by its content — so they should be set in a typographic dress that is restrained and self-effacing. Let the picture do the attention-getting. Set the caption in a pale type — a smaller size of the basic body copy type perhaps, or a pale sans serif. There is no reason for it to be bolder than the body copy type.

## Caption placement

Captions can be used to give typographic variety to the page; this quality should be exploited in a product having a basically rigid, formalized rectangular composition. Where column upon column of type and illustrations prevail, the captions are eye-catching events. An "informal" setting of the captions brings a touch of relief to such situations. The caption should be set with one edge flush, the other ragged. The flush side is the one that must be used to establish a relationship with the picture, while the ragged, feather-edged side floats freely. As a rule, it is wiser to have the left-hand edge as the flush edge, but when the occasion demands it is admissible to use a flush-right alignment, so long as the number of lines treated this way is not too great (a dozen lines perhaps) and the lines are not too wide (not much more than 36 characters). The adhesive quality of the flush edge is shown in the diagram.

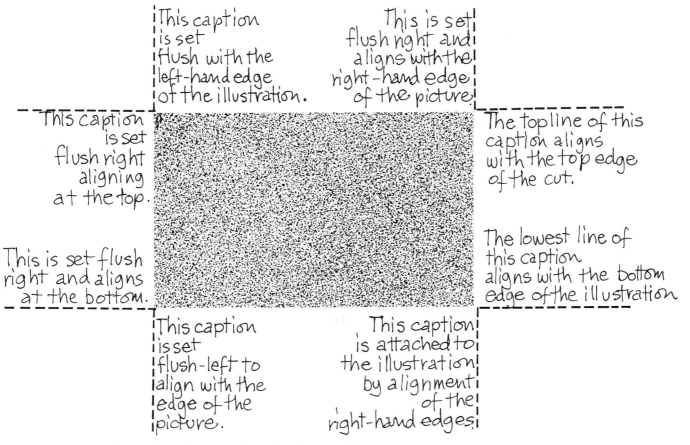

No caption has been placed centered on the picture: this omission is a personal idiosyncrasy based on the view that it is better to concentrate the leftover space into single, larger units instead of halving it, and thereby destroying its potential bigness.

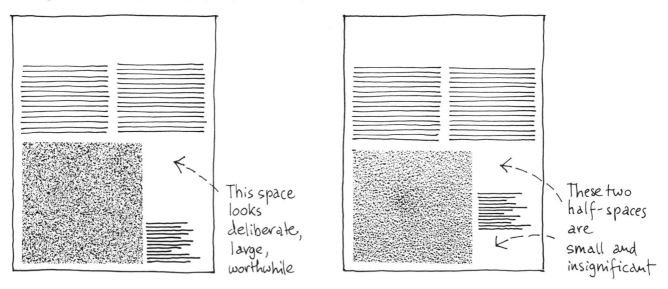

# Runarounds

Use runarounds rarely. Runarounds are variations in column width to allow space for dropping in illustrative material. The simplest runaround is that which is contained within a single column, and merely entails setting several lines of type shorter. Where the runaround bites into two adjacent columns, the finished product

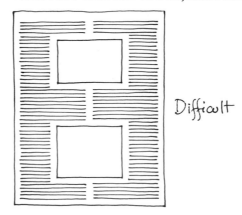

Easy

Difficult

can be very lively in appearance, but it does not justify the difficulties entailed in its manufacture. Fitting the copy and calculating the number of lines are usually enormous problems: the short lines are often so short that they do not allow the typesetter enough leeway to set the type neatly; thus, when he encounters words that cannot be broken from one line to the next (and those words are most often found in copy that has to be set narrow!) he has to open up between words and characters to fill the line with air. It is equally inevitable that paragraphs break and subheads fall at the worst possible place: the area of the runaround. Since the runaround is not going to look comfortable — as it must, in order to come off neatly — in an area that is not surrounded by smooth

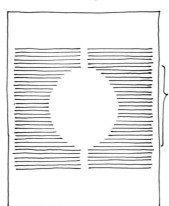

Problematic, since each line must be specified individually for length

color and uninterrupted plain type, it is usually necessary to set the type a second time just to iron out these rough spots. The resetting is time- and money-consuming.

In addition to the smoothness of the runaround's surroundings, uniform clearance has to be allowed around the illustration. For runaround and picture handling to look professionally crisp and neat, the space between the edge of the art and the edge of the type must be kept constant.

Use great care and circumspection in playing tricks with type: any time that a departure from the norm is made (whenever you decide to run type other than black ink on white paper), there is an automatic change in legibility. This change must be overcome if the normal legibility is to be retained. There are instances, of course, where legibility can be sacrificed for effect, but that sacrifice ought to be a deliberate decision on the part of the editor and designer, based on the realization that breaking the rules is liable to provoke retribution. So it is wise to think carefully about

 running type in reverse (white type on black, gray, or colored background)

 running type dropped out from halftones (white type on a picture)

 running type surprinted on halftones (black type on a picture)

 running type on peculiar stock (paper with pattern or texture or hairs in it)

 running type in color, on color, against color, in color on color.

If it makes functional and/or aesthetic sense to break the rules, the danger inherent in the rule breaking can be minimized by adapting the type to the situation: the usual solution is to either increase the size of the type, increase the boldness of the type, or switch to sans serif type. Any one or any combination of these devices may be necessary, according to the circumstances.

The criterion is retention of as strong a contrast between the words and the background as possible. Obviously, the greatest possible contrast is that between black ink and white paper. If the whiteness of the paper is toned down (as by a halftone or by color), a compensating enlargement of the type superimposed on the darker background will effect some of the original contrast, and thus ensure the type's legibility. Then, if the thickness of the strokes of the type is increased, the shape of each letter will be emphasized, and the original legibility will be again brought up to par.

Where white lettering is run against a dark background, especially if the background is made up of solid ink — or of several layers of ink superimposed on each other, as in four-color-process printing — it is important to enlarge the type to offset the fact that the lines of the characters can fill up with ink. That is also why sans serif type is preferable in such cases: serifs are the thinnest and most fragile parts of a letter, and thus the most easily spoiled in printing. One other reason should be mentioned: white lines on a dark background appear thinner and more fragile than the same lines shown in black on a white background.

# 5

# ILLUSTRATIONS: PHOTOGRAPHS AND PICTUR

Pictures attract the eye, gain attention, arouse curiosity. Pictures make the reader receptive to information. People resist the effort of reading: it means work. But they do not seem to mind looking at pictures. So, the more information that can be packaged in non-words, the better. Pictures, by substituting visual images for verbal description, help to short-circuit some of the reading process. But before delving deeper into the subject, it is necessary to define some terms. This is rather difficult, since terminology is inexact and overlaps.

An *illustration* is a visible mark on paper that communicates knowledge without the use of words. In some instances it is pictorial, but it need not necessarily be so; it can just as well be a chart, a map, a graph, a diagram. It can even be typographic, if the type used also transmits a desired visual flavor (in which case type, normally thought of as a strictly verbal medium, becomes a pictorial, nonverbal medium).

A *picture* is an image of something that is usually recognizable and naturalistic. It is a depiction of a scene, a person, or an object; it is a two-dimensional transformation of a three-dimensional original. In the sense that the word is used in this book, it is not a "painting," though paintings are not excluded if it makes sense to include them.

A picture can be manufactured in two basically different ways: by machine or by hand.

If the picture is made by machine, it is called a *photograph* (which should be no news to anyone). The vast majority of the "pictures" discussed in this book are photographs.

If the picture is made by hand, it can be called by a variety of names, depending on the graphic technique used in its making. So it is a *drawing,* if the artist used only lines with which to depict his or her subject. Or it is a *rendering,* if the artist used tones applied in some manner, whether by brush, chalk, spray paint or whatever. (A *watercolor* is a rendering made with water-base paints; an *oil-painting* is made with oil base paints; a *sketch* is made with any technique, but it is made quickly and left unfinished . . . and so on.)

Photographs and renderings (of whatever sort) have several characteristics in common: they are both tonal rather than lineal; they both must be reproduced by some sort of halftone method, and they both must have square edges when they are reproduced. (There are, of course, other edge treatments, but by and large the standard one where the halftone dots stop at a demarcation point is the one that comes immediately to mind.)

So far so good.

Unfortunately, such comparative simplicity does not obtain in the complicated world of publishing. The generic term "illustration," which would be so ideal in discussing visual images in general terms, has been preempted by the journalistic profession to imply "drawing." When editors talk about illustrations they usually mean diagrams or charts or maps. Sometimes they also mean "pictures" of some sort, but that is not always so.

It is therefore necessary to take the word "illustration" and qualify it with the words "photographs and pictures," as in this chapter heading, or with "nonpictorial," as in the heading for the following chapter.

To complicate matters further, the words "picture" and "photograph" are just about synonymous, as used in this chapter. Wherever the meaning calls for it, the appropriate word has been used; elsewhere, however, the words have been used according to the compromise worked out by the author and his editor; much discussion time has been used up in the endeavor to define, as precisely as possible, the specific word in the specific context. Alas, it does not work: common sense is the last resort.

# Two perils in pictures

## Pictures show too much

Every reader can interpret a picture his or her own way, according to his or her background, mood, interest, inclination. A reader does not necessarily share the editor's view or knowledge; therefore, he or she cannot be expected to see the same thing the editor sees in any given picture.

The editor, however, is deeply involved in the story and often forgets that the reader is not sitting right there in the editor's office. The editor must remember to make the effort to explain the meaning of each picture to the reader within the context of the story, so that its salient features are brought out clearly and understood by the reader. To handle the picture correctly, the editor needs to be aware of this necessity and also needs words to explain the picture.

Very few pictures are so clearly focused on a subject that words become superfluous. It is very risky to run pictures without them.

## Pictures are not The Universal Panacea

They are merely one of several different kinds of raw materials used to get ideas off the page and into the reader's mind. Having a good shot or two does not mean that the problems of presentation have been solved for that story. What matters is *how* that shot is used. The art of editing and art directing lies in the ingenuity and skill with which the potential communicating capacity of these raw materials (of which pictures are one) is brought out and applied to tell a story.

yͤ idealle nostrum for yͤ halitosisse, yͤ broken heartes, yͤ splitte personalitie, yͤ sluggish digestion, but — best solution and recommended as such and guaranteed of yͤ manufacturer, for yͤ dulle pagee! (Juste like yͤ this one)

# What is a good picture?

One that helps bring out the point of a story. The *ideas* inherent in the visual image are what matter most. So, although some shots within a group of pictures may be more attractive, better composed, or clearer focused, or may even include prettier models, the pictures that should be chosen for use in the magazine are those that embody most clearly the ideas in the story and help to illuminate, define, and articulate them.

In judging pictures for publication, it is right to think of them in precisely the same terms as when editing words — strive for clarity, meaning, content in terms of the thrust of the story. It is therefore right to ask such questions as, "Does it help the reader understand the story?" "Does it reinforce my argument?" "Does it illuminate the character of the people involved (apart from just showing what they look like)?" "Does it assist the reader in visualizing the interrelationships of the objects in question?" "Does it bring out or reinforce the significant factors under discussion?"

# The danger in pretty pictures

Do not allow yourself to be beguiled by the beauty of a photograph or the attractiveness of its subject. Do not pretend that it is *useful* if it is merely *beautiful,* and so run it among others that are in fact useful — though perhaps less pretty. This is cheating. It cheats the reader, who sees through the deception immediately; and it cheats the magazine, since the reader will have lost some of his or her faith in it because of the deception; and credibility is one of the magazine's most valuable and hard-won assets.

If the picture is irresistibly beguiling — because it is so rare to find such a Great Shot in the context of the subject of the magazine — run it, but run it for its own sake. Run it big, to get as much mileage and attention out of it as possible, and admit to the reader that this is a special situation, and that you are showing the picture in the hope that he will enjoy it as much as you do. But such a gimmick has to be so labeled: Picture of the Month, perhaps. Or perhaps you can use it as a "mood shot" for the frontispiece, or possibly tailpiece, to a story. Just so long as you do not pretend that it is an ordinary informing-kind of picture.

Such an application of a special photograph is justified in that it gives the book an extra degree of delight; it makes the reader feel good for having received that something unexpected; and it probably makes everyone concerned realize, perhaps for the first time, that their particular field has an aspect they had never suspected could be so beautiful.

# An essential investment in time: the story conference

The more illustrative elements a story is likely to have, the more essential a proper story conference becomes.

All too often, in the rush of magazine production, the art director is handed a folder containing a finished manuscript, three dog-eared photos, a small mugshot, and a note stating: "A couple more pix plus type table coming Monday." Of this he or she is expected to fashion a story, arranging it so that it is *"good looking"* (whatever that may be). This is a waste of time, and the best possible way to smother a potentially lively article. It also undermines morale, since the poor designer can't help but be frustrated and bored by that kind of unthinking labor.

Instead, a formally scheduled conference between editor and art director should be held — *before* the editor writes a single word of the final manuscript. All the editor should bring to such a meeting is a story outline, together with the illustrations he or she has gathered and the ideas for illustration that have occurred to him or her in the process of working on the story to this point. One other essential piece of information is needed in the story conference: the total pages allocated to the story by the editor-in-chief. The editor must explain to the art director what the story is about and — even more important — why the magazine thinks it worth publishing. The art director must ask questions, clarify and define points, challenge conclusions, and get involved in the story to the extent of becoming interested in telling it. Only when the art director understands the story and becomes involved in it can he or she begin to contribute knowledge, skill, and talent to the product.

The product? A melding of pictures and words into a unified statement in such a way that the whole becomes greater than the sum of its parts — so that one plus one equals three.

It is highly unlikely that such understanding leading to such melding of words and pictures can be achieved without personal interplay. Ideally, writing and layout would be done with one head and four hands. Alas, we have to accept two heads to go with the four hands. Compromises have to be made. However, there are two crucial decisions that must be reached in the story conference, if the goal of synergistic journalism is to be reached:

*First decision:* what the title (or at least the working title) will be. The final words can be polished later; what matters at the outset is the direction of the story, which is an essential clue to the art director about the flavor, atmosphere, and content. Without such knowledge, it is not possible to translate the literary quality in the words into visual terminology. All the art director can do is play it safe and do a straightforward presentation that says nothing about anything — but is neat. That is no way to achieve a lively magazine.

The second reason for the need of a title: the picture that is picked as the opening salvo must have a clear relationship to the words. The art director has a legitimate stake in the choice of such a picture.

*Second decision:* how the allotted space will be subdivided to fit the component parts of the story. This obvious requirement forces the editor to organize the story, making estimates as to the length of the several subdivisions. These estimates must be co-ordinated with equivalent spaces allocated on the pages by the art director. Naturally, the two must work together to produce an agreed-upon set of thumbnail sketches of the pages, annotated with subject notes or — if possible — coordinated headlines and subheads.

Armed with these preliminary decisions, the editor returns to his or her desk to write (muttering *sotto voce* about unfeeling artists), and the art director returns to his or her cubicle to make preliminary layouts (complaining bitterly about lack of time and/or good material). That sort of disagreement is fine — it happens all the time. The participants may be complaining, but they both know exactly where they stand: the editor knows how the story will break up and how much to write; the designer knows what the story is supposed to be communicating, which pictures are useful for that purpose, and therefore which ones to stress through size and placement and which to play down. He or she can also start thinking about appropriate type handling.

The moment of truth comes when they meet again a couple of days later to coordinate each other's solutions. Obviously the original scheme didn't quite work — it never does. Arguments at this point, however, are highly productive, since both have valuable views to contribute, based on mutual understanding of their mutual problem. Such arguments as "I don't like it" or "This isn't good-looking," which are based on personal, arbitrary whim, can be dispensed with in favor of more realistic arguments based on journalistic criteria: "I don't think the layouts work because the wrong aspect is emphasized" or "That other facet is just as impor-tant as the one you concentrated on, so we've lost balance; sorry, I misled you — you've got to give it more prominence." It is also at this point that the writer can demand more space for the text (writers always do) and the art director can argue against it on aesthetic grounds (artists always do). Then, final layouts are made — and these are such that justice is done to the content of the story.

Emil Weiss

114

# An essential investment of money: photostats

The more illustrations a story is likely to have, the more essential it becomes to work with photostats. Photostats are inexpensive copies of photographs or any other visual material, made on paper to the size specified: blown up or reduced. A negative is made from which the positive is then shot. The positive is then trimmed to size and rubber-cemented or Scotch-taped to the dummy.

In a simple area of the magazine, such as the "news section," where pictures tend to be standardized to one-column or two-column width, an educated guess by a skilled art director can be relied on for appropriate picture sizing. An outline drawn on the dummy sheet indicating the size and position of a picture will generally not result in disaster.

In new-product columns, however, many problems are caused by standardization of picture sizes, since the scale of subject matter can lead to ridiculous-looking situations; for example, a paint can (product A) might be placed adjacent to product B, which happens to be a sixteen-story crane. The two pictures, side by side, result in a maxi-can or a mini-crane. Not advisable, but not the end of the world either.

However, it is most unwise to depend on the art director's guess, no matter how experienced he or she may be, in any situation where some sort of relationship — be it in size, shape, placement, scale, or content — between the pictures is intended. It is necessary that the editor and designer actually see before them the exact effect created by the sizing, cropping, proportion, and interrelation of the pictures *before* the pages get sent to the printer. Photostats should therefore be made of each picture to the intended scale; they must be neatly trimmed and placed in position on the dummy — and then one can see whether the layout actually works or not.

The cost of photostats is not negligible, and the time required for their production has to be worked into the schedule; but the investment of money and extra work pays off handsomely in the resultant improvement in quality of product. The desire to get the scale and size of pictures just right marks the difference between an amateur and a professional appearance in the magazine. Such dependence on a mechanical technique is by no means an insult to the art director's artistic judgment. On the contrary, it recognizes the importance of aesthetic relationships of which he or she is the arbiter. But it also recognizes the fact that it is practically impossible to work out (in the mind's eye only) the precise croppings and exact reductions of a group of pictures and be certain that they will work well together. They are meant to work well together, but they are not likely to do so unless the physical eye can be brought into the production process in a stage intermediate between the mind's eye and the final layout. And for that purpose, the only good way is by using photostats.

A lagniappe of having stats to work with: it often happens in practice that a new and much better arrangement suggests itself from the actual photostats on the table, one that would never have been imagined had there been only a group of rectangles drawn on the layout sheet.

Given a bunch of very normal photos, the normal procedure would be to draw a number of rectangles on the dummy sheet like this ------------

A usable, if undistinguished, result would ensue ----
All the pictures have been used, they are neatly arranged, and there is ample space for head and text.
What is missing?
Interplay between the pictures OTHER than simple alignment of the edges.

If photostats had been available, such interplay could have been achieved. For proof, turn the page...

Photos: Susanna Opper, Abraham & Straus *Spotlight*

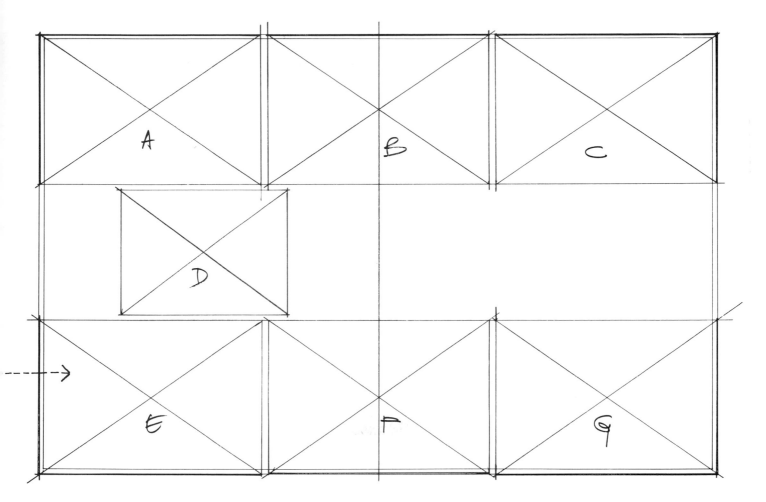

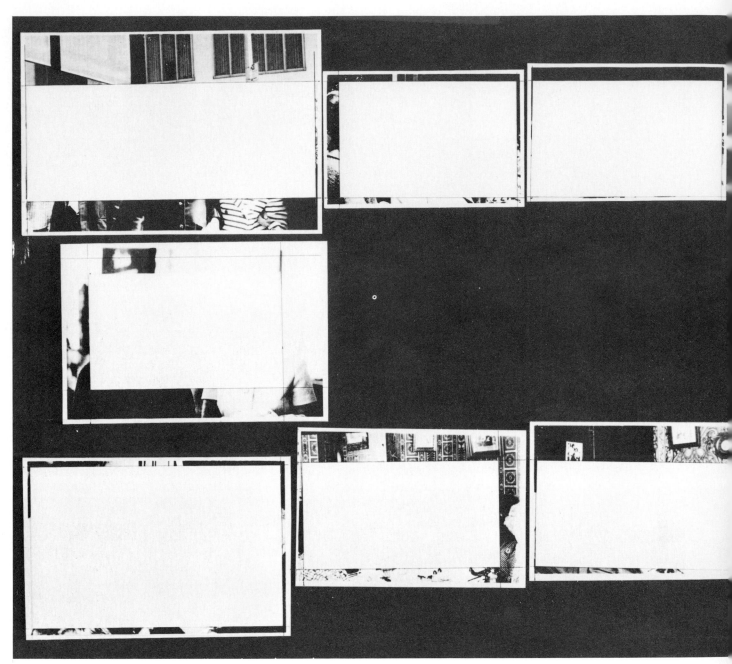

This is a picture of the photostat leftovers, after the useful areas were cut out and used in the assembly of the 'after' version of the scheme. It shows how the stats were made at different sizes, and how the useful areas were cut out at angles, off center etc.

The effect of all this extra trouble →

The three street pictures are allied in position and — more important — in the scale of the peoples' faces and at a constant eye-level. So the impression of a single enormous panorama is achieved. Its horizontality is stressed by the band of white space above.

The restaurant pictures are similarly unified, echoing the horizontality of the strip above.

The focal picture at center is stressed in importance by simple enlargement and cropping-away of uninformative background.

Such refinements cannot be attempted without stats.

↑ This 'before' (same as on the preceding page) is shown here for ease of comparison with the 'after' ↓

# Choosing the right picture

## Seeing what is available

Spread the pictures out, so you can see them and judge them all at once. Never riffle through a stack of photos as though they were playing cards, and never put them on your lap. Instead, spread them out on a large, uncluttered table, without overlapping any. When they are laid out in front of you that way, you can begin to notice differences in quality, similarities in camera angles, and contrast in content. You can also start grouping pictures by subject and so begin coordinating them with your story outline. Then, when the groups have been established, you can weed out the obvious duplications; reject the inappropriate; notice potential mood shots; look for unexpected combinations; find interesting possibilities in cropping of shots — you can, in fact, start the picture-editing process.

## Using the safe shot (or not)

Try not to use the "safe" shot: nothing is deader than the standard picture of somebody receiving an award, or two people shaking hands or posing in front of something, or — worse yet — somebody pointing at something. There are times when such material is inescapable; in that case, if you have a choice, use the picture that doesn't make the person look *nice*. Use the shot that tells more about the subject than the fact that he or she has two ears and two eyes and a mouth that smiles inanely.

People are interested in people, which is why you find so many mugshots published. But if you want a livelier book, you had better use the livelier mugshots. The subjects of those less-than-flattering portraits may get mad at you, but they'll get over it. Besides, the magazine does not exist in order to flatter the people it reports on. It exists to report the truth as the editors see it, and posed mugshots or handshaking scenes fall short of at least one aspect of that truth.

# Just any old picture doesn't help much

Just any old picture does not make a page lively. If the picture is dull, the page remains dull (zero + zero = nothing). This truism remains valid in spite of the design adage that "where an element breaks a pattern, interest is thereby created." A plain gray halftone dropped into a surrounding gray morass of type does indeed appear different from the type, and so "breaks up" the dullness of the type — thus creating a certain degree of interest. But that is not enough.

To pick the appropriate un-dull picture you have to differentiate between the two basic kinds of pictures that are normally used in a magazine: the grabbers and the explainers.

## The grabbers

Just as a headline is an attention-creator, so can a picture be an attention-creator. Every headline is written in as lively and interesting a way as possible, because the editor realizes that a headline must have more quality and polish than an ordinary sentence just set in bigger and bolder type. A picture can be thought of the same way. To create interest with a picture, interest must be inherent in that picture. If that interest is lacking, the grabbing-quality hoped for will not come through. Unexpected words in a headline, polished English — startling images, fine photographic quality — these are exact parallels in the functional aspect of attention-getting.

## The explainers

These are pictures equivalent to paragraphs full of explanatory detail — factual expository material. These are the "one picture is worth ten thousand words" ones, and very useful they are, too. But these illustrations often tend to be workaday, unimaginative, and dull; they are used in the magazine for imparting information. It is unwise to depend on them to create sparkle.

Both kinds of pictures are necessary in a magazine; both kinds have a certain value. It is important to distinguish between their respective functions and not use the one kind of photo in the other kind of application, but instead to become so sensitive to the visual properties of pictures that excitement is noticed and used appropriately where it is already to be found.

Photos: United Nations

# Money and the hard-to-photograph

Spend the bulk of the photographing budget on taking pictures of dull subject matter. It is no great trick to take passable pictures of beautiful or photogenic subjects, but it takes imagination, skill, and expertise to make a cigarette butt or a garbage dump visually interesting. Very often, the talented photographer is hired to shoot the well-known and beautiful aspect of the magazine — and the workaday "uninteresting" stuff is left to the editor-amateur, who has limited equipment and even more limited visual imagination. Editors with cameras are the bane of art directors' lives anyway and should be forbidden, but we live in a practical, money-short world where, alas, art directors are sentenced to finding happiness in spite of having to live with editor/photographers. So — since they are here to stay — at least let them direct their energies to the easier, photogenic matters of the book and let the pros go out on the difficult assignments. If you analyze them, you'll find that most specialized magazines devote as much or more space to the workaday matters as they do to the glamorous material; so if the photographing effort gets reorganized as suggested, it is likely that better (and better-looking) magazines will result.

Look at the same old subjects in new ways. This concept is just an outgrowth of the previous point: to use fresh imagination on tired subject matter. Naturally, not every subject lends itself to experimentation, especially where the straightforward explainer shots are concerned. Wherever it makes even remote sense, however, the photographer going out on assignment should be encouraged to try for freshness, if only for its own sake. He or she should go out and shoot from unexpected angles (from below, from above), through gauze for fuzzy foggy effects, or through a keyhole for an onlooker effect; unlikely lighting should be used; the photographer should spit on the lens. Who knows what trickery a fertile imagination can come up with? The point is that the photographer should be sent out with an understanding that he or she has freedom to do interpretive and creative experimentation — with the confidence that when the contact sheets are brought back to the office, the photographer's attitude will be acceptable and his or her imagination will be appreciated. The work will have a chance of being used in the story *because* it is fresh, not *in spite of* it's being "different from the stuff we usually run." A climate of acceptance is hard to establish because it requires much teamwork and understanding between editors and photographers; but such a climate is essential if the editors want to turn out a product that is lively, issue to issue.

# Questionable quality

Accept — and use — the kinds of pictures that used to be rejected out-of-hand: the soft-focus, rough-grained, doubly exposed, smudged-movement kinds — the sort of material that even the daring photographer in the preceding subsection might not push too hard. There is room in a magazine for unexpected visual images if they are used with subtletly, with awareness of their shortcomings and emphasis on their positive attributes, and in the appropriate place. There is no reason why every photograph on every page of every magazine must be the clearly defined, hard-edged, precisely focused, historically correct equivalent of a new-product shot.

The picture tells its story *because of*, rather than in spite of the smudged action.

Risk going out on a limb: use more symbolism in the pictorial
material. This is just another way of saying that you should have
more faith in the intelligence of your reader's and their capacity for
understanding what you are driving at without it's being illustrated
by an obvious visual image. If something is obvious, then —
however well photographed or interestingly illustrated — it will
remain obvious; and obviousness tends to be dull.

Often a twist can be given to an illustration that can eliminate
this obviousness, can turn the picture into something quirky — and
the reader can be relied upon to understand such a twist, especially
if the words that accompany the image channel his or her thinking
in the right direction.

A picture of an open door does not have to be interpreted as a
closeup of efficient hinges: it can mean "invitingness." The context
within which the image rides will help the reader deduce the
correct meaning of the symbol.

This is indeed a photo
of peeling paint.
But it is also a photo
of aging.

# Mood shots

Use as many mood shots as possible in the book. They intrigue the reader, set the stage, establish atmosphere. Often such shots are symbolic — tangential to the main thrust of the story, yet perfectly appropriate. If symbolic material is not available, and there are no out-of-focus shots anywhere either, the historical context of the subject in hand can always be explored. This is one of the easiest problems to solve, simply by getting in touch with one of the several picture collections that stock illustrative material ranging from ancient woodcuts through the most up-to-date materials from everywhere about everything. The range of material is extraordinary — and it becomes available as a result of a simple telephone call; a clear description of the problem to be solved or, if possible, a specific solution required will bring a batch of pictures on approval in next day's mail. The use of any of the material thus found is paid for by a fee for the one-time reproduction rights of whatever is chosen. Unused material should be returned immediately, and no charge is made for the finding service. Material obtained from these sources is usually of very high graphic quality and so can add immeasurably to the story as well as to the apparent sophistication of the magazine as a whole.

There are also numerous books of old engravings available, from which reproduction is allowed at no cost other than the first cost of buying the book itself.

# Picture files

Establish your own picture file for photos that might come in handy as mood shots in the future, and together with this, establish an idea folder for visual idea starters that you come across, and that you will certainly forget unless there is a specific place for them to be hidden in that you can remember to dig through when stuck for an illustration idea.

## Size as indicator of importance

Signal the Big Idea of the story in the Big Picture — and make that big picture as big and as dominant as possible. Then, reinforce the big idea within the big picture with smaller ideas carried in the smaller pictures, to flesh out the big idea, add details, corroborate the thesis. To pick out the nub of the argument, emphasize it, and bring the readers' attention to the central issue is the essence of editing. In visual terms, such attention-focusing is achieved most easily by the simple expedient of giving the important picture the size that shows its importance.

Never make pictures the same size: doing so implies that you have no preference or opinion as to the relative merits of one over another. It is unwise to abdicate the decision-making process to the reader, and give up the use of one of editing's most effective techniques: the differentiation by size.

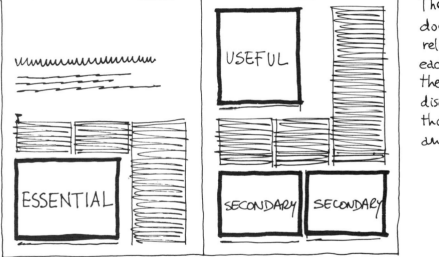

The size of each picture does not reflect the relative importance of each in the story. So the reader has to discover it through thought and analysis and hard, slow work.

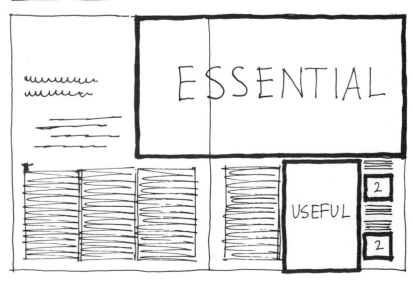

There can be no question in anyone's mind about which picture the editors deemed most important. Not only does the spread communicate more clearly and faster, but it looks better and more dynamic. Yet all the type is in this scheme that was shown in the scheme above.

## Size as a relative concept

Bigness and smallness are relative concepts: bigness exists only by contrast to smallness. In the context of a magazine page's scale, it is necessary to reduce the size of the surroundings in order to achieve something appearing large. Among a number of small elements on a page, a medium-sized one will look enormous (like a bluefish among guppies). Placed among elements larger than itself, that same medium-sized piece will appear small (like that bluefish among sharks). So the secret of lively page makeup, quite apart from the editorial expressiveness of the content (touched on earlier), is the playing off of large units against small units.

As an additional aspect of this largeness/smallness subject: editors and designers are often tempted to make the pictures as large as possible, wherever they can. Unfortunately, this technique does not achieve the desired dramatic quality; instead, it produces an overall bloated look. It is essential that the smallness of the magazine page be remembered; only then can you utilize the smallness of scale of the elements imposed on that page as a valuable display characteristic. Pictures should be made larger than the normal size only where emphasis is needed or justified. What is "normal" size? The size required to make the content of the illustration easily discernible. The dimensions of a photograph — the number of square inches it takes up on the page — is only one factor to bear in mind. Other factors are that elusive one, "scale" — and the picture's quality. Size and scale must be balanced one against the other — and both must be thought of in terms of the overall impact on the magazine page.

Alone, a picture lacks 'size'.

It only looks big next to a small one.

It only looks small next to a big one.

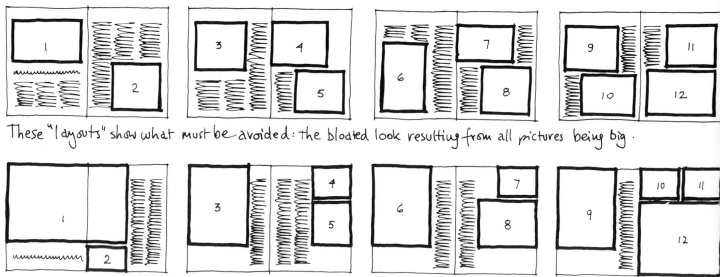

These "layouts" show what must be avoided: the bloated look resulting from all pictures being big.

These "layouts" show the effect of varied picture sizing (using bleed and a base alignment on the page).

Size of pictures and placement of pictures on the page should be thought of as complementary aspects of design. But there is a third necessary element in the equation: the thrust of the story line. (This is a purely *editorial* aspect, since it requires a basic decision of *meaning*.)

Too often, peripheral material is used to "dress up the story" in spite of the fact that the subject of the pictures has only a superficial relation to the main story line. This divergence of meaning will create confusion in the minds of the readers and will leave them somehow dissatisfied. It is true, however, that pictures which don't have very much to do with the story may go unnoticed by the other kind of reader, the one who merely skims through the book. Such "glance-level" readership is important, too, of course: a major goal of editorial presentation is to get the superficial readers intrigued by what they see, slow down their skimming, force their attention onto the page, and start them reading.

Taking all these considerations into account, it is still better to be forthright about it and apply the principle of size-and-placement in such a way that confusion is removed and reader-attraction retained to some extent. How? Simply by splitting the two elements away from each other, leaving the main story alone and adding a separate element — quarantined from the main story by space or lines — as a "sidebar" secondary story. This secondary story should, ideally, have its own small headline and its own descriptive text block, so that it becomes a self-contained element, placed in its self-contained and easily visible bubble of space. The advantages of such handling are several: confusion is resolved; the glance-level-dressing-up effect is not altogether lost, and — most important — a third extra-added-attraction has been created: that of a small story.

Short stories are often the best read in the issue, simply because of their shortness and apparent ease of reading (and the minimal expenditure of time involved). Therefore it is likely that the sidebar itself will attract the attention of the casual reader, who will read it *first* — and thus be cajoled to enter the main body of the text. He or she might not have read the story had not that small sidebar been "broken out" of the main story and run by itself. Thus a mis-sized big picture can well become far more effective than a small picture that is properly sized but handled differently.

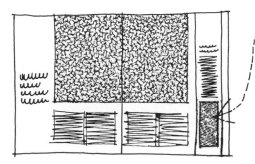

Sidebar matter broken out of the body of the story and run in a clearly defined area at a smaller scale, in smaller type, at a narrower measure.

# Bleeding pictures

Use the "bleed" with discrimination, deliberately, carefully. The normal magazine page has a white margin that frames the "live matter" on all sides. The reader expects to see that white margin as he turns the pages; in fact, that white margin becomes a recognition signal to him that the material seen is editorial rather than advertisement (since editorial margins are — or should be — all of standard width, whereas ads are designed so haphazardly, in comparison to editorial matter, that they appear not to have such standard "edges").

A bleed makes use of that margin for picture, thus destroying a portion of the "frame". As a result, a small portion of the pattern that the reader is conditioned to expect has been eliminated. On the other hand, a bleed calls attention to itself *because of* that destructive act, simply because anything that breaks a pattern tends to call attention to itself. If attention-getting is an editorial objective, then "bleeding" a picture might be a useful tool.

A second positive attribute of bleeding is the illusory page enlargement that results when a picture is brought out to the trim edge of the page. In some way — because the framing has been removed — the picture can be interpreted as flowing beyond the confines of the page in front of you. The subject is broader, wider, more panoramic; and what you see is merely a piece of it. This illusion tends to enlarge the page and thus also to increase the impact of what is shown.

Here again, the decision whether to bleed or not to bleed becomes both a design consideration and an editorial consideration: Is the interruption of flow more important? Is the subject worth the attention? What do we gain by which sacrifice? As a matter of general principle, it is better to restrict pictures to the confines of the live-matter page and *not* bleed. Bleeds should be used only where real emphasis is justified. But when bleed is decided on as a tool, it should be used boldly enough to make it smashingly noticeable. There is no point in pulling a special stunt that nobody sees. Small-scale bleeds are only noticeable as small-scale nuisances.

Pictures should be kept within the confines of the live-matter page

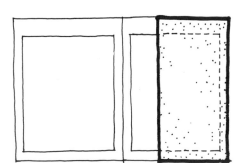

But if a bleed is <u>useful</u>, bleed BIG

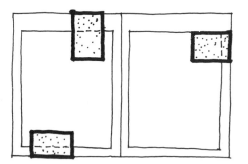

... and avoid mini-bleeds like these

## Relationship of words to pictures

Make the relationship between headline words and the visual content of the picture quite obvious. The train of thought generated by the big picture should be picked up by the words of the headline and sharpened, clarified, honed, and expanded by them. The two must work together and say the same thing — so that the editorial meaning is so strongly conveyed that it becomes irresistible. Only then will the readers' curiosity compel them to read the deck, and then the first sentence. At this point a reader should be hooked by the story's importance to him- or herself and go on and read the rest. On the other hand, if the headline does *not* follow from the picture, but instead starts a conflicting trend of thought, then the entire attention-provoking advantage of the picture will be wasted.

The closer in meaning the headline comes to the obvious interpretation of the picture, the more effective does the blended communication become.

This shot of a square in the Old West seems to say: "The Old West was a busy place". It should not be twisted into saying that Conestoga wagons were well-engineered.

# One picture, one message

Never try to tell two stories from one picture. Each picture should be chosen to convey a primary point, and ideally there should be as many pictures as there are points. If that many pictures are not available, then those points that are not illustrated should still be run — as separate, unillustrated points. For it is very dangerous to use one picture for more than one editorial purpose: such duality of purpose is difficult to make clear, and if the editor finds it hard to make clear, then certainly the reader will be confused. There are special situations, however, where such trickery is appropriate.

What does this picture say?
Ancient Roman entertainments?
Fashions in Old Rome?
Outraged Innocence?
(Gérôme painted it as that).
It should be made perfectly clear
which meaning the editors choose.

Whenever there are enough pictures available, try to make the material fit a picture-caption story rather than the more usual essay-with-pictures presentation technique. Such a journalistic form is often harder to do, since it is a less usual — less familiar — pattern. But it can often be more inviting to the reader, and thus more effective in getting ideas off the page: the comic-book format gives the impression of being "easy to read" — a minimum-effort presentation to which the reader responds positively. Of course, a picture-caption story has a different flavor and so has a built-in obvious advantage as a change-of-pace story within the issue.

The story concerns a flow of processing — a subject that lends itself to visual description. The captions, arranged in obvious series, reinforce the sequential presentation, while reporting the necessary facts not seen in the photos.

# Making the most of the available material

## Combining small elements into groups

Avoid peppering the page with little dark spots. It is better to pull
the pictures together, whenever doing so makes editorial sense.
Such a conglomeration of small elements increases their impact.
Here are the commonest (simplest) ways to make such agglutinations:

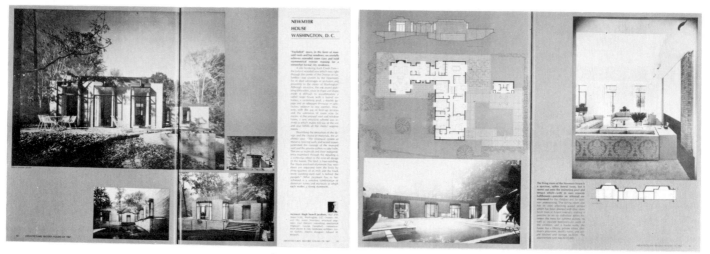

Placing pictures on a background tint of gray or color.

Putting the elements inside a box.

Placing pictures very close together — possibly even butting them — so that their proximity welds them together.

Large picture in color, small ones in black and white.

Small picture in color, large one in black and white.

(NOTE: this works perfectly well where no color is available — but color makes it more visible as a separate technique).

Making one picture dominant, and superimposing the other, supporting, ones over it. This ruse is useful when color budgets will not allow all the illustrations to be run in color, but a colorful atmosphere is wanted.

Placing pictures within a grid of strong vertical and horizontal lines, in which the lines are so strong that they become the dominant tying factor. The spacing can be regular (as in a net) or irregular (as in a Mondrian painting).

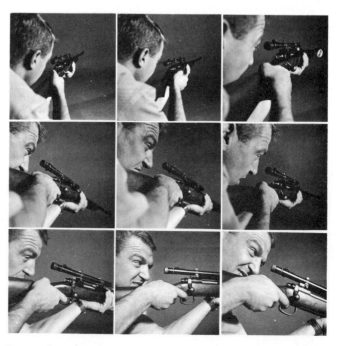

Repeating the shape or size of a number of pictures, so that the common element of shape or size becomes the unifying force.

Using the subject matter of the pictures in such a way that elements in them (such as the horizon, scale, and direction) work together in conveying meaning and the visual expression of that meaning.

Picture sizing, placement, scale, horizon alignment combine to emphasize the vastness of the interior spaces — the whole point of showing the pictures in the first place.

Overlapping the corners and placing the pictures in a shape vaguely similar to a clock face brings out the purpose of the pictures: to show the effect of passage of time in one Italian market square.

Overlapping edges of pictures in a montage.

Cropping the pictures in a startling way, so that the peculiarity of handling becomes the unifying characteristic.

# Placement of the picture in imitation of the angle of the shot

For instance, an aerial photograph normally appears most natural and most comfortable when it is placed at the foot of the page, reinforcing the illusion of "looking down" into the view. Conversely, a picture of a seagull soaring overhead in the sky is most effective when placed at the head of the page, since such positioning carries the illusion of space into the miniature world of the magazine. The reader perceives the picture by looking upward, in the same direction that the photographer pointed his camera.

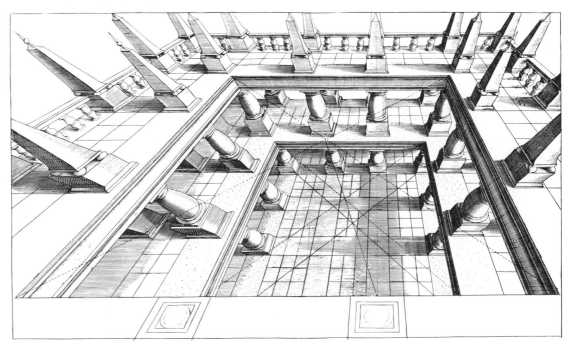

# The direction in which the people in the picture are looking

Curiosity always compels people to glance up at the sky when they see someone else on the street doing it. This same curiosity carries over into photographs, but in this instance, the readers do not actually follow the photographed person's gaze — they are merely made comfortable or uncomfortable by it.

As a general rule it is better to have mugshots of people "speaking to each other" on the page. Also, it is usually better to have the people in the photos facing into the spread rather than out of it.

But, as with all generalizations, situations can come up where an inherent liability can be turned into an asset: that curiosity-generator can be used to carry the reader from spread to spread by placing an obviously outward-looking picture in the far right-hand edge of a page, in place of a carry-over line, perhaps.

Looking into the spread:

from the left

...from the right

Emphasizing the relationship of the characters on the spread

PRO!   CON?

The direction in which the subjects are looking put to use on the publication pages.

Utilizing the pull of curiosity to make readers turn the page

# People pictures

"Mugshots" deserve special coverage because so many are used in publications, and because imagination and ingenuity often become paralyzed when the editor or designer confront them. The simple point to remember is this: people pics are no more sacred or untouchable than any other kind, and like all other kinds, they are raw material to be manipulated for editorial ends. Here are a few ideas on what to do with them. The ideas may not look all that innovative; their efficacy comes into its own when applied to *groups* of mugshots.

Try to pick the unsafe image, the one that illumines the character inside the physical shape, instead of merely showing what someone looks like.

← Comparatively dull.

Thinking, scratching, alive →

Home in on the personality by tight cropping, thus allowing enlargement and more impact within the same overall space.

The brooding beauty of the face is less striking here,
← than it is here →

Crop into unexpected proportions: ordinary shapes emphasize the ordinariness of the original. But unexpected shapes bring out some startling qualities →

Concentrate viewer's attention onto the face by silhouetting out the background distractions. A serendipitous advantage: the random outline of the silhouette adds informal visual relief to the squared-up rigidity of the surrounding page. For maximal effect: cut away all but the face itself;

To retain the geometric precision of the page, yet use silhouetting, enclose the portrait in a box

All sorts of variants are possible. One of them → a box too small to contain the depicted personage.

Shape the picture into an unusual form, when such a trick might be appropriate and not undignified.

←
Safer: see the photo as an object reproduced on the page → casting a shadow.
(See page 161)

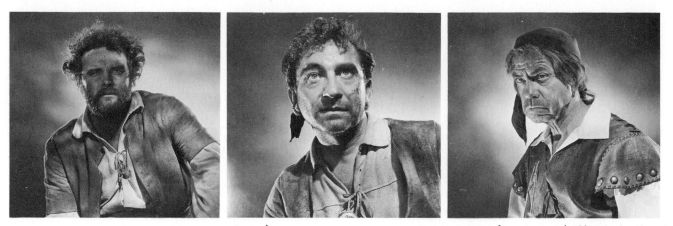

Mugshots in groups: typical (good) originals varying in head sizes, facing in different directions, lit from various angles, but seen against similar backgrounds. The formula-solution to running them as a group would be
to make the faces all
the same size...
Crop them into the
usual vertical
rectangle... display
them in precise,
shooting gallery
alignment ———→
(How dull!)
Here, blown up for
drama, the identical

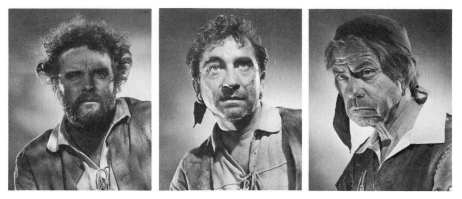

shots: silhouetted, overlapped, but retaining their variety of head sizes. A much more human group. How to make it? EASY! Cut out the figures carefully, compose the group and glue down. Shoot the halftone as a single unit.
(True, his head is a little too large for credibility. He ought not to be "behind" the fellow in the
↓      middle — but who noticed? This overlapping was
          dictated by available
            shoulders in the
              originals.)

Present sequences in clear flow — from left to right, the way people are used to reading. Too often sequences are placed in such a way on the page that readers have to puzzle out the direction of flow before they can follow the story line: vertically? horizontally? left-hand page first and then the right-hand page? or right across the spread?

A horizontal flow is usually better than a vertical flow, since we are trained to read from left to right, and so automatically assume that relationship unless other elements are present to persuade us of another direction. To package our product — the magazine — so that it is of greatest service to our readers, we must make use of all such available habit patterns: anything that helps readers get through the material faster must be used.

A horizontal sequence should be as broad as possible, and the number of pictures packed into the left-to-right direction should be as large as possible. The gutter between the pages is not an insuperable obstacle and should be ignored, so long as the clarity of the horizontal flow is retained. In saddle-stitched or perfect-bound magazines the gutter can be safely disregarded, but in side-wire-bound magazines, special attention must be paid to the obviousness of the gutter-jumping direction.

The simple trick here is to divide the space that separates the pictures *un*equally: bunch them up tight — practically butting them side-to-side — but separate them as widely as possible from each other up-and-down; the purpose is to create as self-contained horizontal "strings" of pictures as possible.

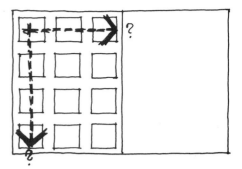

Equal space between pictures gives no clue about the direction in which the sequence has been arranged.

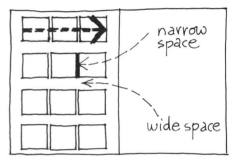

narrow space

wide space

Unequal spacing between pictures implies more intimate relationships one way, and thus leads to an understanding of the direction.

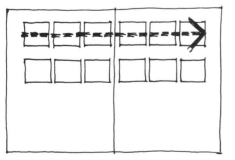

Using the full width of the spread helps to make the sequence more of an important event in the issue; the gutter can safely be ignored if the spacing between the rows is strong enough to weld them into obvious rows.

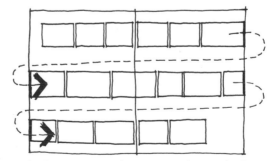

As long as the horizontality of the rows remains dominant, variations in picture widths and bleeding of the rows can add to the visual interest and editorial expressiveness of the presentation.

# The horizon

The horizon should always remain at the same level in neighboring pictures, because the pictures "work better" together that way, and because the views look more interrelated and natural that way. Besides, the magazine appears more sophisticated because of such a simple trick. It is, however, essential that photostats be used in the design of the pages, in order to accomplish this goal.

Horizon alignment is a principle that becomes most important when the subject matter of the pictures has any architectural or landscape components. Imagine a blank wall, represented by the blank white page, into which holes are punched (where the pictures are). If the window-pictures are conceived of as looking out at a view beyond the wall, it becomes quite obvious that the horizon should remain in a constant position if you want to create a grandiose vista with the several photos.

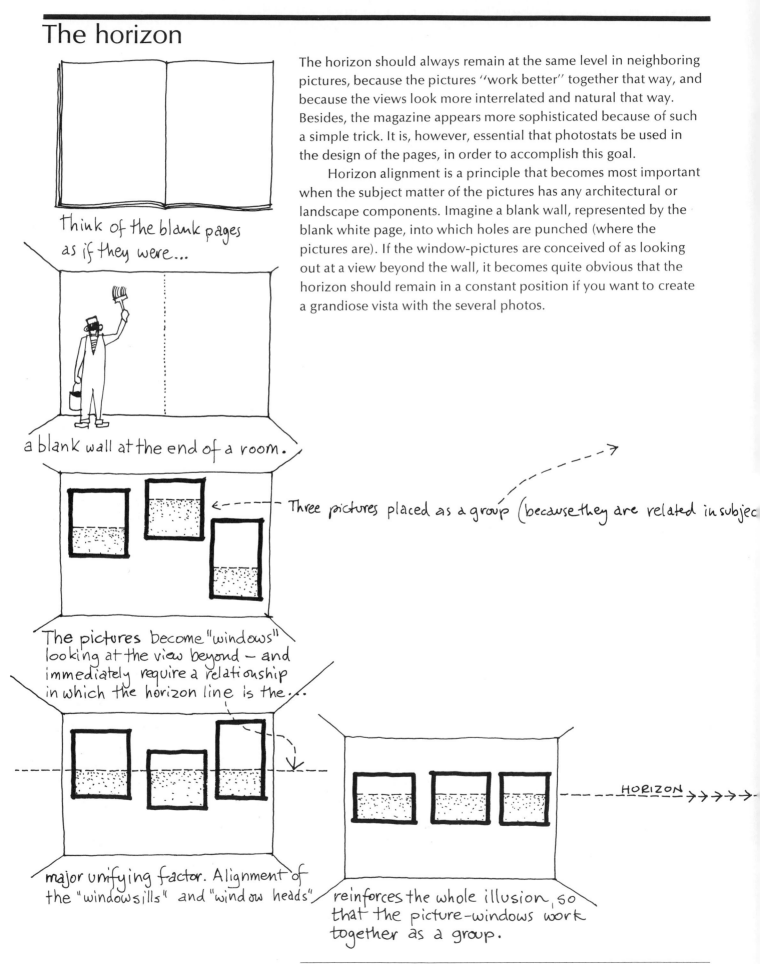

Think of the blank pages as if they were...

a blank wall at the end of a room.

Three pictures placed as a group (because they are related in subjec

The pictures become "windows" looking at the view beyond — and immediately require a relationship in which the horizon line is the...

major unifying factor. Alignment of the "windowsills" and "window heads"

HORIZON

reinforces the whole illusion, so that the picture-windows work together as a group.

.... but ignoring their visual potential.

The same three pictures, cropped and aligned on the horizon. A coherent group — a grand view.

# Focusing attention onto the critical area

Home-in on the image in the photograph; make the most of a picture's point-making capability by focusing the reader's attention on the element of the picture that you want him or her to perceive. This can be done in three ways:

## By words

Tell the readers what to look for; they will do so, and (maybe) find it. This is where well-organized and well-edited captions come in: in order to make quite clear what the editor wants to point up in a picture it is wise to emphasize the point in the very first few words of the caption (commonly known as "hot words"). These words are, in effect, a little label or headline that immediately gives the clue to the picture's thrust in the story. Too often the opportunity for exploiting the hot-word capability is lost by using those words as plain description of the image instead of as the meaning-to-the-story of the image.

The first words of the caption are crucial in explaining what the picture is about:
is this a picture of

Broken windows

or is this a picture of

Vandalism

or is this a picture of

Classical clichés

or what?

Cropping can change the feeling of a picture and can clarify the picture's meaning. It can help the picture to communicate faster by editing out (cutting away) extraneous, disturbing, surrounding images and thus showing only what the editors have in mind.

If the purpose of this melodramatic picture is to show public consternation at the Bad News, then the full image is correct.

If the purpose is to show a simple scene of delivery of a message – then the surrounding crowd can disappear without regret.

# By manipulating the image

Often it is inadvisable to cut away surrounding areas in a picture, since they are essential to an understanding of the subject within its own context — yet there may still be a specific small area to which it is necessary to draw the reader's attention directly. (In a story about a newly invented cog that is part of a larger machine, it is necessary to show the entire machine in order to place the cog in its surrounding and show how important it is; yet the reader should not need to study the whole machine in order to find the little cog in question.) In such cases, it is often good to *dull down* those essential-yet-secondary surroundings, so that the sparkling area that remains undulled draws attention to itself by virtue of its liveliness.

This dulling can be accomplished relatively easily and inexpensively by several means, the commonest being retouching. The photograph is given to a photo-retoucher, who mounts it on a backing and then airbrushes (sprays) appropriate paint onto the areas to be played down.

A second way is to make overlays, showing the edges of the darkened areas, which the engraver can follow in the mechanical stages of the preparation of the printing plates.

A third, simple, do-it-yourself way consists in purchasing overlay material that carries a transparent film of gray, placing it over the photograph, and scratching away the gray paint from the areas that you intend to keep unchanged. The engraver then makes the plate from the photograph with the overlay on top of it. Various degrees of whiteness or grayness are available, expressed as percentages of solid (100%) black or of solid (100%) white. The advantages of this method are that you can control exactly what you wish to see as bright areas, and you can see what you will get right in front of you.

The most important factor, however, is that the editor must regard a picture as a piece of raw material that may — and easily can — be manipulated to achieve greater expressiveness. Editors must be aware of this capacity of pictures; they must demand greater clarity, because only when they demand it will they get it.

Mass assault, organized mayhem, lots of things going on — and it is a picture of ACTIVITY.

But here is a detail seen in its context: teamwork by a small group, surrounded by essential background information.

# Multisubject pictures

## Splitting the caption

A picture that shows several different elements, all of equal interest, all of which need to be touched on in the caption, will probably require a long and unwieldy caption. To avoid such a monster, it might be worth exploring the possibility of breaking up that long caption into several smaller ones, each dealing with a separate aspect of the picture, and running them separately disposed around the picture. Not only does this help the readers by lightening their apparent workload, but it is also an unusual technique for the normal magazine page — and as such it can inject unexpected interest.

Rejected suitor searching for strong-enough limb to use as a gibbet.

Dignified gentleman ignoring the whole demeaning scene.

Dejected suitor number two. A voyeur.

Members of Pompeiian Jet Set unable to keep confidences to themselves.

High spirited Pompeiian lady currently in a depression.

Where a picture shows several interrelated elements that need discussing, a variant of the technique described in the preceding paragraph might be used: the picture (rather than the caption) may be split up into its component parts. A picture may be dis-membered to show its elements — yet by proper positioning those picture sections can remain recognizable as a single complete photo.

Temptation to riotous living    wistfully    repudiated.

# Labeling the elements

Where a picture shows a number of elements that require labeling to make them intelligible, there are two basic ways of solving the problem:

*Printing the labels directly on the photograph.* The arrows or numbers or labels or whatever must be "dropped out" in white in areas that are dark, so that they can be read; in light areas of the photograph, they must be "surprinted" in black. If color is available, it is often a good idea, in order to achieve maximum contrast, to "drop out" the words in white and "surprint" them in color in the voids thus created.

The drawback of this technique is that such radical manipulation can ruin the artistic quality and integrity of a picture. Besides, the result can also look awfully messy. So before the decision is made, it is necessary to evaluate the importance of the picture both in itself as well as in its relation to the story and to the issue as a whole. If it is a plain, informing-kind of picture, such violence may not be harmful. But it may be unwise to subject a picture that has special value to this technique.

*Drawing a miniature diagram of the photograph.* In this case, the salient points of the picture are indicated on the diagram rather than on the original photo. This daintier technique leaves the original image unharmed, but it, too, has a serious disadvantage: it obliges readers to undertake quite a job. They have to translate a photographic image into a miniature outline image; notice the appropriate key letter; remember it; find the explanation of the key letter in the caption; then inspect the original photo again. Quite a process, when compared to the simple label slapped onto the picture itself!

a  Upfront Foster
b  Rumkeg di Vicenzo
c  Doubloons McNamara
d  Topside Frankenheimer
e  Legs O'Neal
f  Hair Lips Grosshan
g  Black Sheep de Noël
h  Pilchard McGee

# Getting extra mileage from one picture

## Repetition of sections

Split the picture into subcomponents and show them in sequence — to indicate movement across the stage.

## Repetition and superimposition in varied sizes

Superimpose the same picture in increasing-size versions, to show growth or shrinkage.

Overlay corners of the picture — coordinating this device with an increase in size, to indicate motion toward the viewer.

Use the picture twice, once the normal way, the second time
flopped left to right, to indicate two sides to a question.
Flop the picture and turn it upside-down, to create an illusion of
reflection.

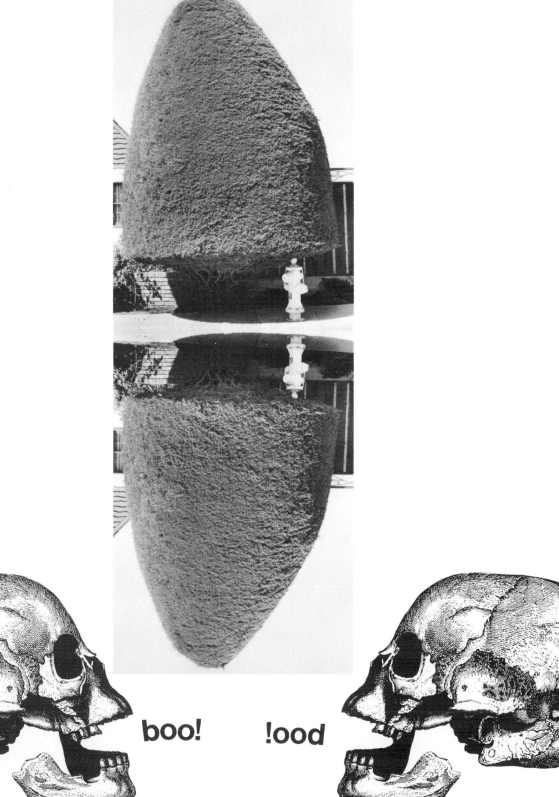

boo!    !ood

# Dismembering into patterns

Superimpose on the picture a graphic pattern that will allow elements of the picture to be taken out and used elsewhere in the story as recognition symbols.

# Using the negative

The negative version gives a picture a ghostly quality that can be used to convey to the reader an implied editorial comment or attitude. ("The editors don't like this," perhaps.)

# Cutting the picture into strips

Cut the picture into a series of parallel strips and then glue them back together again, staggered a little bit, so that you retain the recognizable image, yet gain a shocking expression of vibration, or earthquake, or even regular motion.

# Pictures of pictures

Instead of merely reproducing the image shown on a photograph, draw attention to the fact that the image is captured on a piece of paper — see the object as an object in itself — and then reproduce a picture of the entire object. To create this illusion, concentrate on showing the *paper* in some way. Below: tearing off an edge and reproducing it implies an astonishing sense of urgency. On the opposite page, three other techniques to accomplish the same thing are discussed.

John Castellucci

Casting a shadow gives the illusion of a piece of paper floating above the surface of the magazine page. Shown here in its simplest technique: a fat black rule butted against the halftone, indented at the top and right. Obviously there are more elaborate ways to render the basic idea: with shadows varying in tonality, with a white strip of paper surrounding the image, with curved shadows, etc. Below: the deliberate dog-ear. Here, too, the rendering and draftsmanship can yield more realistic results. Third technique: simply imposing the picture on the page at an unexpected angle.

# Partial silhouetting

The rectangular edge of a photo can limit the potential impact of the subject matter. Clearly, there are some photographs so masterfully taken that any tampering would destroy their artistic value. Yet most don't deserve such respect; and remember, it is the *story* that matters, not the integrity of the original photo used to illustrate it! It is therefore legitimate to improve on the storytelling capacity of the original, increasing its impact for editorial purposes. Here is a technique that allows the inherent drama to burst out of the picture into the reader's consciousness. At left, a good, simple shot. Below right, the identical shot — still apparently a rectangular halftone, except that it has been enlarged and the important elements have been silhouetted to make them appear as though they "poked out of" the rectangle. The rider is no longer contained in his valley but is riding right into the reader's lap. That's impact!

Silhouette the subject and let it float; or silhouette the subject, but enclose it in an overall box, so that it floats in an articulated rectangle of space.

An example of the
usefulness of silhouetting:

From this unlikely-appearing
original...

... can be extracted...

... a perfectly usable mugshot.

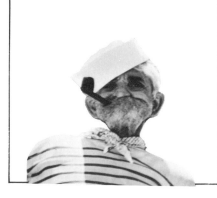

The thin line articulates
the space within which
the head appears and
formalizes the image into
a true mugshot illustration.

# Vignetting

Vignette the whole photograph so it appears to float away in undefined mists around the edges. This storybook quality may not be appropriate very often, but is worth remembering for that special occasion when you can make a stronger editorial point by an unusual device such as this.

# Nonrectangular shapes

Give the photograph an unusual shape — anything but rectangular or square. The same note of caution applies here as in the immediately preceding point.

# Picture frames

Combine pictures and ruled lines in some way; surround the photograph itself with a line of appropriate thickness, and adhere to that thickness of line for all the photos within a specific story to differentiate them from all the other material in the issue. Or place a "shadow box" frame on two sides of the photo, making it appear to be on the front of a box or deep within a tube of space. Or combine rules around the photograph with a second set of lines that surround both the photo and the caption beneath it. The possibilities are endless. This is a good area for collecting idea-starters for that swipe-file suggested earlier.

# Rounded corners and photographic realism

Give the pictures rounded corners, to create the impression of a group of transparencies. Naturally, it is necessary to keep the proportions of 35mm transparencies, or the illusion will not work. To reinforce it, place the pictures within a square box that resembles the cardboard carrier in which transparencies are usually enclosed.

Photos: John Castellucci

35 mm. transparency proportions are long and thin, as these uncropped photos show.

To create the illusion of 'pictures of pictures' it is necessary to round the corners the way they appear in the sleeve.

## A **NEW** LOOK AT AN OLD VIEW

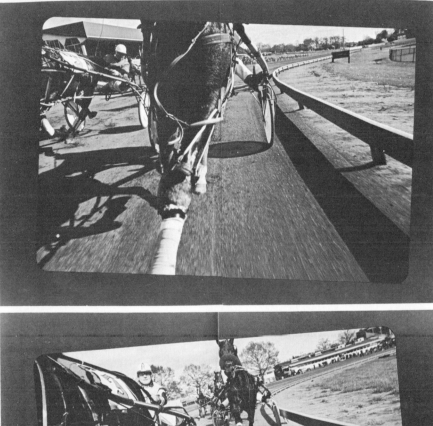

Example of a picture story about pictures: the gist: a wide-angle lens camera attached to driver automatically photographs the action during the race. The dramatic pictures were enlarged to full-spread size, shown against a black background, their corners were rounded — and they were placed on the pages at random angles to increase their surprise value. For a closeup of one spread, see the frontispiece to this chapter.

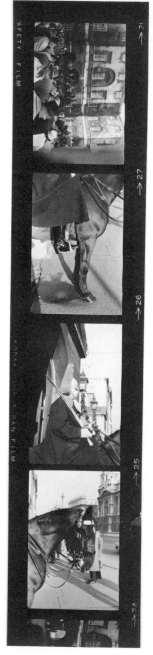

Showing the image inside the frame can help emphasize its origin or enhance its storytelling capacity: sprocket holes of motion-picture film imply sequence; side-bearer lettering on film implies uncut 35mm snapshots; the notched frame of a 4″ × 5″ piece of sheet film implies careful studio conditions . . . interpretations, of course, varying with the circumstances.

Further: show the picture as an image on the television screen  or a view outside a window. Thinking of pictures this way opens up a whole series of variants to enliven the communication value of a publication page.

# Blending words with pictures

Sometimes (rarely, though all the more valuable for that) situations arise where it is useful to call attention to verbal/visual interdependence. The standard way to do that would, of course, be to surprint the words over the picture in black, or drop them out in white, if the area of the picture is dark enough to do that. Here are two slightly more imaginative versions. Clearly all sorts of variants on such techniques are possible, limited only by ingenuity, budget, and editorial restraint.

The picture flows into the words

The words invade the picture

Use the photograph as the reality of an image — and by extending drawn lines from it, show how that reality is constructed.

Do not assume that the pictures available are irrevocably destined to be used as plain square halftones — the way pictures always seem to be. Pictures are just raw material, ready to be developed into something more interesting to look at or more expressive to communicate with.

# 6

ILLUSTRATIONS—NONPICTORIAL

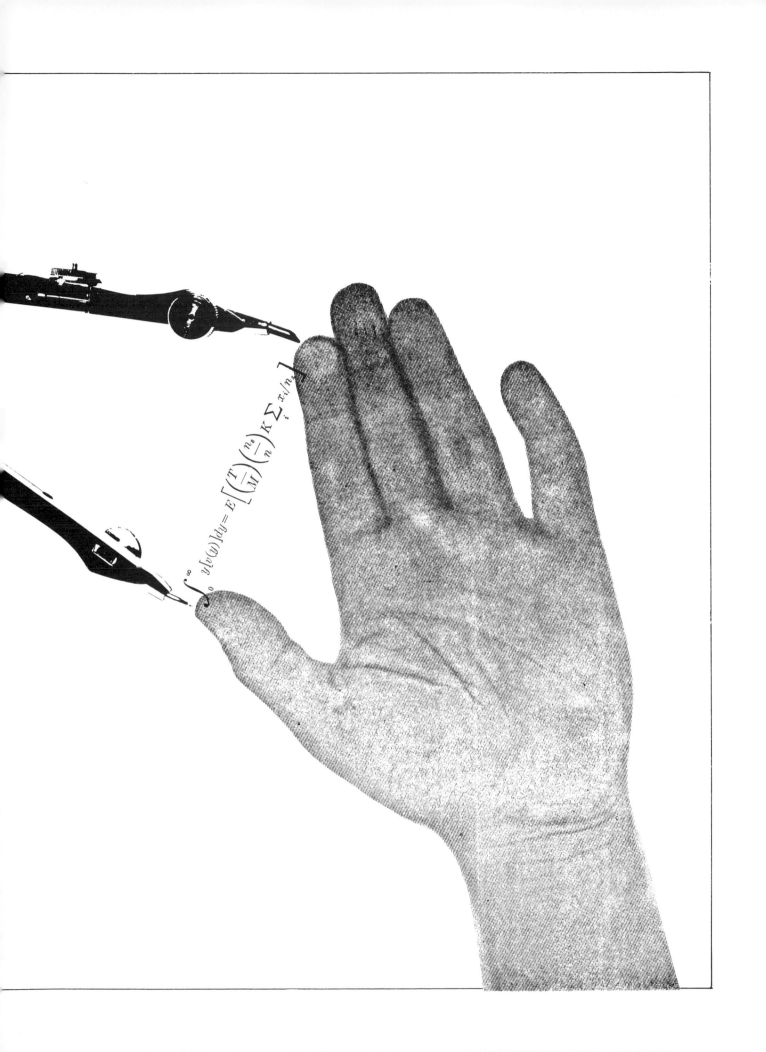

Three distinctly different sorts of elements get printed on the white page:

the words (in type of various kinds, arrangements, and sizes)
the pictures (photographs, renderings, drawings)
illustrations — that is, everything else.

This chapter is concerned with the many various kinds of "everything else" that exist. But they all need to be touched on, since there is no logical way to determine preference for one sort of illustration over another. Each story demands specific solutions to its specific problems, so each magazine differs from all other magazines in its normal mix of illustrative techniques. It even differs from issue to issue. A story-to-story difference is actually advantageous, in order to create the variety that holds audience interest. There are, however, two factors that must be borne in mind when "illustration" is being invented:

*The editorial content* — the purpose of the illustration — must be clearly visible. There is no room for art-for-art's sake here. Speed of communication (and therefore incisiveness of graphic thinking) is of highest value.

*The overall style of the magazine* must not be violated by adoption of graphic techniques that are unsympathetic to it. In fact, quite to the contrary, much of the visual character of the magazine can be *created* by the style in which the illustrations are done. Because most drawings, charts, graphs, tables, etc., are custom produced, they can be specified to conform to predetermined patterns. For magazines that use a great deal of such material, it is necessary to have a graphic style book, similar to the typographic style book used to set up the parameters of verbal/visual possibilities.

# Charts and graphs

## Effectiveness

The impact of a chart — its effectiveness and usefulness — depends on how much you are trying to say by means of graphics and how succinctly you have contrived to say it. As in all things editorial, an art director cannot design a successful chart unless he or she understands what it is about *and* knows what emphasis the editors wish to place on the material's meaning. Only when both these things are understood can they be expressed graphically (by exaggeration of scale, weight of line, choice of color, placement of elements in relation to each other, and so on).

How exaggeration of scale can affect the "meaning" of a graph:

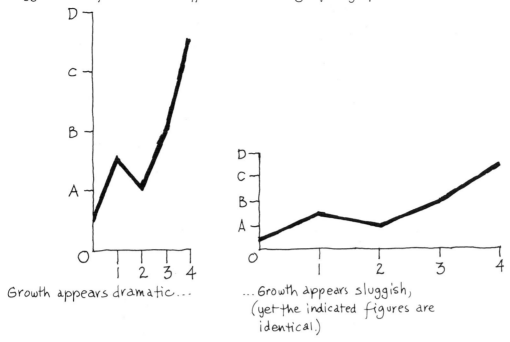

Growth appears dramatic...

...Growth appears sluggish,
(yet the indicated figures are
identical.)

Charts should always be as simple as possible. They should never compare more than three elements with each other, and then only if the elements are reasonably clear and far apart. If they overlap, it might be wise to consider breaking the single chart into two individual but interrelated ones.

Where the lines are clearly separated, several lines can be run in one frame:

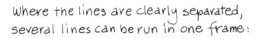

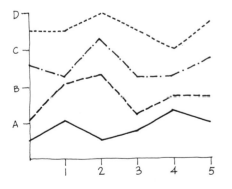

...but when a spaghetti situation occurs:

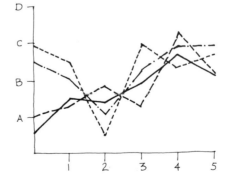

it is clearer to break the material apart:

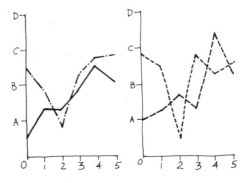

# Headings and titles

The readers should never be forced to draw their own conclusions from a chart: it is better to bring out the significance of the figures or trends or conclusions or interrelationships — by means of a good headline (not a label headline, but a sentence that says something), or by means of a caption (where a group of charts makes it necessary to run a label atop each one in order to permit fast identification of the individuals in the group).

— It is not enough to say

GROWTH (in tons)

... it is much better to indicate the significance of the chart or graph in a non label title

IN TWO YEARS OUTPUT WILL DOUBLE

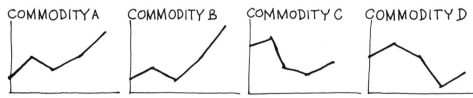

Simple labels are appropriate when fast recognition of categories is needed

COMMODITY A   COMMODITY B   COMMODITY C   COMMODITY D

THE OVERALL PICTURE INDICATES SUSTAINED GROWTH.....

...and when the significance of the GROUP of charts is brought out in the caption

Where there are several correlated charts, it may even be possible to skewer them together in meaning by a single headline broken by leaders.

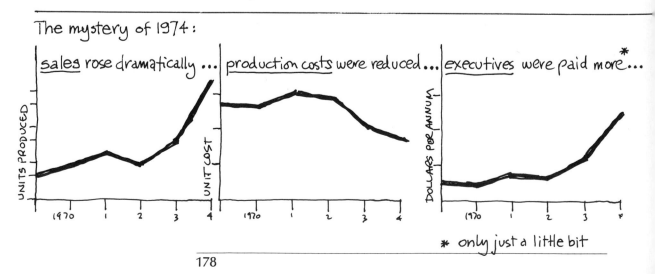

The mystery of 1974:

sales rose dramatically ... production costs were reduced... executives were paid more*...

* only just a little bit

Eliminate as much work as possible for the reader by getting rid of complicated keys and labeling the various elements themselves. Insert the source of the raw data into the chart in an inconspicuous place, and make each chart as self-contained a unit as possible.

Diagram showing the elements that have to be taken into account in producing a typical chart illustration

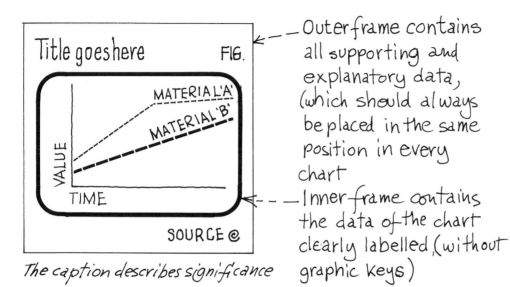

Outer frame contains all supporting and explanatory data, (which should always be placed in the same position in every chart

Inner frame contains the data of the chart clearly labelled (without graphic keys)

Such material varies — of course — and the graphic handling may also vary (the "frames" are NOT the only or even the ideal solution in all cases) but the principle of standardization of solution applies in all cases. A "style" must be established — and adhered to.

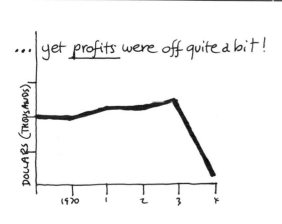

...yet _profits_ were off quite a bit!

# Grids and graphics

Reduce the grid lines behind the figures to an irreducible minimum, leaving just sufficient to allow the numerals to be read. The grids tend to camouflage the "trend" shown in the chart, since they set up a confusing subsidiary pattern of vertical and horizontal lines.

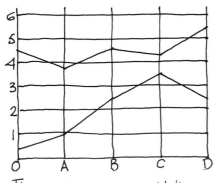

There are so many grid lines here that they overwhelm the plotted lines and the graph becomes illegible.

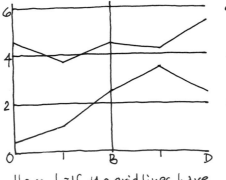

Here, half the gridlines have been erased — and so the plotted lines are more visible.

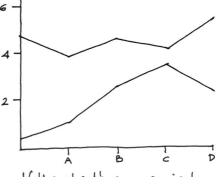

If the chart's purpose is to show general TRENDS (rather than scientifically accurate data), the clearest way to discern them is by clarifying the background altogether, leaving vestigial forms of the grid along the chart's edges only as reference points.

But common sense may dictate caution in throwing out *all* background lines in *all* cases: it is perfectly possible that a scientific subject shown as a graph requires great accuracy in plotting and reading. The purpose of the chart is to show the detailed relation-

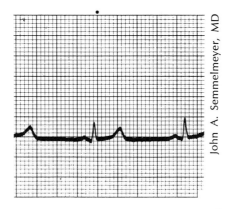

John A. Semmelmeyer, MD

ships between the wiggly line and its background grid. In that case, forget about simplification and show the whole thing. But it must be reproduced large enough to be discernible.

Simplify the graphic rendering of the charts in such a way that there is no duplication. For instance, where there are areas shown in tone, be sure that they are not outlined with a line as well, since that outline can easily be confused with other lines. Try to eliminate

Unnecessary lines like these outlines should be eliminated

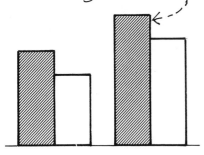 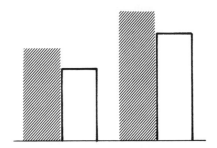

("coloring-in" should be
left to childrens'
coloring books)

Graphic simplification results
in a clearer statement:
the gray bars contrast better
with the white ones when their
outline has been removed.
That is because the outline is
a graphic characteristic that
both bars have in common —
but it is only essential on
the white one.

as many elements as possible without jeopardizing the legibility or accuracy of the data.

Dress the various elements in graphic clothing that will make each one individually expressive of its relative importance: contrast the crisp black line of the major trend with the fat, chunky tint background information; contrast the fat black line with the thin secondary ones. But all this requires editorial judgment and decision: What are we trying to stress? What is the purpose of the chart? What are we saying with it?

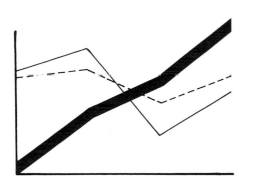 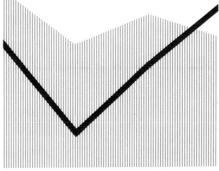

## Varieties

Do not accept the obvious handling of the three types of chart: the pie, the bar, and the mountain; encourage imaginative graphic variations that will be more interesting and appealing in themselves and statistically just as accurate in their plotting.

# Pie charts

The common pie chart is not terribly interesting — even if it is dressed up with tones or textures:

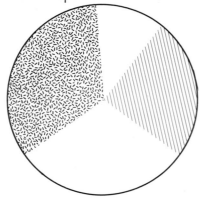

The dry statistics have to be given a little sparkle: by graphic color

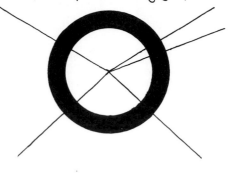

or by taking the obvious, flat circle and doing something with it (like laying it down on its side and three-dimensionalizing it)

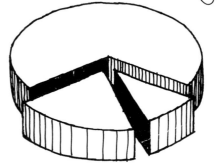

... or by using an appropriate circular image that is both a chart and illustration.

But why must a pie chart be circular? The percentage scale is just as accurate in a SQUARE frame as in a ROUND one.

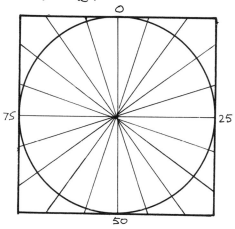

So...

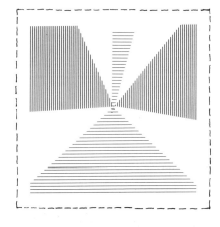

Why **must** percentage proportions be shown radiating from a center? Why is it not far more accurate to show 100 spots — and change them in some clear way so the reader sees the proportions AND can <u>COUNT</u> the actual figures?

Two versions:

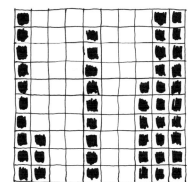

(... and think how color would help).

# Bar charts

Here is a typical, static bar chart:

...it is a little different from the most ordinary because the bars are shown with a gradation of tinting — lighter at the top — and the base line is wiggly. But that is not enough to give it life.

Here is the self-same set of statistics graphically arranged to underscore the concept of "growth".

(The curved bases of the bars and the darkened tops of the bars work to emphasize motion upward.)

Here is an equally typical bar chart showing two elements that make up a whole — compared as trends.

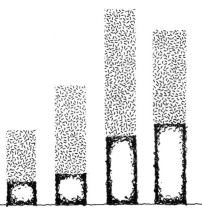

...the draftsmanship is deliberately scraggly and hairy — to show that accuracy can be conveyed by means other than hard-edged crispness like this

Taking the material in the bar-chart opposite, and giving it a "dimension" transforms the bars into skyscrapers - solid, dignified, heavy objects. By careful handling of proportions, handsome compositions can be created (something that is far more difficult when the "plain" bars are the only graphic material at hand)

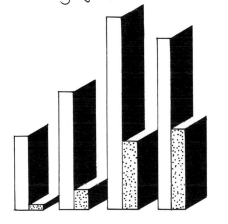

This is a bar chart that organizes its basic comparisons about a watershed line — a demarcation line above which are plotted positive figures, and below which go the negative figures. (Yet the overall totals can still be compared, though not as easily.)

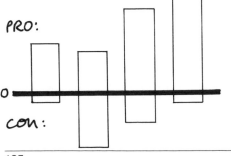

PRO:

0

CON:

If the subject matter of the chart can be sensibly expressed in terms of graphic units, every effort should be made to use such pictograms. This is a version showing "UNITS" of something (crates?) which can be counted by the reader.

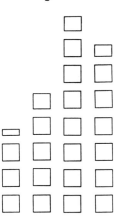

Here is another version of the same principle, but the "UNITS" are more abstract: plain typographic material. The printer can make such bar charts very easily.

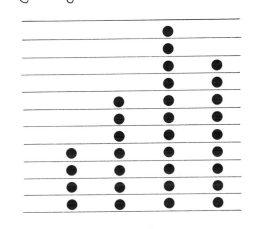

more about bar charts →

This version of "UNITS" goes to the opposite extreme of literal realism. So long as the subject matter is NOT coins, the technique is "different" (coins are so hackneyed that their use is likely to be counterproductive)

Bar charts can be laid on their side. They will probably use up less space on the page this way, since the column into which they fit will allow good length for each bar (and there are often just a few bars that need to be accommodated, so that no exaggeration in width of bars is needed.)

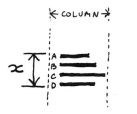
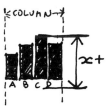

This is the same chart broken into "UNITS" — in this case typographic symbols ( one "E" = 1 elephant ). A tabulation like this can easily be set by the printer, and the reader can count all the elephants he feels like counting.

```
A EEEEE EEE
B EEEEE EEEEE  EEEEE EE
C EEEEE EEEEE  EEEEE EEEEE EEEE
D EEEEE EEEEE  EEEEE EEEEE EEEEE  EEE
```

The simple graph:

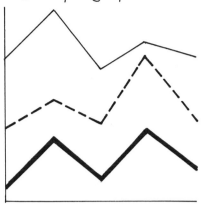

No matter how the lines are drawn (light, dark, dashed, or patterned) it looks dry.
It is not much wetter (?) if tints are inserted:

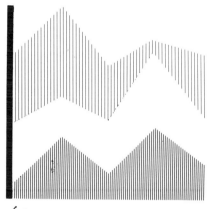

(this tint-mountain failure happened because of the lack of relationship between the tint areas: they are purely arbitrary)

Here the tints follow an orderly progression from dark to light — making it easier for the eye to follow.

In this version of the graphs, the tinting is reversed, with the "sky" being the darkest, and the closest "mountains" the lightest. Harder to read, but more startling.

The same old graph, but given a (phony) shadow edge which gives the appearance of dimension but which is an illusion: the indices are all statistically correct.

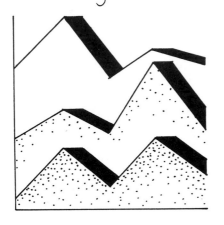

A slightly different approach:

While total annual sales steadily rose overall profits unaccountably declined

letting the line of words be the line of the graph --- the medium becomes the message.

This three-dimensionalization allows direct comparison of two trends, emphasizing the disparity of the two subjects. It only works for two subjects, since the grid must be placed "between" them:

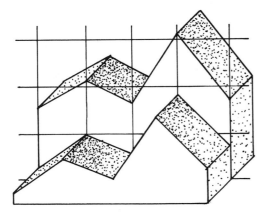

Applicable to all chart forms:

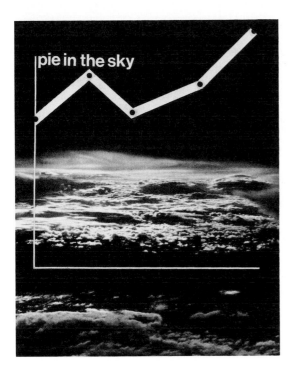

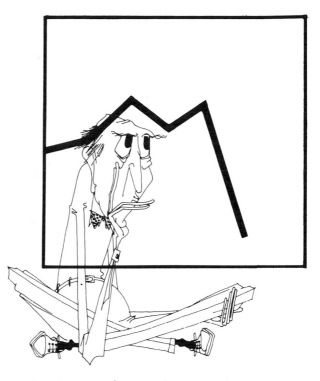

Background illustration symbolic of the subject covered by the chart. The photo can be used as shown here, where the chart is dropped out in white, or the photograph can be "ghosted" as a very pale image over which the chart is printed in black. Color is potentially very useful for this kind of trickery.

Background illustration that comments on the message of the chart, or that interprets the editorial significance in some way. This does not imply that it must be some sort of cartoon — the illustration can be any kind of picture that will be recognizable by the reader FASTER than the statistical matter that requires study.

# Tables and typographic "illustrations"

The principle of Differentness applies here: anything that breaks a pattern catches the eye (like the solitary lit-up window in a sky-scraper in the evening, or the out-of-step soldier on parade). It does not matter whether the variation is large or small — wherever there is a discernible pattern, and it is broken, that break will call attention to itself.

Dull ...          ... un-remarkable          ... but this is startling

That is why a type table, which is also made up of plain type, will become fascinating when it is shown in the middle of a plain type page; it will be the first thing the reader sees because it is different in texture and color. It is because of this quality of noticeableness in a context of text that we can think of tables as "illustrations" — and why such a prosaic element as a type table can, indeed, break up the text and be thought of in terms of visual interest.

The same principles of simplicity and clarity promulgated in the "Charts and graphs" section, above, apply to type table as well (as they do to almost all journalistic presentation — but it never does any harm to repeat the point). Tables, however, entail an extra problem that charts and graphs do not present to the same degree: type tables need s p a c e . They simply cannot be squeezed below a certain size and retain their legibility, whereas the artwork for a pie or bar chart can be made to cover almost any size area. It is therefore necessary to do considerable calculating in sizing a type table, or to supply the printer with good samples to follow. It is always wise to build in a safety factor of 25% more than the minimum area guessed at, because the typesetter cannot do a neat job in congested space. To achieve clean alignment of vertical and horizontal rows (and clean alignment is crucial for both legibility and looks), the typesetter needs room to maneuver.

As in charts and graphs, a useful headline and/or caption that explains the *meaning* of the table to the reader is of greater value than a plain take-it-or-leave-it label that just defines the area from which the raw data are culled.

To enhance the clarity of type tables, use as many horizontal or vertical rules between the elements as is practical. If actual rules are not possible or not appropriate, then use space to separate the rows from each other. Naturally, second color in the rules or in

every other line, or in every other group of lines, is an ideal tool to
clarify type-table material and should be used functionally that way.
But the plain type table should not just be printed in black ink over
a pink-screen background; nothing is duller or more useless. But:
if parts of the pink background tint are dropped out in white, so
that the crucial row of figures is printed in black on a white
background, and so stands out immediately as the major element
of the type table, then that maligned pink screen is another matter
entirely.

| Project | Square feet | | Estimated construction cost | | | Time sequence | | | | |
|---|---|---|---|---|---|---|---|---|---|---|
| | Net | Gross | Building | Site | Total | 1972 | 1973 | 1974 | 1975 | 1976 |
| ministration and Student Center .... | 78,455 | 144,828 | $ 6,951,800 | $ 153,200 | $ 7,105,000 | 7,105,000 | | | | |
| rary, Humanities, Social Science, d Student Center ................. | 293,924 | 469,774 | 21,139,800 | 1,049,100 | 22,188,900 | 22,188,900 | | | | |
| tural Science and Mathematics ..... | 169,337 | 284,624 | 14,800,500 | 181,800 | 14,982,300 | 14,982,300 | | | | |
| e Arts—Theatre ................. | 78,260 | 119,752 | 6,107,400 | 653,300 | 6,760,700 | | | 6,760,700 | | |
| ditorium ...................... | 25,850 | 38,775 | 1,977,500 | 148,300 | 2,125,800 | | | 2,125,800 | | |
| ysical Education ................. | 94,145 | 137,962 | 6,208,300 | 468,900 | 6,677,200 | | | 6,677,200 | | |
| Classroom space distributed: | 739,971 | 1,195,715 | | | | | | | | |
| dge ......................... | | | | 720,000 | 720,000 | | | | 720,000 | |
| rage ........................ rking .....................Cars | 226,080 250 | | 4,747,700 | 246,000 | 4,993,700 | | | | 4,993,700 | |
| rmitories, Commons .............. rage ........................ | 282,580 97,920 | | 12,794,300 | 276,000 | 13,070,300 | | | | | 13,070,300 |
| hletics  Tennis Courts ............. Fields — Acres ............. | 9 5 | | | 599,000 | 599,000 | | | | | 599,000 |
| rking .....................Cars | 350 | | | 475,000 | 475,000 | | | | | 475,000 |
| ving—Planting—Acres ............. | 3 | | | 270,000 | 270,000 | | | | 270,000 | |
| | | | $74,727,300 | $5,240,600 | $79,967,900 | $44,276,200 | $15,563,700 | $5,983,700 | $14,144,300 | |

Horizontal lines are easy to set in type tables, but vertical lines are essential
in organizing the material and making the table intelligible. So the vertical
lines must be inserted as artwork — or run in color as a separate operation.
(The typesetter can be persuaded to insert them, but it is a slow, expensive job).

| Project | Square feet | | Estimated construction cost | | | Time sequence | | | | |
|---|---|---|---|---|---|---|---|---|---|---|
| | Net | Gross | Building | Site | Total | 1972 | 1973 | 1974 | 1975 | 1976 |
| ministration and Student Center .... | 78,455 | 144,828 | $ 6,951,800 | $ 153,200 | $ 7,105,000 | 7,105,000 | | | | |
| rary, Humanities, Social Science, d Student Center ................. | 293,924 | 469,774 | 21,139,800 | 1,049,100 | 22,188,900 | 22,188,900 | | | | |
| tural Science and Mathematics ..... | 169,337 | 284,624 | 14,800,500 | 181,800 | 14,982,300 | 14,982,300 | | | | |
| e Arts—Theatre ................. | 78,260 | 119,752 | 6,107,400 | 653,300 | 6,760,700 | | | 6,760,700 | | |
| ditorium ...................... | 25,850 | 38,775 | 1,977,500 | 148,300 | 2,125,800 | | | 2,125,800 | | |
| ysical Education ................. | 94,145 | 137,962 | 6,208,300 | 468,900 | 6,677,200 | | | 6,677,200 | | |
| Classroom space distributed: | 739,971 | 1,195,715 | | | | | | | | |
| dge ......................... | | | | 720,000 | 720,000 | | | | 720,000 | |
| rage ........................ king .....................Cars | 226,080 250 | | 4,747,700 | 246,000 | 4,993,700 | | | | 4,993,700 | |
| rmitories, Commons .............. rage ........................ | 282,580 97,920 | | 12,794,300 | 276,000 | 13,070,300 | | | | | 13,070,300 |
| letics  Tennis Courts ............. Fields—Acres ............. | 9 5 | | | 599,000 | 599,000 | | | | | 599,000 |
| king .....................Cars | 350 | | | 475,000 | 475,000 | | | | | 475,000 |
| ving—Planting—Acres ............. | 3 | | | 270,000 | 270,000 | | | | 270,000 | |
| | | | $74,727,300 | $5,240,600 | $79,967,900 | $44,276,200 | $15,563,700 | $5,983,700 | $14,144,300 | |

# Illustrations the printer can supply

If we stretch the definition of the word "illustrations" to include not merely the usual graphic clarification of visually representable subjects, but also the wider sense of the adornment and breakup of a page by graphic means, then we find that the printer can do a great deal for us — so long as we recognize his capacity and ask him to use it. So here is a list of quite a few pieces of what in theatrical parlance would be called stage business. That term is appropriate to graphic presentation of editorial matter: the function is similar in each instance: to build character, provoke interest, enrich presentation.

## Rules

Short rules, long rules, thin rules, fat rules — the variety of their application is almost endless (and they are very cheap). Thin lines run vertically alongside the columns of type (like railroad tracks) are a contrapuntal design element, useful as decoration or for character creation within a specific story or section of the publication. Heavy lines run horizontally across the page split segments of the story from each other, articulating separate elements on the page.

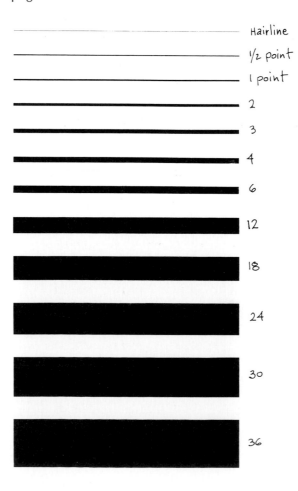

Hairline

½ point

1 point

2

3

4

6

12

18

24

30

36

All typesetting departments (whether part of a printing plant or an independent specialty shop) are equipped with rules and borders of various designs. Design possibilities are almost infinite, since each supplier of type has wide selections .Thus, Linotype has its group of designs, Monotype has its, Ludlow has yet another; designs are available in film and as preprinted artwork in wax-backed sheets of various kinds. It is necessary to have a catalog from the printer supplying the typesetting, in order to ascertain what he has available. But the variety is usually great. Here are a few typical examples.

But it is not necessary to be confined to the material used "as is": with a little imagination, the graphic can be used to primary editorial purpose, not just as secondary background decoration.

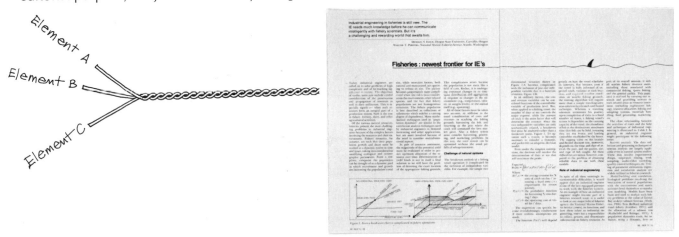

# Boxes

If the box is self-contained with rules all around, and if (as would be ideal) the corners of the box are rounded, then the self-contained quality of the box is emphasized and irrefutable. The boxed material becomes a framed element and as such, *different*. If the boxed material is typographic, like its surroundings, it is advisable to drop the type size down a step, to alter the "color" and "texture" and thus emphasize its differentness even more. (The same effect is achieved by reducing the size of type in plain copy, as in a type table.)

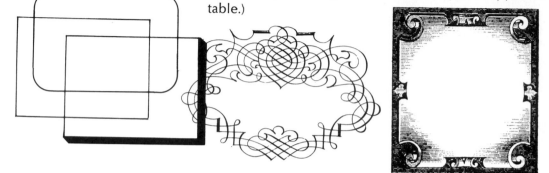

# Ornaments

Here are a few of the typical typographic materials available from printers that can be used to great effect with a little imagination and care. But they must be *remembered* as being there.

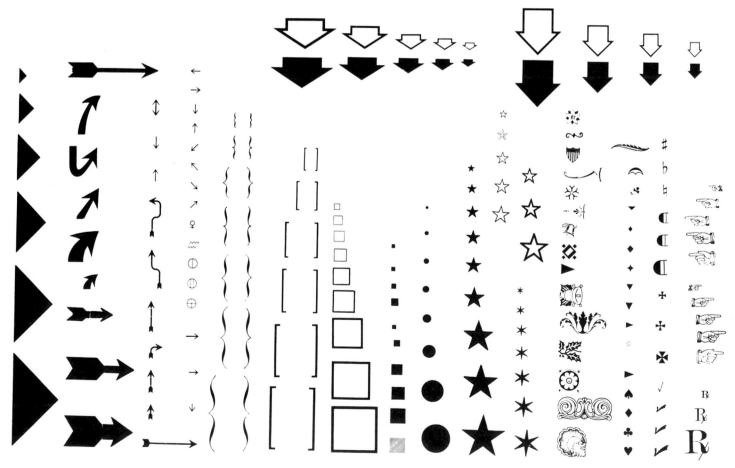

It is hard to say where "initials" end and out-of-scale type begins. Perhaps it doesn't matter. What matters is that startling effects can be obtained by using them. Here are a bunch of typical attention-getters.

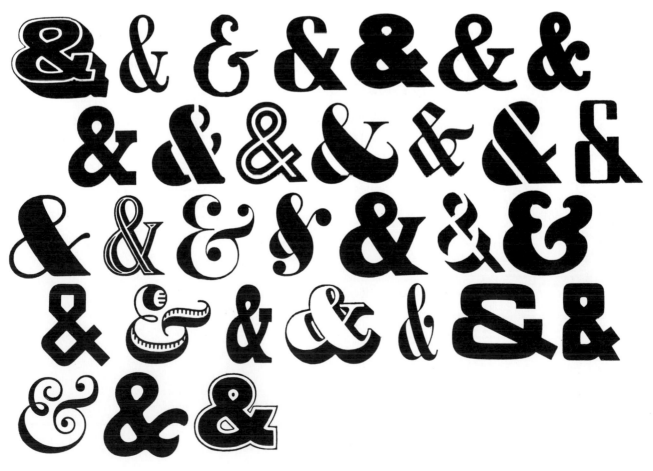

This is a group of ampersands, to bring out the point that the actual design of each individual character can vary enormously — and that the effect it is capable of producing can vary equally. So the point is not merely that you will use a great big Q and A, but that your choice of what *kind* of Q and A will be used will determine the quality and flavor of the achievement.

# Free-floating sentences

The visual grayness of the text page can be effectively broken up by dropping in (in some arbitrary way) a provocative statement, run in large, bold type — and placed in space that will assure its being noticed. The statement can be a quotation from the text, a summation of it, or a disagreement by someone else — it does not matter what, so long as it is interesting and will catch the reader's attention. It must be short to be effective. It can be placed at the head of the page, the foot of the page, or somewhere in the middle; but the placement must appear to be deliberate (most deliberate place: plumb in the center of the page), so that the sentence is not mistaken for a dropped-in subhead. (Its positioning is obviously unrelated to the particular place in which it happens to fall in the text.) This technique, used freely and with great variety in literary magazines, is well worth studying.

Sentences as "illustrations" : five possible solutions (of a total* of 1,764,923)

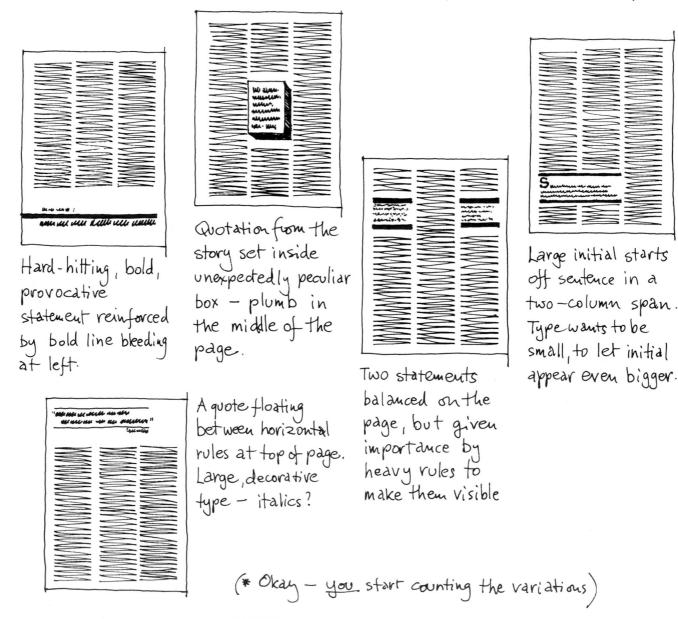

Hard-hitting, bold, provocative statement reinforced by bold line bleeding at left.

Quotation from the story set inside unexpectedly peculiar box — plumb in the middle of the page.

A quote floating between horizontal rules at top of page. Large, decorative type — italics?

Two statements balanced on the page, but given importance by heavy rules to make them visible

Large initial starts off sentence in a two-column span. Type wants to be small, to let initial appear even bigger.

(* Okay — you start counting the variations)

An obvious way (seldom thought as being "illustration") to break up the pages is by using display type deliberately as though it were a design element. Naturally this can only be done if the story itself is broken into component parts, topic by topic (and subtopic by subtopic), each signaled by a fresh heading. If this editorial segmentation of the story allows at least three major-appearing headlines per spread, then the technique will probably work; so long as the headlines are each handled graphically in a similar way (i.e., two-liners, or five-liners all flush left in a column, or underscored, or however else you please). The great virtue of headlines as art (in fact, of any type as illustration anywhere) is that the words themselves are of interest to the reader. It is very likely that he will be grabbed by them far more positively than by a much more decorative but much less meaningful piece of artwork. BUT: those fascinating words had better be big enough, bold enough, in enough white space to make them unskippable.

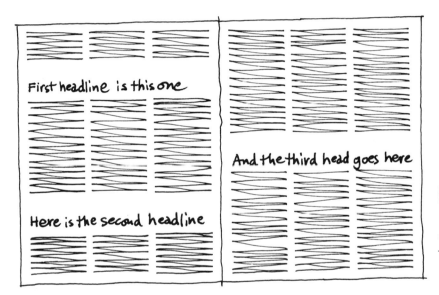

Headlines-as-art are not very exciting here, since they are not artfully placed or arranged on the page (in spite of plenty of white space and boldness of type).

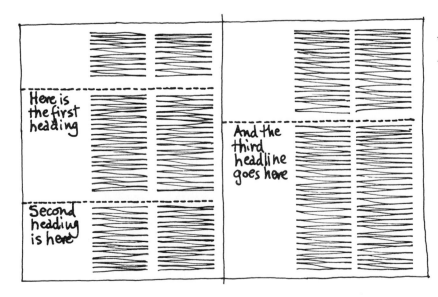

Headlines-as-art are used better here. There is greater contrast between the two kinds of type on the page (i.e., text and heads) since the heads appear massed, alone.

*Variation in type size in headlines:* If there is a key word that is particularly interesting to the readership, then it is a good trick to pop it up in size or color. This is, of course, a blending of the designer's and editor's art, for the designer can do nothing with words that do not lend themselves to such treatment. But if the editor can tailor the headline (or subheads) to allow such a manipulation, then the designer can make much drama from very little raw material. It is useful, often, to repeat the decorative key word as the continued line throughout the story, thus tying it all together neatly and simply.

Masthron osllewtry sletoh nndisi  danw sesouh tseug sniep

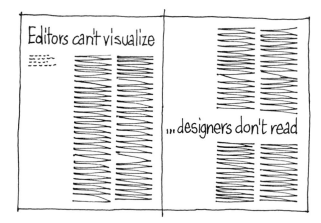

*Split Headlines:* If the headlines allow themselves to be split by phrases, it is possible to place the phrases in separate positions on the spread, and thereby achieve unexpected results. An even better (because more functional) application of this principle is to allow the headline to flow from one spread onto the succeeding one, thus forcing the reader to realize that the story continues.

Another (smaller-scale) application is to break the headline into components that tie in with a cataloging of elements on display:

The headline becomes the visible catalog of the subject matter. Its graphic strength (the strong horizontality) allows the text to be of unequal lengths, and yet the spread appears organized.

## Variation of type size in body copy

To achieve clarity and breakup in running copy, it is often possible to set part of it in one size — to signal its major importance — and another part in a smaller size — to signal its relative unimportance (and thus its potential skippability). The reduction in type size is also often accompanied by a reduction of the column width — by indenting right and left, or by doubling up two narrow columns under the wider big one.

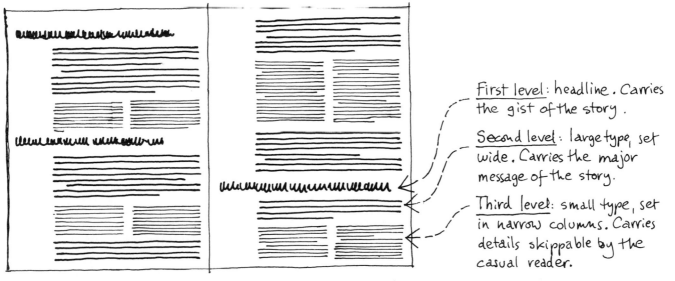

First level: headline. Carries the gist of the story.

Second level: large type, set wide. Carries the major message of the story.

Third level: small type, set in narrow columns. Carries details skippable by the casual reader.

Naturally, this can only be done when the copy is organized for such "two-level readership," so that the type dress can express the content correctly and usefully. Much discussion about typographic esthetics results from the application of this expressionist trick: it is undoubtedly true that the smooth texture of the type is destroyed; but it is precisely the destruction of that smoothness that can result in effective communication in a story structured to take advantage of the technique.

## Variation of type color in body copy

A much more often used variant on the two-kinds-of-body-type technique comes into play when a more obvious sense-breakup is to be expressed: when there are, for instance, a list of questions and answers, or pro and con views; in such cases the questions can be set bold (or italic, or bigger, or in color), and the answers can be set in the normal body copy type. Since the column alignment usually remains inviolate, this textural variation is only superficial — and is therefore much less "ugly" and causes less aesthetic pain.

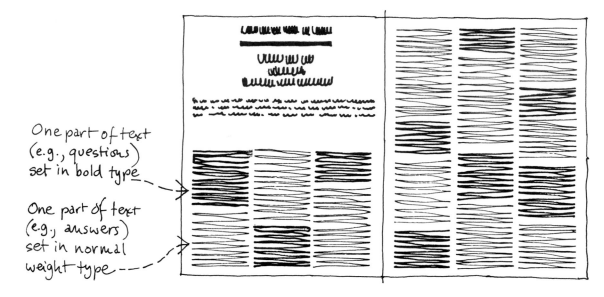

One part of text (e.g., questions) set in bold type

One part of text (e.g., answers) set in normal weight type

## Floating subheads

Placement of subheads — if the page structure allows it — need not be confined to the column of type. It may be advantageous to place subheads outside the column — in the margins of the page — so that they pop out and catch attention (in much the same way that the headlines discussed earlier do). In this placement they are

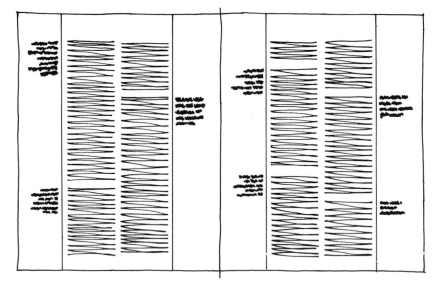

Hairline rules, bleeding top & bottom, split text away from subheads.

Subheads set in margin flush left or flush right.

much more visible and can therefore be used to more purpose than just "breaking up the text" as subheads usually do. They can be summings-up for fast reading (if the text is organized that way), and they can be very useful reference points if there are many pages of text and much cross-referencing needs to be done.

## Repeated words

There are words that can be manipulated typographically in such a way that the word itself becomes a picture of the meaning. However, such playing with type can only be done by the typesetter with great difficulty, because of the technology involved (but can be done very easily by hand using rub-off lettering). One capacity, however, which is distinctly type*setting* as opposed to type playing is that of repetition. It is very easy indeed for the typesetter to set and reset words, especially on the linotype; so, where repetition helps create a word image (visual glyph) it is appropriate to have it set by the printer: **REPPPPETITION**
**REPPPPETITION**
**REPPPPETITION**
**REPPPPETITION**
**REPPPPETITION**
**REPPPPETITION**
**REPPPPETITION**
**REPPPPETITION**
**REPPPPETITION**
**REPPPPETITION**

## Words and lines

If the combination of words and artwork is very simple, it is easy for the printer to provide the "art" at little or no extra cost. But it is necessary that the lines he is asked to scribe be straight and either vertical or horizontal (i.e., boxes). If, however, the boxes can become symbolic of the meaning of the words, the whole becomes greater than the sum of its parts — and may even add a little wit to the dry material. For instance:

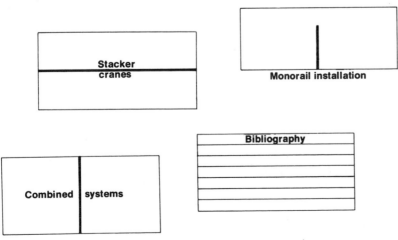

## Text set in shapes

This is a very expensive and difficult trick, since it requires much setting and revised setting to get the lines to come out right (without too much shoddy-looking letterspacing or bad word breaks at the ends of each line). But every so often it may come in handy. It requires considerable preparation on the part of the type specifier, since each line length must be separately specified in picas (which tends to be a boring job). So the concept had better be good enough and important enough to offset such a nuisance factor.

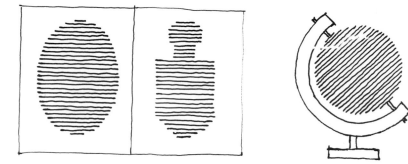

## Type as pictorial image

It is not necessary to have a picture of the Eiffel Tower to communicate the idea of "Paris." All you need do is set the headline in a typeface that has a recognizable "Parisian" flavor — voilà!

# FRANCE

But as in all such potentially cliché situations, unless this technique is used with taste, discrimination, restraint, and finesse, embarrassment can result. Nevertheless, it is worth showing a few examples as thought-provokers for those times when such a technique can be legitimately (and cleverly) employed.

The type-as-image characteristics can be applied to three basically different areas of meaning in the story:

> allusions to the geographical area of the story (as in the France example);

> allusions to the historical time period of the story;

> allusions to the subject matter of the story. This then subdivides into two subcategories: the hard physical material that is under discussion, and the more abstract idea inherent in the story.

The examples shown opposite cover all of these fronts.

irish

RUSSIAN

CHINESE

AMERICAN

German

INDIAN

GREEK

HEBREW

ORIENTAL

ART NOUVEAU

PICTURE

BUBBLE

HURRICANE

SNOW

RAIN

ANTIQUE

ART

CONIFER

MONSTER

DIGNITY

TENSION

Finest Craftsmanship

MONUMENTAL

with~it

BUILDING

STOCK TICKER

NOBEL PRIZE

COMPUTER

NEEDLE POINT

classic

ACRYLICS

ELECTRIC

Memorandum :

STENCIL

CIRCUS

BROADWAY

sculpture

WINTER

# Illustrations bought at the store

Much useful material can be had for pennies — plus a modicum of imagination. Here is a short list of the most obvious, just to start the ball rolling.

## From the stationery store

Rubber stamps with appropriate wording; the impression then reproduced as faithfully as possible to give the illusion that the poorly inked stamp made an actual imprint on the page — reproduced as a dropout halftone, run in purple ink. Additional wrinkle: photograph the stamp itself together with the imprint.

Mailing labels, prescription labels for bottles and jars, booklet labels, labels of various kinds.

Stickers for various sorts of jobs, such as mailing instructions (Air Mail, Special Handling, etc.); also stars, notarial seals, etc.

Preprinted forms, such as bills of sale, legal agreements, leases, financial-looking stuff. Business forms, tax forms, and whatnot, for background atmosphere. (There is also always the stock table from the newspaper for that perennial financial problem.)

Envelopes of various distinctive shapes, with windows, die cuts, peculiar closures, etc., all of which can be photographed — like this plastic binder spine.

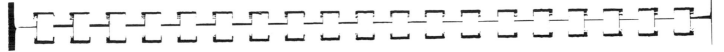

Drawing tools, from pencils to electric typewriters; designers tools; drafting equipment, etc.

# From the art supply shop

Textured papers or patterned papers run as backgrounds (for instance: to give the illusion of blueprints, take a sheet of cheap tracing paper, make a bad Ozalid print of it — blank — so that the mottled spots come out; photograph the result, engrave as a halftone, and run in blue-black ink in the magazine). Do artwork on graph paper.

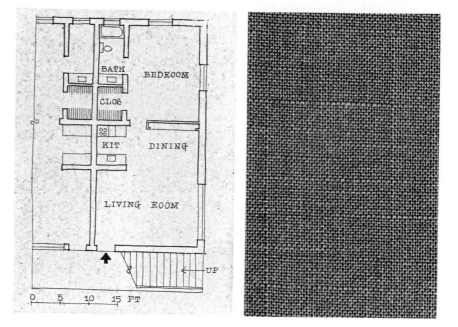

Ready-to-use illustrations available as rub-off sheets so that complex pictures can be made from subunits.

Rub-off type to make into word/pictures.

Miniature model-making materials (usually at H-O scale) that can be used for background effects or photographed with surprising result, since the combination of life-size elements and subminiaturization can be startling.

Preprinted sheets of architectural or mapmaking symbols (such as brickwork or trees) ready to cut out or rub off and use as original artwork.

Emil Weiss

## From the Post Office

All sorts of fascinating rubber stamps and images are to be had if you look for them. Stamps may not be reproduced except under very strictly controlled circumstances — but no law says anything about the rest of the mailing paraphernalia!

## From the bank

Money. Coins may be photographed and reproduced any way you see fit. Bills are much more tricky: the law keeps changing — it is safest to check with the Post Office about the latest interpretation of the law. But it is now possible to reproduce bills face-on (not just as stacks seen from the side) if the reproduction is not in full color or life-size (i.e., if it is reduced or blown up).

## No illustrations at all

Just using white space as an element of the design. Here is a graphic material you can always be sure is there — and it costs nothing extra. Why not use it?

# Homemade illustrations

Ink blots — very useful for running in red ink and pretending they are blood (assuming you have a bloody story to work on).

Photograms of recognizable objects, such as drawing instruments, simple tools, earrings, pocketknives — anything that is recognizable in silhouette. Such objects are placed on the sensitized paper by the photostatter and exposed to strong light — resulting in simple silhouettes. Think small: such objects tend to be most effective when reproduced life-size.

Thumbprints — or prints of other printable things.

Electrostatic impressions of objects done on a Xerox machine.

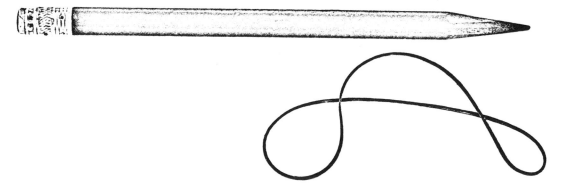

Rubbings of coins, reproduced as halftones.

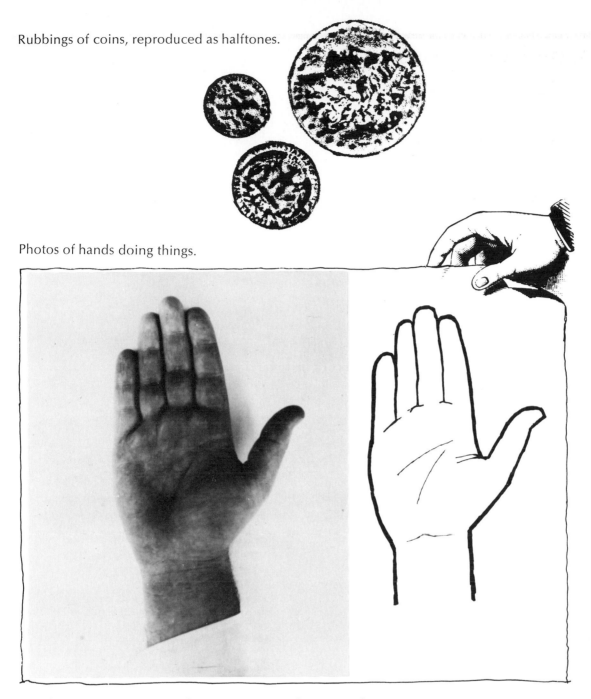

Photos of hands doing things.

Handwritten comments in the margin — or other sorts of handwritten annotations of the text. If second color is available, it is very easy to make <u>underscores by hand</u> in the text itself, or arrows from one part of the text to another — and run that in color. It is more difficult in plain black because of the production problems involved.

*That's a good idea!*

# Photomechanical variations

There is another aspect to the subject of illustration that must be remembered as a potential tool for magazine enlivening: this aspect is based on the realization that a photograph is merely *raw* material, and that it need not necessarily be handled as an ordinary halftone just like all the other photographs. Instead, it can be manipulated by mechanical processes that can change its look — and its meaning. However, such manipulation of image should be done only when it is *editorially* useful and appropriate, since every time a change is made in the image, something has to be given up — and usually, it is detail that is traded off for graphic texture. To understand the technique, it is necessary, first, to understand what a halftone is and how it is made.

## Halftone screens

A halftone is made from any original copy (such as a photograph or a rendering) that has a continuous gradation of tonal values ranging from light to dark. This original material is mechanically transformed from the continuous tone into a similar-appearing pattern of closely spaced dots of varying sizes. The dots are larger in places where the original appears "darker," and they are smaller where the original is "lighter" (bigger dots carry more ink, thus creating an illusion of "darkness"). This effect is achieved by rephotographing the original through a mesh screen. The fineness of the screen (i.e., the number of lines per inch) determines the number of dots that will appear. The more dots there are, the more faithful the reproduction will be to the original, and therefore the greater the quality of the detail in the reproduction. Conversely, the coarser the screen, the fewer dots, the fewer the details. Newspapers use a 65-line screen. Normal screen for letterpress printing of magazines on coated stock is 110 lines to the inch. Offset lithography uses a 133-line screen. Fine printing starts at a 150-line screen and goes on up from there. The screen used depends on the quality of the paper stock , the technology of the printing, the inks, and money.

But the normal screen is not the only screen that must be used to shoot a piece of continuous-tone art through. There are many other screens available (at modest extra cost) that can be used to change the texture of the subject matter. Here is a group of the most widely used "special-effect" halftone screens in which the same original subject has been treated, each with a five-times blowup of the detail to show the textural makeup of each screen.

When any of these screens are combined with color in some way, fresh effects can be achieved that lend sparkle and surprise to an otherwise normal (dull?) issue. But even by themselves, run in plain black ink, pictures run in these screens are attention-getters — *as long as they are large enough and the screens are coarse enough to be noticeable.*

Normal halftone (133 line screen)

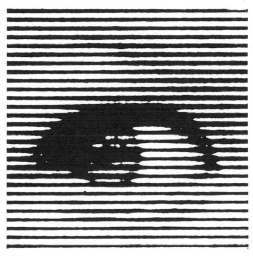

Horizontal line screen

Photomechanicals: Norwalk PhotoGraphics

Mezzotint screen

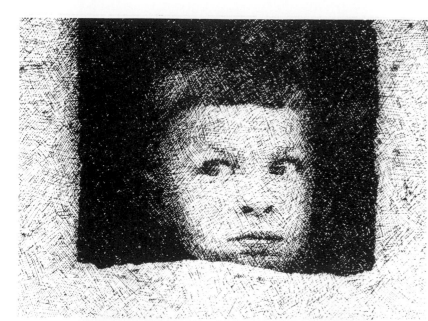

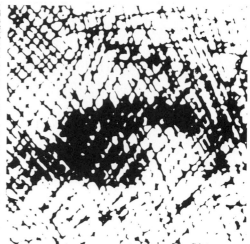

Steel engraving screen

Concentric circle screen

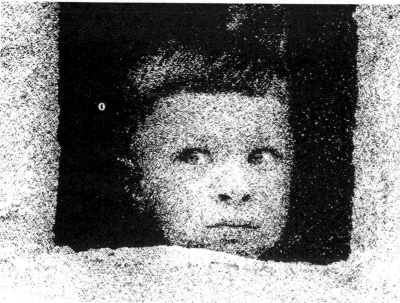

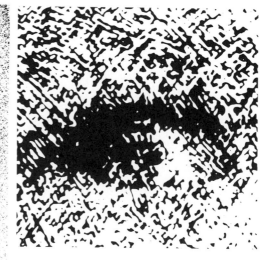

Steel etch screen

Another halftone technique that can be most usefully employed in reproducing that special-situation material is the "dropout halftone" (known as a "facsimile halftone" in letterpress parlance). This is a specially handled halftone in which certain unwanted areas of the picture are removed by hand-silhouetting or photomechanical masking during the manufacturing process. The result is that there are no halftone dots visible in the masked-out areas. Such a reproduction technique is especially useful in showing pencil drawings, for instance, where the dark-and-light quality of the linework must be retained (to get across the character of the original pencil artwork), yet where a background is undesirable (to make it appear as though the pencil lines had been drawn on the actual magazine page itself).

Emil Weiss

Straight, square, halftone

Dropout halftone

# Linecuts

Linecuts are reproductions of original material that have no tonal gradations but are made up of plain black/white marks throughout. Pen-and-ink drawings are perhaps the most common material for "linework."

An important advantage that linecuts have over normal halftones is that they do not need to have a hard edge to box them in, as halftones do: a photograph has to end somewhere (and it is usually a rectangular image). A "drawing" ends where its individual lines happen to stop. That irregular outline of the linecut can be used as a design foil for the hard-edged halftone or the equally hard-edged columns of type that surround it.

But running a drawing in plain straight linework is not the answer every time. Here are the commonest variations:

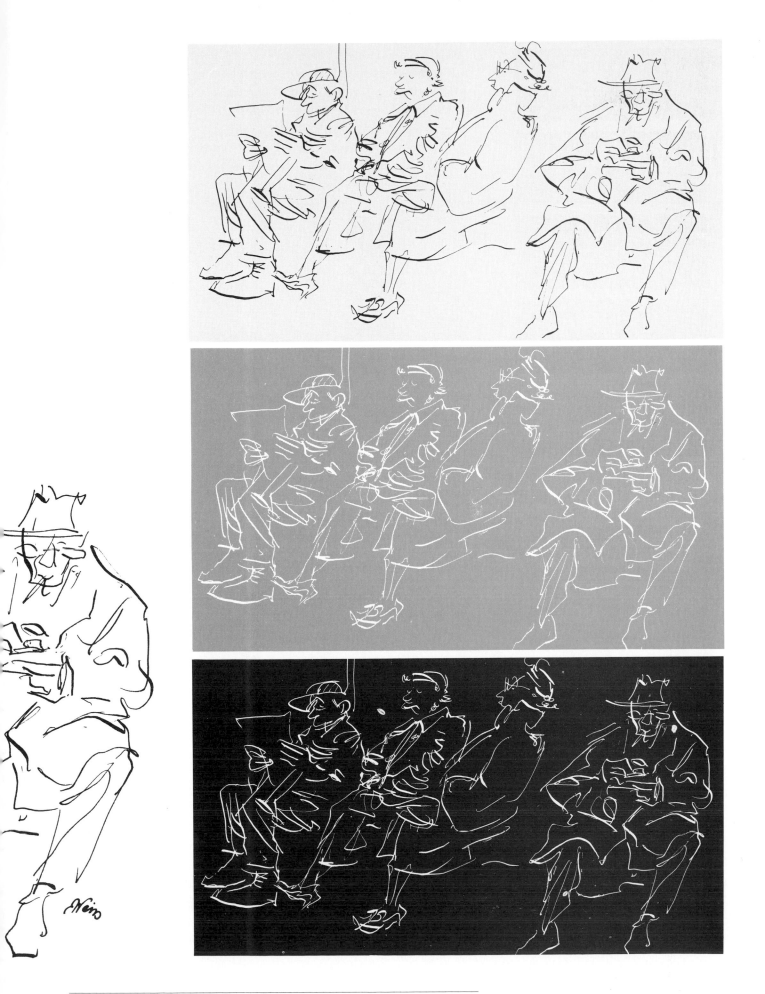

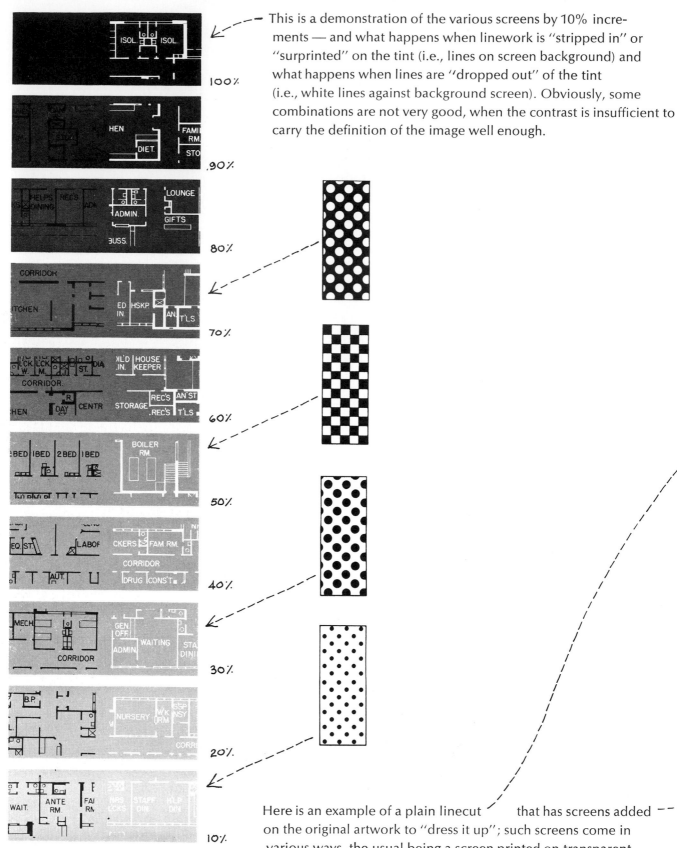

This is a demonstration of the various screens by 10% increments — and what happens when linework is "stripped in" or "surprinted" on the tint (i.e., lines on screen background) and what happens when lines are "dropped out" of the tint (i.e., white lines against background screen). Obviously, some combinations are not very good, when the contrast is insufficient to carry the definition of the image well enough.

100%
.90%
80%
70%
60%
50%
40%
30%
20%
10%

Here is an example of a plain linecut that has screens added on the original artwork to "dress it up"; such screens come in various ways, the usual being a screen printed on transparent cellophane-type material with a pressure-sensitive wax adhesive on the back. The required piece is cut out and simply pressed onto the artwork. The screens undoubtedly add texture, flavor, color to the piece.

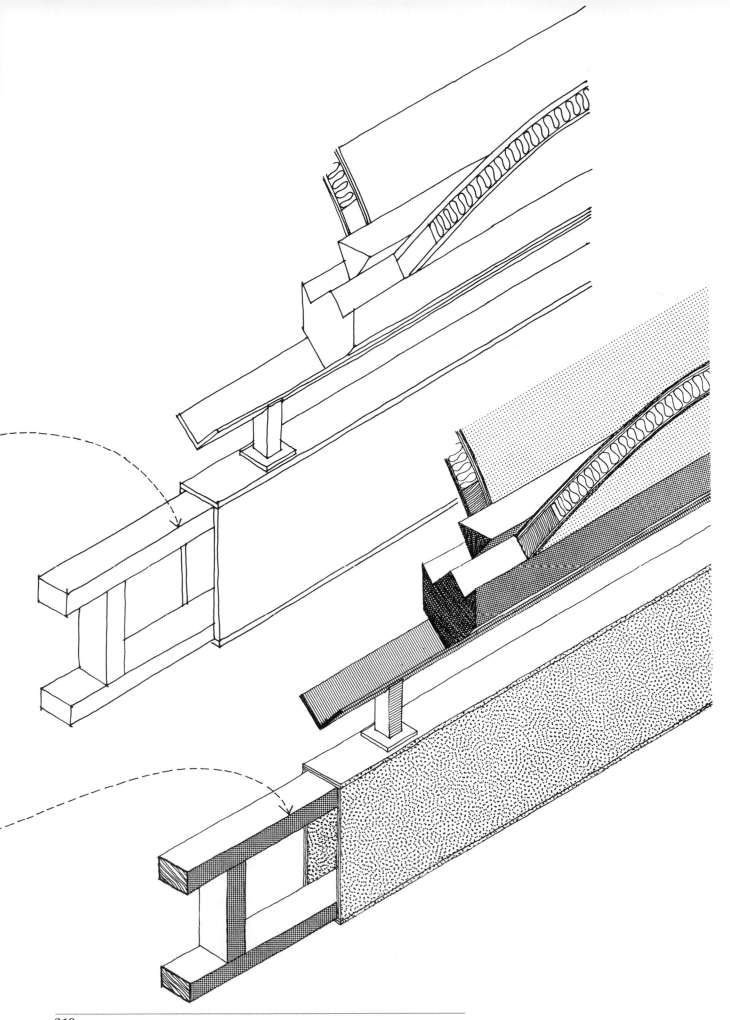

# Line conversions and posterizations

Line conversion is a combination of techniques: taking an original (with continuous tone) and shooting it as linework. In this process, which *pretends* that the original is not halftone material but line material, the artwork is photographed on high-contrast paper. The effect of this trickery is that all the areas of the original that are paler than 50% disappear, because they are not picked up by the sensitized material. Conversely, all the areas darker than 50% become solid black. The resultant line version of the original has much poster quality, with unexpected contrast and graphic excitement. Naturally, most detail has disappeared; hence, such stylized artwork should be restricted to use where it is appropriate as mood setter (as in frontispieces) or attention-getter (as in "break pages" in a series of subchapters) — where detail is unnecessary or possibly even undesirable. Often the same photograph can be used twice: once for its inherent shock value as a line conversion, the second time (elsewhere) as a straightforward information-carrying halftone. The only restricting criterion that must be borne in mind: the subject matter in the picture must be simple and recognizable by shape alone.

This technique can be carried a step further (usually by specially equipped studios and at not inconsiderable expense) into highly decorative areas of "photo-posterization" in which two or more shades of gray are superimposed one on another. In such cases the simple 50/50 black/white line conversion just described is not used, but two or more intermediate degrees of grayness are defined. Naturally, gray-on-gray can be further enlivened by substituting colored ink for the black — with unexpected and often highly decorative results.

"Tone-line" reproduction: the most subtle line version of a continuous-tone original.

Line conversion: this is the commonest, simplest to produce — and the crudest in effect. But it can be very useful.

In "posterization", it is combined with,

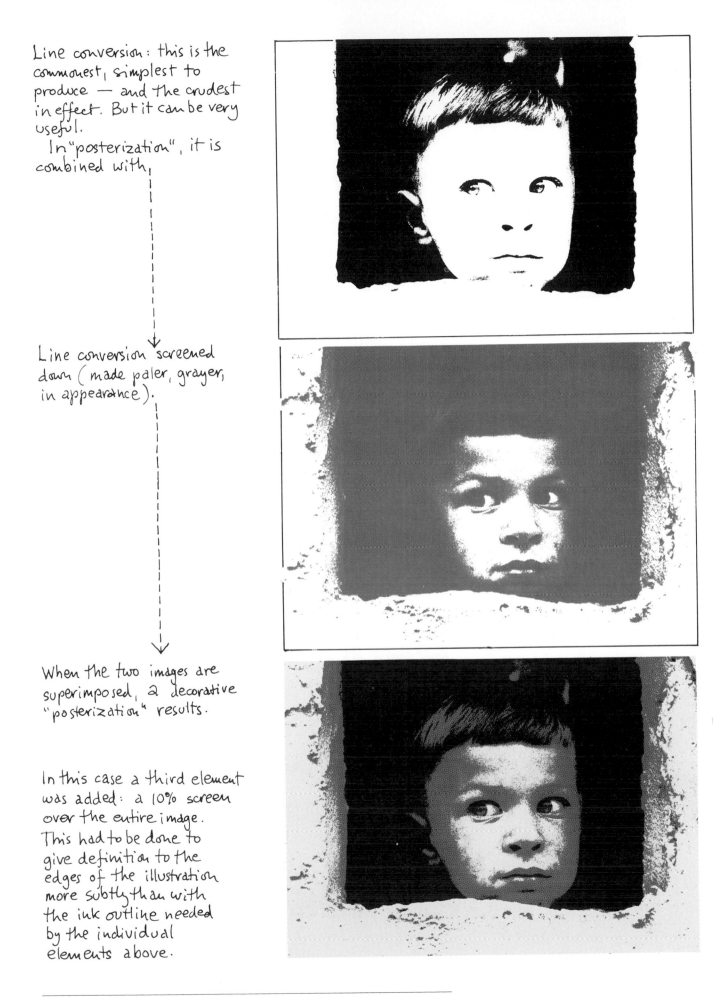

Line conversion screened down (made paler, grayer, in appearance).

When the two images are superimposed, a decorative "posterization" results.

In this case a third element was added: a 10% screen over the entire image. This had to be done to give definition to the edges of the illustration more subtly than with the ink outline needed by the individual elements above.

## Photographic distortions

Cameras and lens attachments are now available that can distort and change original copy in almost any way the imagination might require. It is not a technique to be used lightly (not only because it costs a lot), because it should be reserved for the situations that deserve and can gain impact from such imaginative solutions. Here is just one example:

**pennies**

*Original type*

Duostat Corp., Statmaster Division, Kenvil, N.J.

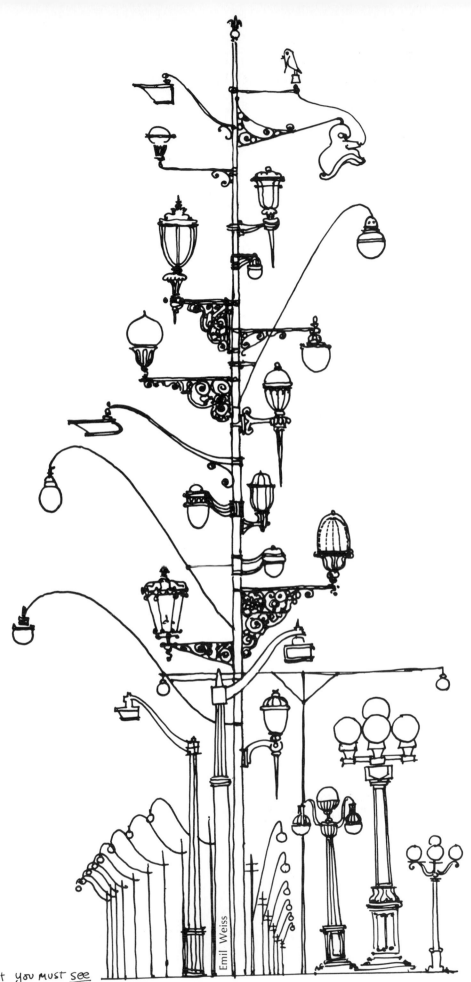

... but in spite of all the technology — first you must see

Emil Weiss

223

7

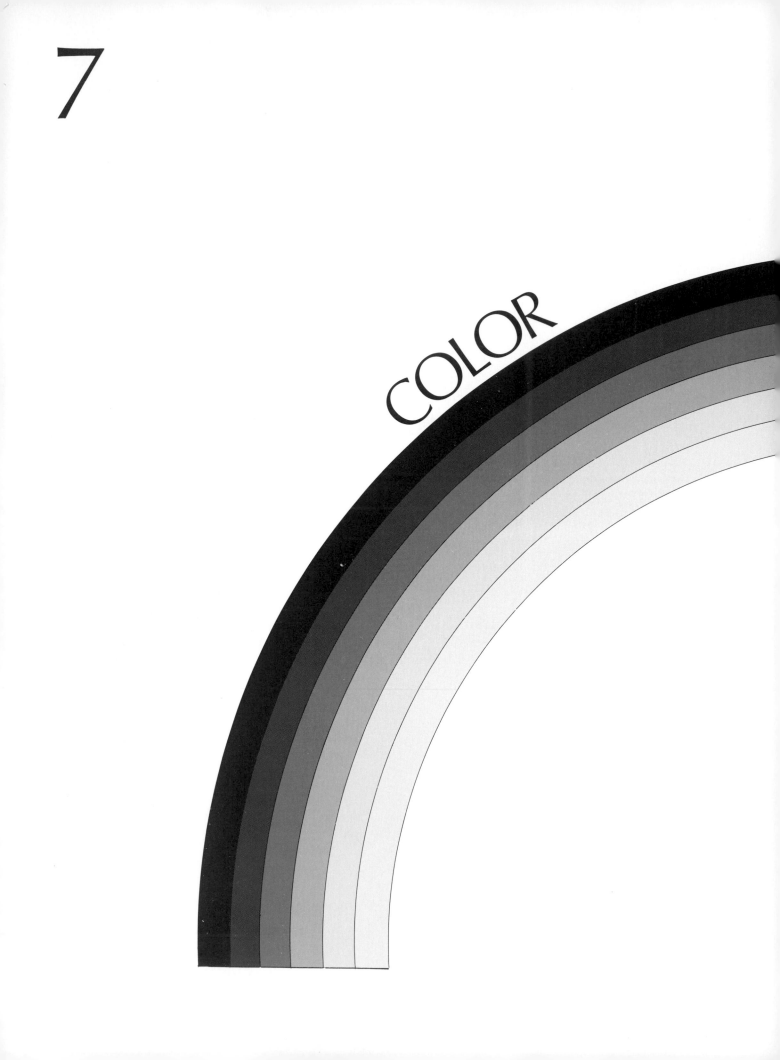

COLOR

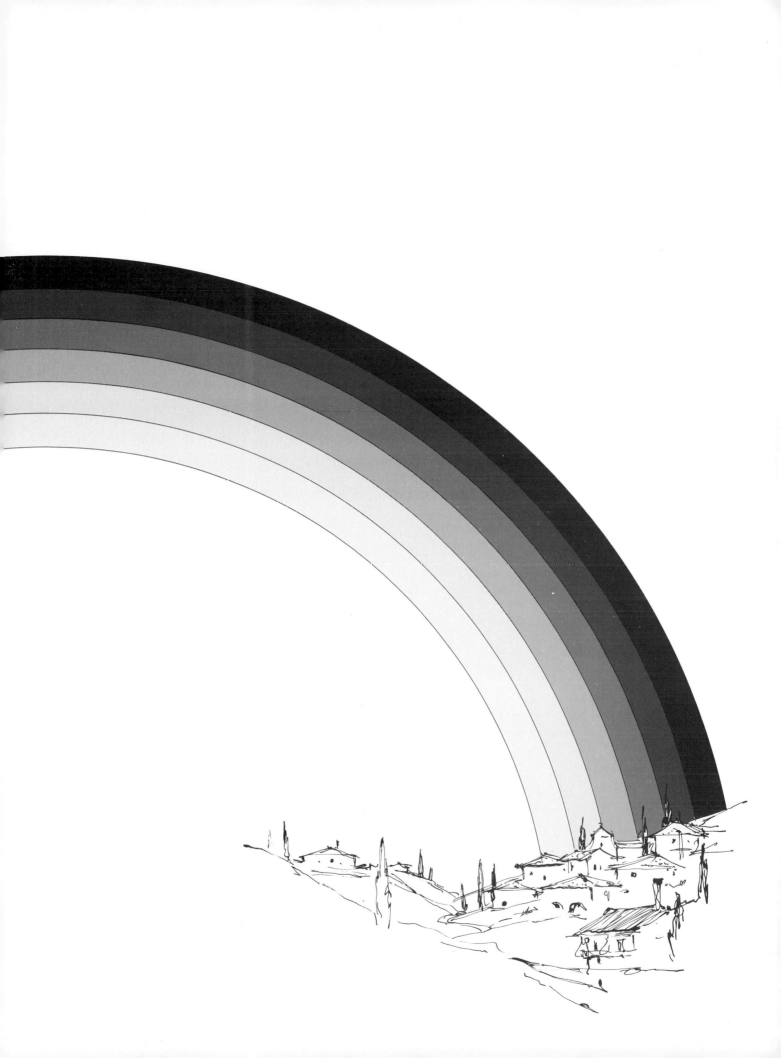

There is no question but that a picture in color is more realistic than the same subject in black-and-white. Dogs see the world in shades of gray — people see it in a spectrum of hues. But photography started as a monochromatic technology, mass reproduction techniques followed, and so people have become used to a monochromatic world in their publications, are not startled by it, and are perfectly ready to accept it as a convention of communication technology. Black-and-white also costs less to produce than color does. Until the cost of color reproduction is brought down to a competitive level with black-and-white, it is wisest to think of the bulk of our illustrative capacity as being restricted to the plain old one-color — usually black — range.

By implication, however, when a situation arises in which color becomes available (because the publisher succeeded in getting more pages sold than anticipated, or because the production manager has found a way of printing the forms so that a "free ride" in a color form is available to several editorial pages, or because the editor insists that color must be used for overriding editorial reasons) then it follows that the investment in color must be handled in such a way that it pays off: it must be used splashily, visibly, boldly, inescapably. It must look as though it is supposed to be there.

But: *color per se* is not half as important to the reader as it is to the editor. The reader sees color in most ads, and ads tend to be so violent in their effort to outshout each other that their very colorfulness tends to work against them: a sense-dulling garishness overwhelms the reader. As a result, a little color in the editorial pages tends to be overlooked by the jaded reader. It is insignificant in the context within which the reader sees the editorial product. The editor rarely gets the opportunity to use color because it costs so much. So he or she thinks its rarity makes it wonderful — ascribes all sorts of marvelous capabilities to it. Alas, by itself it won't fly anywhere — unless the editor knows the magic words.

# Buildup

The same three-dimensional/time-sequential technique must be brought into play: flow across a space; flow from space to space; repetition in some recognizable rhythm, and — as always — simplicity in handling shapes.   A one-shot effect is nigh-on impossible to achieve: look how hard the ads try, and how few succeed, despite all the thinking and money invested in them. The editors must use their one great attention-getting advantage: multipage space that they control. Within that space they must manipulate color in such a way that its effect grows cumulatively from page to page, in a sustained and thought-through effort — so that the resultant richness is inescapably communicated to the reader.

If such wide-stroke color application is added to the even more important technique of color-used-functionally-as-an-editorial-tool, you have a combination capable of tremendous impact.

# Color used functionally

A cliche — like any good principle — it simply means that color is used in some symbolically appropriate manner or with a rational purpose. Alas, there are as many rational purposes as there are post-facto rationalizers or designers with a gift of the gab. There are, however, four basic functions that *can* be defined:

> Color used as background tint — organizing small elements into bigger units (medium-size areas).

> Color used as decoration to dress up the book — point up an article, make the issue appear richer (large-size areas).

> Color used as articulator — to pick out small elements (small-size areas).

> Color used as a tool for emphasis (small-size areas).

If color is used to help get the *idea* off the page into the reader's mind, then its use is justified in the functional sense. If it helps the speed of comprehension (by pointing up the important areas under discussion), or if it helps to clarify complex interrelationships (by showing how one element here corresponds or reacts to another element over there), color is used functionally. If it helps create a mood appropriate to the article (by being properly brownish and yellowed to signal old-fashionedness, or crisp and blue with white lines to signal blueprinting, or whatever), or if it helps to create continuity within a special story in the magazine, it is used functionally. Or if it is used for specific tasks, such as highlighting key words, relating copy to illustrations, focusing attention on important features, dramatizing product operation, diagraming structure or design, distinguishing special elements in graphs or tabular matter, then color is being used functionally. BUT: there is a nonfunction of color, too:

Never should color be used in a place where black ink would be the norm; in such instances, it simply becomes obvious to the reader that the color is used just because it is available — and that's editorial cheating. Frivolous use of color weakens its impact elsewhere, where it is really needed.

# How the four basic functions affect color choice

## Color as background tint

The primary job that color has to perform is to tie things together (not tear them apart). So you need restrained, well-behaved colors that don't scream and take away attention from the units that they are supposed to be subservient to.

They should be pale in tint; the trick is to choose a hue that will have a basic tonality that blends with the tonalities of the halftones , so that the two meld into one in the eye. The percentage of darkness of tint of the color should not exceed the average percentage of the darkness of the halftones. How do you measure percentages? Well, there are instruments that can do so accurately, but the precise measurements are totally unnecessary — the percentages mentioned here are just guidelines to an underlying principle.

If a color is used solid (100%, not broken down into a screen to appear paler), then it is wise to choose a pale color to start with.

If, however, the capacity to run type or line art in color is also desirable, then pick a darkish color to start with (to get the type and linework definable enough), and use tints of the color in the large areas. The danger here is that — for some reason — many colors in the red, brown, orange, purple range turn pink when they are screened down into a tint, often causing the designer to turn equally pink with embarrassment. It is wise to check ink charts carefully before plunging ahead into unknown territory — but wiser still to spend the extra money and superimpose the color tints on tints of black. The latter trick, of course, opens up a new array of interesting possibilities of color mixing.

## Color as decoration

This requires bold strokes. Directness and honesty are essential here — without fear. But (and there is always a but) restraint is the essense of elegance. However much one might be tempted to throw caution to the winds and be direct and honest and have some startling fun, it is essential that the editors remember the context in which they are working, and that they remain within the limits of the self-imposed discipline of the magazine. The purer and cleaner the color, the more strident its effect is likely to be. Within the context of the magazine (which is the antithesis of a poster) it is wiser to pick the dusty earth colors — even in situations where richness or the startling quality of colorfulness are desired. Further-more, since the ads are garish, it is important to choose editorial color that will enhance the subtlety and sophistication of the editorial product in restrained contrast to the ads.

## Color as articulator of details

The smaller the area that color will fill, the greater our freedom to use whatever color we feel like using, and in such situations, the brighter, the better — with the stipulation that brightness increase as size decreases. Most "AAAA second colors" (those standard color inks used by the majority of two-color advertisers) fall into the ugly-but-bright category. Naturally they are the colors that editorial pages can get a "free ride" on as a result of the way in which the printed form is arranged and run off on press. As is often the case, not even the production people can foretell precisely which color will be available for use on the editorial pages — and if they do know ahead of time precisely which hue is running in that particular channel, there is often little they can do about it, since their ad placement and their form arrangement have to be done in the most efficient and economical way possible. It therefore follows that any use of color that will be dependent on the exigencies of unforeseen or uncontrollable ads should be restricted to the small-spot category.

## Color as a tool for emphasis

It is important that one danger of color be recognized: whatever we may be used to thinking, we are wrong if we believe that color ink is more visible on the page than black ink. It is not. Black has the maximum contrast against the white page. As such, it is the easiest to discern — and therefore the easiest to read. If color were better, we would most probably have red newspapers or blue newspapers or purple newspapers. We seldom run type in color — and when we do, it is precisely because of the gentler effect of color against the background white stock. So: it is folly to expect the same startling effect from color against white paper that you get from black against white paper (if the ink areas are of equal size and shape).

And this is the point: if you want an equivalent smash from color, you have to increase the size of the color-carrying element to compensate for the decreased contrast. The factor by which you have to increase the size varies in proportion to the brightness and darkness of the color chosen: the closer the color is to black, the smaller the size increase necessary. The paler the color, the bigger the area in which it must be run.

# Process colors and second colors

There are two basic sets of colors available to editors.
*Process colors* are the four color elements of "four-color process" reproduction and are used by all but the most specialized publications to present their color pictures. Since only some of the pages of a magazine carry such material, the pages on which it is run are printed on separate sheets or forms. (Because printing in four colors is obviously more expensive than printing in one or two colors; not just because of the extra printing plates involved, but because each color requires a separate ink-roller, and only big presses have the four or five rollers required; and big presses command more fees per hour than little ones do.)

The process colors used are special hues developed to complement and balance each other. The color original is "separated" into its four component color segments (through one of several different processes which define the comparative value of each of the four colors — black, yellow, red, and blue — over the entire picture area and make a printing plate of the original in each of the four colors). When those four color elements are printed on top of each other, the tiny dots meld in the eye and produce, as faithfully as possible, the color values of the original.

Individually, the four colors are not terribly beautiful: the black is not black but grayish. The red is not red but magenta — which turns into a particularly unpleasant pink when screened down to a tint. The blue is not blue but cyan, a pale turquoise, and possibly the most useful as a color by itself. The yellow is an acid pale yellow, practically invisible by itself on the white page except in large areas or tintblocks. It is surprising that such individually unlikely colors can create the effects they do when they are printed in screened form on top of each other.

Through trial and error, and through the need for a workable standardization throughout the printing industries of the world, the four colors have evolved over the years and are now so deeply ingrained and there is so much investment in their use that they are likely to be with us for years to come. Besides, the four-color pictures they produce are of eminently successful quality, taking economics into account.

Only when they are used by themselves are they less than satisfactory. The secret for editors to remember here is always to think in terms of *combining* process colors in some way: one color with black, or two colors, or three colors. It is, indeed, more expensive to proceed this way, but the resultant effects are more colorful and subtle.

*Second colors* are of two different kinds: the "standard" colors (standardized by the American Association of Advertising Agencies for use in all publications), and the "special" (matched) colors that can be specified by swatch or by number from an ink manufacturer's catalog. The standard AAAA colors are bright, cheerful, and ordinary. They are not exciting simply because they are standard.

To build in surprise with crude raw material like this, it is necessary to combine screens of the color with screens of black in order to achieve more subtle results. Unfortunately this is not always possible to do, since the imposition of pages on the printing sheet often changes at the last minute, as paid-space positions are amended and the edit pages more often than not are the victim of an unforeseen switch in channels. So, where a particularly strong red had been planned for, and a pale tint plate had been made, we now find a pale second color to work with — and a pale tint plate of a pale color might just as well have not been run at all, the color becomes so light and insignificant. As a result, if the risk of waste is considerable, editors tend to resist potential subtlety (which costs money), hope for a break, and use the color that happens to be available, solid, raw, and undoctored — out of the tube. This is an understandable practice in the practical world — but it certainly doesn't do the image of the publication any good. Often it does it considerable harm, since the crude color *by itself* makes the editorial page look — at first glance — like an ad. This is emphatically not what should be happening. In cases such as that, it is far wiser to eschew the use of second color altogether and stick with undangerous black ink.

The matched colors are, of course, the ideal editorial tool, since they are, by definition, under the total control of the editors, both as to hue and as to their disposal on the pages of the printing form. For the sake of economy, production managers often try to limit the way color should be imposed on the sheet — and their advice must be followed because they have the responsibility of spending money in the wisest way possible. Moreover, compromises are always possible. In the past, specification of color was a hit-and-miss affair, unless one could point to specific precedents in the magazine. Color is a very personal vision, impossible to describe in words. Interpretation of instructions often resulted in misunderstanding and dissatisfaction. Now, however, a standardized system of ink-color identification has been published by an ink-manufacturing association, and the system is being widely accepted. It combines a very large palette of colors with an equally large range of available art materials for designing with — and the whole is based on precise ink-mixing formulas. As a result, it is possible to foretell, more accurately than ever, exactly what the final result is likely to be. (Though there are often surprises in store nevertheless, especially in the area of running color on colored stock, or even color on white stock of different surface properties than the available sample indicates.) So you need only specify the simple code number to the printer, who can refer to his ink guide and know exactly how many pounds of purple he will need to mix in with his dark base toner to manufacture the brown the editors seem to favor.

# How and where to use color

Given the infinite variety of effects color is capable of producing, it is impossible to make an all-inclusive list of color applications. A short listing of the most obvious applications follows, with some pros and cons. No distinction is made between process colors and the two varieties of second colors, because it is unwise to make hard-and-fast distinctions that might mislead or restrict thinking. Intelligent application of judgment and taste, plus considerable experience from past mistakes, will ensure success. Maybe. (Keep a file of past color specifications to refer to, both to repeat successes and to avoid failures.)

## In pictures

Running a photograph in a second color is very dangerous, since the color is paler than black — and the resultant image appears to be washed out. For special effects, this may make sense — but it is not to be done lightly. The darker the color, the less risk involved. Dark browns and blues are the safest. Anything with red in it blushes pink.

When running a photograph in black ink, with flat color on top of it, if the color is pale enough not to swamp the picture, it can be solid color, but if it is a dark color, a screened tint must be used (with an angled screen to prevent a moire pattern). This does make the picture colored, *but* it also robs the picture of sparkle and crispness, because the highlights (pale areas) in the photograph are the areas in which the color is most visible (since the black ink doesn't cover it up) and the color is darker than white paper. Thus the contrast between the darkest part of the photo and the lightest part of the photo is reduced considerably — through the addition of the darkening effect of the color — and the result is a "flat" photo. If details are not important, this may not matter very much. But it must be considered a detrimental factor, and must be balanced with the fact that this is the cheapest way of coloring a black-and-white picture.

Running a photograph as a "duotone." In this technique, the photograph is made as a black-image halftone and as a colored-ink-image halftone. The two are then printed on top of each other. In both plates the dark areas have the heavier concentration of ink and the light areas have less ink (so that filling up of highlights does not occur). In this process the darks become even darker, and a deeper, richer picture results — one that is not only more eventful, but also colorful. Startling variations are possible in varying the degree of intensity that either of the plates is carrying — so that unnatural, unbalanced images can be created by underdeveloping the black plate and overdeveloping the color plate, for instance. Naturally, the plates and proofing of such illustrations can be considerably more expensive than for a plain black halftone.

Running a photograph as a "triotone." If four-color process capacity is there, but the original material exists only in black-and-white, the art can be shot as a plain duotone, and then printed on top of a tint of a third color, to give it an extra quality of colorfulness. A black-and-blue duotone on top of a 30% tint of process yellow can be most exciting, as can a black-and-red duotone on top of a 20% background of process blue. This is an area where much experimentation can be done, and startling, fresh effects can be achieved at a much lower cost than for full four-color-process separations.

Running a photograph as a four-color-process illlustration. This is the most expensive, but, of course, the most naturalistic and informative way to present visual material. As the process becomes ever more widely used, and because it behooves each publication to keep up with its competition, more and more full-color reproductions are finding their way into even the most modest of magazines. Printing by offset lithography (as compared to the use of letterpress printing), has made it far cheaper to switch to color, since making separations on film is far less costly than making engravings on copper.

Running photographs in color, using various trick screens, mezzotints, polarizations, overlaps, superimposing one unexpected color atop another, probably off-register, etc. This is an area fast developing in the category of more specialized publications, such as annual reports, where originality, freshness, and startling graphics are valued and encouraged — at a premium, and hang the expense. It is important that everyone in the graphic communication field be aware of this trend, collect samples that particularly excite them, and apply the ideas when the right subject and time come up.

Running photographs in double-dot impressions. This is basically a duotone technique, which substitutes a second black color for the color plate. The purpose is to create an illusion of extra depth in the dark areas and extra highlights in the light areas, so that the resultant reproduction is as rich in contrasts as possible. A subtle variant of this is to use a second black ink to which a "toner" has been added to give the photograph a slight color cast: blue/black, reddish/black, greenish/black, brownish/black. As in the technique described in the preceding paragraph, this procedure is seldom used in mass publications — at the moment — but will come into its own as time goes by, for special stories with special illustrations that justify such quality in handling.

## In words

*Headlines and display type:* Realizing that color is less visible on white paper than black ink, and realizing that it is necessary to compensate for this fact by enlarging type size or boldening the type itself, we have no reason not to use color in titles, or blurbs, or the subheads of the piece (so long as the color remains the same throughout the story, to avoid confusion).

Run the entire headline in color.

Run part of the headline in color, picking out special words for emphasis in color (and then, perhaps, using those words as the jump line on succeeding pages?); or better still, run the major part of the headline in color and pop out the important words in black, since black is more visible.

Run the headline in a screen of black with color superimposed — creating an unexpected blend — strengthening the color if it is pale to start with.

*Body copy:* Unless the color is good and strong, it is unwise to run standard reading matter in color; it is undoubtedly harder to read. But short pieces, such as an important introduction in large type, are eminently suitable for color treatment. Color is even more suitable in type when a functional purpose can be found — for instance, in a question-and-answer story where the questions are run in color to split them away from the answers. Similarly, picture captions make sense in color — to contrast them with the main body copy. So:

Run the type itself in color (if it is a strong color and if it is a logical trick to play).

Run the type in black over a screen of color background.

Run the type in color over a light screen of black in the background.

Run the type in white, dropped out from a background color panel.

Note: the last three suggestions are given for the sake of inclusiveness. They should be used with great care, as they are fraught with danger: illegibility may result because the serifs in the type get messed up with the screen dots; the white reverse areas may fill up when a lot of ink is put on the printing plates and the type is small — all sorts of disasters can happen. Best rule of thumb: when in doubt, leave it out.

# In panels

The magazine world has lately passed through an antipanel period. This is an irrational fashion trend. There is no reason why color panels should be avoided IF they are used intelligently. What does the "intelligence" boil down to? Simply this: if the page is as intelligible without the color panel as it is with it, then the color panel is merely window dressing and probably should be thrown out. If, on the other hand, the editorial material is helped by the color panel in being obviously better organized (by pulling together elements that ought to be pulled together), then color is being used functionally, and it makes sense to use it.

A word of warning, however, about color panels on the page

— in context of the editorial package as a whole: avoid overly startling panels — panels that are so strong that you don't see anything but the panels. If the color is to act functionally as an editorial tool, it must be restrained and made to do its editorial organizing job — period. It must remain in the background, not usurp the foreground. This misuse of color is the basis for the antipanelists' campaign; and they are right. But if the color panels are quiet enough in color to blend with the halftones as an overall image, then there will be no such trouble.

Use solid color (if it is quiet enough) as background into which elements are dropped — by surprinting in black, or dropping out of the color in white, or both.

Use as background a screen of strong color into which elements are dropped — by surprinting in black, or surprinting in solid of the same color, or both.

Use a screen of color combined with a screen of black, with elements surprinted in either black or color, or perhaps dropped out from one or other of the two screens, leaving a paler, ghosted image as well.

There is one special use of color panels that needs mentioning as a separate subcategory: full-page color over a number of pages to separate the story from the rest of the issue. This can seldom be accomplished unless it is carefully planned in advance and the makeup of the magazine can accommodate it. In such instances it is wise to use a matched second color, to be sure that the trick will be under the editor's control, and will work. If the color is pale enough, it is often advantageous to cover the entire page with the color — even under the halftones — though (it may well be argued) if you are going that far, you might as well print the special story on special colored stock, bind it in as a separate form, and have a guarantee of excellent color coverage, since the color printed over a number of pages may vary in intensity from page to page. Naturally, if the story needs eight pages, and can start on a right and end on a left (to accommodate the eight-page form), such special stock makes sense. Be that as it may, the purpose of the color — the editorial purpose of the color — is to give the *entire* story a special treatment. If it is possible to take the color decision one step further and give it some symbolic meaning as well, then an effective piece of communication in which visual presentation helps to give it life has been invented. (The obvious examples again: brownish for oldness, silver for astronautics, blueness for aeronautics or the sea, etc.)

## In line art

Greater freedom of handling is possible in this area than in any other, where color is concerned. But successful handling is achieved only when color and subject and treatment work together harmoniously. Thus, for instance, it is unlikely that a pen-and-ink illustration drawn in fine lines will have much personality if it is printed in pale yellow — nobody will even see it. On the other hand, if it is printed in black ink on a pale yellow background, great richness of effect is possible. As a second example, will it do the magazine much good to overlap a simple drawing of an automobile with bright purple brushmarks — to "liven up the page"? The element that is noticed will be the purple splotches; the well-drawn automobile will be secondary (assuming that anyone will want to look through the purple to find it). But perhaps a screen of purple coordinated with the shape of the automobile, indicating shades and shadows — with white highlights dropped out from the screen — could help the reader comprehend the shape of the automobile more clearly; and the color could be working for the drawing rather than against it. Again, color must be used with finesse — for a purpose. With that in mind:

Use artwork run in color (if the color is strong enough to sustain it).

Use artwork designed and prepared to be run partially in color and partially black. (The two elements must be prepared on separate sheets of paper, one overlaid on top of the other; or a tissue overlay must be prepared that shows in outline "keyline" which parts are to be run in color and which in black. The engraver then prepares the two separate plates by masking out the inappropriate areas in each.)

Use artwork run in black or in color (or both), employing additional tint screens of black or color (or both) over it. This can get complicated — especially if you add a further possibility of dropping out shapes from the screens to your already complex group of techniques. It is perhaps useful to point out that it is advantageous to have the artist do as much of the technical preparation of the drawings as possible, since he or she is likely to be less expensive by-the-hour than the engraver, who must charge at a higher rate by-the-minute or by-the-process.

## In charts, maps, graphs, plans, diagrams, tables

Here, the use of color is restricted only by the manipulative ingenuity of the art director or artist preparing the artwork. Since most of these illustrations tend to be smaller-than-page size, and since color tends to be used in small areas, it is safe to assume that disasters are not likely to happen *because* of the color. If the color used is very bright, it should be restricted to small areas, or it should be tinted down to pale screens or combined with screens of black, so that it is not out of balance with the feel of the magazine as a whole. It is of little value to list the possibilities specifically one by one. They all derive from the basic principles of:

running elements in solid color;

running elements in solid color with black;

running elements in tint of color;
running elements in tint of color and tint of black;
running elements with dropout in white from the color;
running elements with dropout in white from black.

These can be combined in endless varieties, to clarify, simplify, draw attention to and in general help the point of each illustration to come across. This is an ideal area of interest for which to establish an example file.

## In rules and decorative elements

These constitute an easily applied color use — somewhat overdone (since it is so easy) and not very startling (since it is so obvious). Nevertheless it has its place as one of the weapons against dullness, if not a very sharp one.

Rules can be used as separators — walls — to split one area of the page from another. They succeed in this best when they go all the way into bleed, so that there is no question about their intended use. Equally successful are rules that box in an element completely — on all four sides, and the most successful boxes (the ones that are most immediately recognizable as corrals) are ones with rounded corners.

Rules can be used as combiners — as a graphic device to unify elements on a page or pages in a story. Again, they must extend beyond the type or illustration and bleed off the page in order to be fully obvious.

Rules can be used for purely decorative purposes, to add a simple graphic element to an otherwise plain text page (running thin vertical rules between the columns, for example). Or decorative rules available from the printer can be inserted to add appropriate graphic flavor. Often double rules can be run part in color, part in black — as an extra touch.

Rules can be used as emphasis creators, by underscoring important passages in the type, or by vertical scoring alongside important passages.

Where rules in color are concerned, the color must be strong to give clear visibility to the linework. If the color is not strong, the lines it is used on must be made heavier (fatter), to increase the area that the color will cover.

# GLOSSARY

Ascender: That part of a lowercase letter that protrudes above its main body, such as the upper stroke of a letter *b*; the geographic opposite of the *descender,* q.v.

Bleed: "To bleed" is to run an illustration or any printed image off the edge of the page; "a bleed" is the item that is to bleed.

Blow up: To enlarge the size of copy (usually an illustration) by mechanical means; the opposite of *reduce.* The engraver or photographer receives the instruction to enlarge or reduce the size of an illustration in one of two ways: (1) by the desired dimensions that the editor or designer has drawn on the original artwork or (2) by being told the percent of enlargement or reduction required. The latter instruction indicates to the engraver or photographer the enlargement or reduction setting — the *focus* — for the camera. The technique is based on the accepted fact that the original size of the illustration equals 100%. Thus a twice-the-original-size blowup would be identified as a 200% enlargement and diminishing the original to half-the-original size would be labeled a 50% reduction. A scaling ruler or proportional scale must be used to determine the precise percentage figures, or "focuses," that are not the simple "twice-up" or "half-size" kind.

Blurb: In book publishing, the descriptive "selling" talk on the inside flaps or the back of a book jacket. In periodical publishing, by extension, the "selling" words run in conjunction with the headline and intended to persuade the reader to read the story — by pointing up its importance, usefulness, or other attribute. If the blurb is run before the headline, it is — or it can be — called a *precede.* If run after the headline, it is likely to be called a *deck.* If it is written so that the words do not flow in a continuous sentence either into the headline or out of the headline, the blurb may well be placed independently somewhere on the spread.

Body copy: The words of the story — the meaning, content, thrust of the story. Not synonymous with *body type,* q. v.

Body type: The type used in the main part of the story — the text — as distinguished from the *display type,* q.v. Not the same as *body copy,* q.v.

Bullet: A black dot used for emphasis. Printers have available for setting in type bullets ranging in size from a practically invisible 1 pt. to a Brobdingnagian 36 pt. spot. Too often used too large. Too often used, period.

By-line: The credit line given to an author.

Carry-over line: The words, usually run in the top left corner of a page or spread, that identify the story of which the page or spread is a part.

Cartouche: An ornamental frame, border, box reminiscent of a partially unrolled scroll (or other such formal graphic flourish).

Continued line: The words, usually run in the lower right corner of a page, that tell the readers the page on which the story is continued. The direction may be simply to the next page overleaf, or it may be a "jump" to a page elsewhere in the issue.

Cropping: Cutting a portion, or portions, of a photograph or other illustration either (1) to make it fit into a given space, (2) to concentrate attention onto an important area of it, or (3) to accomplish both objectives.

Cuts: Illustrations, pictures, photographs printed in a publication. In letterpress printing, the word *cut* also describes the actual engraving plate (copper or zinc mounted on a wood base) from which the illustration is printed.

Dead matter: Type or cuts no longer needed for printing; it is put into the *hellbox* for melting down and reuse. The opposite of *live matter.* (See Live-matter page.)

Deck: *See* Blurb.

Department slug: *See* Slug.

Descender: That part of a lowercase letter that hangs below its main body, such as the lower stroke of the letter *p;* the opposite of *ascender,* q.v.

Die-cut: To cut a shape out of a sheet of paper; die-cutting can be done either on press, as part of the printing process, or separately, as an independent operation.

Dingbats: *See* Printer's flowers.

Display type: A general term for the large, heavy, bold type used for headlines, blurbs, etc., as distinguished from *body type,* q. v.

Dropout halftone: Sometimes called a facsimile halftone, an ordinary *halftone* (q. v.) doctored — by hand or by mechanical filters or masks — to remove the halftone dots in the highlights or unwanted backgrounds, thus allowing the white paper to shine through brilliantly. A dropout halftone is similar to a *silhouette halftone* (q. v.), but not the same in that it may or may not cut away the entire background surrounding the wanted image. A dropout halftone is more selective in the areas removed, and it is a more expensive process because of that selectiveness.

Dummy: Sometimes called a *layout,* a dry run of a proposed piece of printing. Dummying, or a layout, is done on dummy, or layout sheets: preprinted forms showing the full-size page and all its regular subdivisions of columns as well as page number locations, etc. The degree of finish to which dummies may be brought depends on the given publication's *modus operandi* and may vary from a few scraggly pencil lines indicating type areas and rectangles showing size and position of illustrations, to carefully pasted compositions that make use of dummy type (i.e., type of the size, weight, shape and kind intended for that particular purpose and usually preset and preprinted in sheets) and photostatic reproductions of the illustrations in the proposed size, shape, and cropping. Obviously, the more elaborate dummy offers a keener visualization of the printing project and can prevent mistakes before they are multiplied on press. Equally obviously, the more elaborate dummy costs money in staff time, production time, materials used, etc. Is it worth it? Decidedly.

Flush: Aligned with, even with, coming to the same edge as. "Flush left" usually designates type set with an even left margin; "flush right," with an even right margin.

Folio: Page number. *See also* Footline.

Footline: Name of the publication and date of issue, placed as a small line of type somewhere in relation to the folio. The *folio-and-footline* is an important element on every page, usually placed in a lower corner, but often nowadays placed elsewhere, to give the publication an up-to-date quality with little effort.

Form: In printing, a *form* is an assembly of pages printed simultaneously in one pass through the press. Usually it is a group of eight or 16 pages, but four-page forms are common; so are 32-page forms. It is wise always to think in terms of eight-page forms, since they tend to be the most economical to print and bind. When a form has been printed on both sides of the paper, it is folded, and the resultant unit of pages is called a *signature*. When the signatures are assembled, that is grouped in sequence to make up a complete publication, they are said to be *gathered*.

Format: The makeup of a publication — its size, shape, typography, margins, binding, headline handling, etc. — all elements combining to give the product an individual character.

Gather: *See* Form.

Gutter: The inner space between two facing pages. Crossing it by running an element from one page onto the facing page is called *jumping the gutter.*

Halftone: The reproducible (printable) version of an original piece of continuous-tone artwork, such as a photograph. The original is rephotographed through a *screen* (q. v.) to break up the continuous tones into a series of closely spaced dots or other patterns, depending on the sort of screen used. The dots then become the printing surface.

Hanging indent: The first line of a paragraph set longer than the succeeding lines, so that it cantilevers out beyond the left edge of the type column (like this paragraph). The opposite of regular *indent,* q. v.

Hellbox: *See* Dead matter.

Indent: "To indent" is to set a line of type shorter than the other lines in a piece of typography. This is usually done in the first lines of paragraphs or to draw attention to quotations, lists, or other special material falling within the flowing text. *Indent* used as a noun is the short form for *indention* and describes the little bay of white space created by indenting a line of type.

Insert: A specially printed piece, usually on stock other than that used for the publication as a whole, prepared separately and bound into the publication. Inserts usually are four-page forms and inserted between *signatures. (See also* Form.)

Justify: To create an even alignment in lines of type so that both left and right margins for all the lines are even. Justifying a line of type necessitates "opening up" by *word spacing* (q. v.) or *letter spacing* (q. v.); justifying a column means inserting extra space between lines to make the top lines and the bottom lines of neighboring columns of type align. This is an execrable practice — except in newspapers, where pressure of time is used as an excuse.

Lead time: Pronounced leed time. Time required for preparation. In magazines it is *never* enough.

Leaders: Pronounced leeders. Dots or dashes set in succession, so as to lead (leed) the eye from an element on the left to one on the right. Leaders are often used in tabular matter or tables of contents. *Fill with leaders* is the usual specification. Usually the leaders are in fact periods — and in that case they tend to appear somewhat crude, since the period, seen in series, looks surprisingly large. The typesetter can help in getting smaller dots — but that accommodation is likely to add to the cost.

Lead-in: Pronounced leed-in. The first few words in a piece of copy. Most often used to describe the first few words of a picture caption, which are usually set in a contrasting type size or weight. Thus: a boldface lead-in.

Leading: Pronounced ledding. Space inserted between lines of type. Type without leading is said to be *set solid;* with a single point of leading it is called *one-point leaded;* with two points, *two-point leaded,* etc. The term comes from the original practice of actually inserting a piece of metal, usually two points in thickness, between the lines of type. Since the metal alloy used contains a proportion of lead, the name "lead" was given to the material.

Letterspacing: Inserting extra space between the characters in a word, l i k e  t h i s ,  to stretch the words in order to make them fit into a line of desired length. This regrettable practice should be avoided wherever possible, since it destroys the texture and color of type, and thus its visual quality as well as its legibility. Letter spacing is useful, however, when all-capital letters are used, since "optical letterspacing" (i.e., spacing done by eye, so it looks right) improves legibility considerably. *See also* Wordspacing.

Line: Line art, linework, linecut, line engraving, line drawing — all refer to a method of drawing, or of reproducing that drawing, in which there are no middle tones, only pure black and pure white. Such original artwork can be made into printing plates without the use of a halftone screen. *See* Halftone; Screen.

Line screen: A screen made of closely spaced parallel lines running in one direction, used in lieu of a halftone *screen* (q. v.), through which continuous-tone original artwork can be photographed and thus become both printable and startling.

Live-matter page: The area within the margins in which type may be placed. To extend beyond the area with a picture, to the edge of the page, is to *bleed,* q. v. Not to be confused with *dead matter,* q. v.

Logo: A specially designed trademark, hence, the name of the magazine as run on the front cover. Sometimes also used to denote the department headings or *slugs,* q. v. The word derives from *logotype,* which describes a group of characters cast together on one piece of metal.

Mezzotint: A textured screen used in lieu of a halftone *screen* (q. v.) to turn continuous-tone original artwork into printable form. It is similar (though cruder and coarser) to the method of handcrafting copperplate engraving widely used in the days of yore.

Mugshot: Standard photograph of a person showing the head and shoulders; derived from police jargon for identification (ID) photographs of evildoers.

Ozalid: A form of blueprinting in which the background is pale and the lines are dark; usually bluish, but brownish and blackish are available. The background has a slightly mottled texture, which is the imprint of the imperfections in the tracing paper of the original drawing; the original is placed onto photo-sensitized paper and light is shined through to create the print.

Perfect binding: Binding a publication by means of glue applied to the spine edge of all pages, the pages having been pretrimmed and roughened to accept the glue. Although this method allows the pages to lie flat when the publication is opened, the binding method is somewhat fragile, and unless it is well produced, the pages can fall out. But perfect binding allows greater freedom in organizing an issue of a publication, since inserts and gatefolds and special-stock pages can be accommodated more readily in this technique of gathering and binding than any other except mechanical spiral bindings.

Photostat: Usually shortened to *stat.* An inexpensive photographic process by which original graphic material of all kinds may be copied, reduced, or enlarged as required. The first copy produced is a paper-base negative showing the image in white on black. From this a right-reading positive may be made. *Photostat* is a trade name that has, through common usage, become the standard term for the output of cameras made by other manufacturers. The competitive products that have become available in recent years have some advantage over the reliable stat equipment, in that they by-pass the negative stage and make direct positives. Furthermore, they make copies faster since they do not have to go through a time-consuming developing-fixing-drying process. Naturally, the copies cost more, but they could be cheaper in bulk; the choice depends on availability, economics, work habits of the people involved.

Precede: *See* Blurb.

Printer's flowers: Ornaments in the shape of flowers or leaves or other *dingbats* (bullets, stars, etc.), naturalistic or abstract (disrespectfully known in the vernacular as cabbages or vegetables), available as decoration in most printshops, but seldom used unless specifically called for. It is useful to get a "showing" (a visual catalog) of what the printer has available; everyone might be pleasantly surprised.

Reduce: To decrease the size of an illustration; the opposite of to *blow up,* q. v.

Saddle stitch: Binding a publication by means of staples placed through the fold at the spine. Pages lie flat, but there is a limit to the thickness of a publication that can be stapled that way.

Screen: Used in making a printable *halftone* (q. v.) from original continuous-tone copy, such as photographs. It is an actual screen on glass or film, through which the original material is photographed.
   *Screen* also denotes the tones of dots or lines or other textures added to the page or to artwork by one or more techniques: the benday process; wax-back, pressure-sensitive cellophane sheets for cutting out and do-it-yourselfing; stripping in ready-made screens available to the printer. How the screens are applied depends on the given publication's normal production process as well as on the capabilities and preferences of the people involved. For the safest and probably cleanest result: let the printer do it.

Serifs: The little cross lines at the ends of the strokes of letters. Type without serifs is known as *sans serif, sans* being the French word for "without."

Side wire binding: Binding a publication by means of staples driven through the signatures near the spine. This is the most permanent and safest of all binding methods, but the pages do not lie flat, and the *gutter* (q. v.) is a major obstacle in creating spreads that look like spreads.

Sidebar: A separate but related story, usually short, run in conjunction with the main article. It is usually boxed or separated visually and bears its own headline.

Signature: *See* Form.

Silhouette halftone: A normal halftone in which the major element of the picture is shown and the nonessential background is cut away. *See also* Halftone; Dropout halftone.

Sinkage: The point at the top of the page where the *live-matter page* (q. v.) begins. If the head margin (i.e., the margin at the top of the page) is not unusually wide, the term *sinkage* cannot apply, since it only describes the result of unusually wide head margins.

Slug: In hot metal composition (Linotype, Intertype, Ludlow, etc.) one line of type set in the form of a single metal bar. Also, like *leading,* (q. v.), a bar of metal used as spacing material between lines of type.

    Used as a verb, *slug* means to hit hard or suddenly, and by extension, in magazine terminology, to inform the reader unequivocally, clearly, and fast as to the area of interest that a story falls in; this can be done many ways, such as by placing a *department slug* (or name) at the head of the page or by running a dateline or other defining element as the first words of the story.

Small capitals: Capital letters smaller than the regular capitals in a font. They are usually the same height as the type's *x-height,* q. v.

Spine: The backbone or bound edge of a publication that has a square back. The square back is a result of binding by *perfect binding* (q. v.) or by *side wire binding,* q. v. The spine usually carries the name, date, and volume and issue number of the publication and is also often used for running the title of the major story in the issue — to take advantage of the part of the product that is visible when several copies are stacked on top of each other or are placed vertically on a shelf.

Spread: The two facing pages apparent when a publication is opened up. Often called a *double spread,* which is saying the same thing twice, like "pizza pie." A spread is sometimes called *double truck,* but this term takes the concept a step further, however, since it implies material that covers both pages, making one unit of them, and jumping the gutter.

Surprint: To print one graphic element atop another. Usually it implies printing type on top of a halftone background, such as a headline over a photograph. Unless this technique is handled with great care it may produce problems of illegibility. The wisest course is to avoid surprinting when only one color is available, although it becomes safer when more than just black is to be had.

Tombstoning: Undesirable alignment of elements horizontally across the page so that disparate elements, which are not supposed to merge, become visible as one. Commonest of such disasters: the alignment of three subheads in three adjacent columns.

Uppercase:  CAPITAL letters. The term derives from the old practice of putting all the capital letters in a box — or case — *above* the box containing the small, or *lowercase* letters.

Vignette:  An illustration whose background appears to fade away on all sides until it disappears into the white space of the page.

Wordspacing:  Inserting extra space between words in a given line of type in order to stretch the available words until the desired line length is attained. This is an inevitable outcome of the practice of making all lines in a column of type of equal length, so that even edges are achieved. *See* Justify; *see also* Letterspacing.

x-height:  Also called the body of the type; the height of the main portion of the lowercase letter. Since the term *x-height* is used because the lowercase x has neither *ascender* (q. v.) nor *descender* (q. v.), it could just as easily be stated as the "n-height" or the "w-height," but not the "i-height."

# INDEX

The Contents shows a detailed listing of general subjects. It is suggested that it, rather than this index, be used as the primary reference source for broad areas of interest. The index is intended as a detailed locator and cross-reference guide; therefore, to avoid duplication, broad topics as well as glossary citations have been omitted here.